Elephants Don't Snore

Portrait of the author by Life *Magazine's photographer Al Fenn, Antarctic 1956.*

Elephants Don't Snore

Leverett G. Richards

Rose Wind Press
Vancouver, WA

ISBN 0-9631232-4-6
Richards, Leverett G. 1908-
Includes index: p.325
1. Aviation - Polar Exploration - Pacific Northwest - History-
   Journalism

Other books by the author:
Ice Age Coming "The Story of Glaciers, Bergs and Ice Caps"
TAC "The Story of The Tactical Air Command"

Book Design by Mary Rose
Cover photo of musk ox bull "Oomingmak" by L. Richards,
1977.

TABLE OF CONTENTS

Section II — *To The Ends of the Earth*

SECTION III — *Drama of Disaster*

FOREWORD

Adventure is not an equal opportunity experience. Sure, everyone has some adventures thrust upon them, like getting caught in a tornado or earthquake or a train wreck. But for most adventures, we have a choice, and most people choose not to climb that mountain or bulldog musk ox or babysit a very pregnant elephant. We opt not to go looking for that tornado or earthquake, and we lead a safer but duller life for it.

Lev Richards' stories are about one of those rare people who leaps at every possible adventure. He does things we might label as stupid or too risky, but then our inner selves secretly wish we had been at his side.

His recollections are not like the fishing stories that get better with the telling — when he started doing his 50th anniversary stories, such as the Indian pact of 1932, or the arrival of the Russian aviators in 1937, he first dove into the files in his basement, emerging with clips and large format negatives from the first time he had covered the events.

Stories about his exploits are legend — and legion. I had heard tales about him but most were so outrageous as to be unbelievable. My first encounter was in keeping with his myth.

On May 18, 1980, as Lev likes to tell it, he wore out three photographers while flying near Mount Saint Helens, documenting the explosive volcanic blast. I, too, was in a small plane, reporting for another newspaper on the devastation, the mud flood, the boiling salmon. The north side of the mountain, where the death toll would eventually reach 57, was in shambles. But emergency officials feared that mud slides and flooding might be occurring on the south side, too, so a radio message asked us to scout that area before heading home.

On that day, a huge military plane was orbiting somewhere high above the mountain, using its radar to police the 20-mile no-fly zone around the now missing peak. During the day we had heard several warnings to aircraft that they were entering the exclusion zone, to leave or face action against their pilot's license.

We swung south to the string of lakes at the south side of the mountain, and with the air controller plane's permission, started east into a scene from hell. There was a relatively low ceiling of clouds and ash. The afternoon light was normal at the horizon behind us, but ahead was a fence of bright purple lightning, flashing through a backlit sky that changed colors from brown to white to red to white.

We pressed on, trying to see what bridges might remain, and whether the forests had been obliterated. But as we got nearer to the wall of purple lightning, the pilot started to drift south, toward clearer air. In addition to the lightning, visibly swirling up-drafts and down-drafts, and the possibility of falling pumice bombs, who knew how long it would take the sandy ash to grind through an aircraft engine's guts?

Just as we decided we had gone as far as we dared, we heard the airborne traffic cop above us tersely warn a small plane that was much closer to hell, unseen, somewhere ahead of us, deep in the no-fly zone.

Back came a polite acknowledgement that the other plane would obey.

I can remember our pilot muttering something to the effect: "That damned Lev Richards."

WILLIAM J. STEWART

This book is dedicated to
Durkee, Mary Jeanne, Bradley and Trevor.
They are the future.

INTRODUCTION

Why write a book? Because I can't help it. I write out of desperation. I am a compulsive writer, a storyholic. When I see a story that cries out to be told, I am compelled to try and tell it.

In 70 years of reporting and writing I have had a ringside seat at a lot of history in the making. I have been to the ends of the earth, quite literally. I helped drop supplies to Fletcher's Ice Island near the North Pole in 1952. I was on the crew of the plane that made the first air drop at the South Pole and covered the first landing at the South Pole in 1956.

I made a modicum of history when I arranged and participated in the first fully documented man-made rainstorm in 1947 and again when I helped capture the first flock of Antarctic penguins for the Portland zoo in 1957.

I spent the night in a leper colony at Molokai, Hawaii where Sammy Koahine strummed the guitar with his stump of a hand and sang sad songs of his own composition, hoarsely, through an artificial larynx.

Four high school friends and I made our own skis and pack sacks and were the first to ski through Yellowstone Park in the depth of the winter in 1925. We nearly froze to death. We did it again 50 years later. I served as a summer ranger naturalist in Mount Rainier National Park and climbed Rainier and all the major peaks in the Cascades. I climbed Fujiyama in 1986 when I was 78.

I have piloted planes 100 feet below sea level and up to 52,000 feet above sea level. I have ridden covered wagons and broken the sound barrier in a supersonic jet fighter. I helped to cover the landing of the Russian pilots who were the first to fly over the North Pole nonstop from Moscow to Vancouver and covered the return of copilot Georgi Baidukov 50 years later. I saw a city die during the Vanport Flood in 1948. I covered the Columbus Day Storm of 1962; the Alaska earthquake of March 27, 1964, and other big stories, ranging from the Space Shuttle to the capture of musk oxen on Nunivak Island for the Portland zoo.

In 54 years of flying I have logged more than 11,000 hours and never scratched a passenger. Never bitten one either, although I have been tempted. In line of duty I have been bitten by a duck, kicked by a reindeer, mistaken for a penguin's egg and slept with a passel of pachyderms.

I was raised to respect and protect women. I remember when Fanny was a girl's name, and when drugs were something you bought at a drug store. Gay was a happy word, as in "young and gay." Sex was a noun, and it wasn't discussed in public. I was graduated cum laude in 1932, in the depth of the Great Depression. I lost $7.50 in the bank holiday. It was a whole different world out there.

I was lucky enough to get a job as a reporter, later editor, on the *Clark County Sun*, a weekly that covered Clark County news.

The lead pencil was the reporter's best friend. Hardest part of my job was to decipher the news notes from country correspondents, scribbled on the backs of envelopes with dull pencils.

John Lownsdale, the market editor of *The Oregonian* wrote his copy and his stock market tables with a soft lead pencil. Only one printer in the back shop was able to decipher his copy, which read like a doctor's prescription. He was the last of the pencil pushers.

A few enterprising reporters were beginning to use typewriters. We had to provide our own. I left mine in the city room one day and someone took it.

On a breaking news story you made your notes with a heavy lead pencil in the rain, stood up to a pay phone in the dark and dictated your stuff off the cuff to meet a deadline. No cellular phones, no laptops and no fax machines — probably the most useful reporting tool ever invented until the computer burst on the scene. Not all reporters could stand that pressure.

But the smartest thing I ever did, 62 years ago, was to marry a rhododendron. The Virginia Richards hybrid rhododendron. It's one of the most popular on the market developed by the late Bill Whitney, one of the world's top hybridists. (I can never get used to overhearing someone asking the price for "that Virginia Richards in the window.")

Born and reared in Battle Ground, Washington, she has been the accountant, the architect of the family's future, the tower of strength as well as teacher, aerial navigator, gardener, seamstress and homemaker. There is an old Chinese saying: "Women hold up half the sky." Virginia holds up more than her half.

I learned to fly in an old Bird biplane with a Kinner engine in 1938. When the Japanese bombed Pearl Harbor, I volunteered for (unpaid) training as a flight instructor. Virginia took over my job as a Southwest Washington correspondent and photographer for *The Oregonian* to keep beans in the pot until I got on the Air Corps payroll ($75 a month). I was privileged to serve 26 years in the Air Force, retiring as a lieutenant colonel.

But Virginia also served. She led the life of a camp follower during World War II, dragging our children with her, and endured the hardships of an Air Force widow when I was called to active duty during the Korean conflict and other overseas tours of duty.

I grew up in the wilds of Montana. I was shy. Women frightened me. I would cross the street to avoid encountering a girl. We had no television or radio. We depended on books, games like "Authors" and the occasional chautaqua for entertainment and education. Travelling shows and rodeos provided excitement. My favorite book was *The Three Musketeers* by Alexander Dumas. Actually there were four musketeers and I can still name them all — D'artangna, Athos, Parthos and Aramis.

I have always loved words, especially long, pretentious words like hypomonstrosesquepedelianism. I was compelled by curiosity, but plagued by shyness most of my life. I remember pacing the halls for 15 minutes before getting up nerve enough to knock on the door of Professor Hugo Winkenwerder, Dean of the School of Forestry at the University of Washington, for an interview.

Schools of journalism 50 years ago emphasized the duty of the press to print the facts, or at least the arguments on both sides of any issue. That was the price we paid for freedom of the press. That was the very foundation of democratic government. Editors were free to criticize in the most outrageous language in the editorial columns, but news was to be reported objectively.

The first story of mine to see print was written when I was

17 for the *Bozeman Chronicle*. I interviewed Miss Miles, the first white woman to see Yellowstone National Park. Her name was Cecilia but everyone called her "Miss Miles." She looked and dressed like Queen Victoria and was just as prim. I became acquainted with her when I used to help her clean house. I would hang her big feather mattresses on the line and beat them with a rug beater, raising clouds of dust. I would haul stuff up and down the long flight of steep stairs that lead to the basement, helping her with her spring house cleaning.

Her father was U.S. Army General Nelson A. Miles, hero of the Civil War, commander of the District of the Yellowstone, based at Fort Keogh, Montana, on the banks of the Yellowstone River at its intersection with the Tongue River, about 150 miles northeast of Bozeman.

The army was responsible for exploring and administering Yellowstone National Park, the country's first national park. When General Miles organized his first expedition to explore and enjoy the vast reaches of the park in 1878 he took his wife Mary and his daughter Cecilia with him.

The expedition resembled an armed invasion more than a peaceful outing. The party included 10 officers, 100 mounted soldiers, 4 civilians, 5 ladies and 3 children.

Miss Miles recalled the beauties of the scenery, untouched by man. The weird and wonderful geysers, hot pools, thermal terraces and mud pools.

There were no roads. The company rode west through picturesque country, followed for a ways by a train of military wagons loaded with camping gear plus rifles, ammunition and emergency rations. Pack trains later replaced the wagons.

"We were scarcely ever out of sight of wild game, and the streams were alive with beautiful speckled trout," Miles noted in his official journal.

The peaceful picnic mood was soon shattered. Scouts reported that a party of Bannock Indians had left the reservation and gone on the warpath out in Idaho. They had stolen horses, attacked ranches and were moving through Yellowstone Park. Miles promptly sent the civilians, women and children to Fort Ellis, Montana, the nearest army post. He split his meager forces into two patrols and moved to intercept the rebel warriors. The renegade Bannocks were taken by surprise, 14 were killed, the rest captured and sent to Fort Custer.

The women and children rejoined the column at Mammoth Hot Springs, which later became the Gardiner entrance to the park. They continued on their leisurely exploration with pack trains for 12 days, following old game trails through the heart of the park.

General Miles (then a colonel in the Union Army) was wounded in the Civil War at the Battle of Fair Oaks and four months later wounded again at Chancellorsville. A few months later he was "shot out of his saddle while defending his lines against a strong force of the enemy." For his bravery beyond the call of duty he was awarded the Medal of Honor.

Miles served as commander of the Department of the Columbia with headquarters at Vancouver Barracks from 1881 to 1884. He and his family lived on Officers Row, now a National Historic Site, virtually in my backyard.

Miss Miles died not long after the story was published in the *Bozeman Chronicle*. She was in her eighties and becoming unsteady in her gait.

One day she was found dead at the foot of her basement stairs. She had been killed instantly when she fell down those steep stairs and broke her neck.

My family moved to Clark County, Washington not long after my friends and I trekked through Yellowstone. I attended the University of Washington where British professor Dean Vernon McKenzie, strict in the rules of English grammar, cemented my writing style for life.

No really hep reporter would be caught dead using schoolbook shorthand. But I used shorthand all my life. So did Vern Haugland, aviation editor of the Associated Press. We both learned Gregg in high school in Bozeman. We were the only outlaws in the Aviation and Space Writers Association. I learned in self-defense. No one could read my longhand, including me; whereas my shorthand was textbook stuff. Besides, any spy who tried to read my notes was doomed to frustration.

Reporting has changed over the years. We used to phone in our stories to the newsroom where a clerk typed every word we read to her. Styles change, too, from a time of flowery prose and verbosity (we were paid by the inch) to a tight, concise, even cryptic style as news space shrank and the cost of newsprint soared. The brass didn't think I would ever master an electric typewriter. Neither did I, until I discovered the automatic eraser. Then I was hooked. The computer was a bigger hurdle for one who never figured out how to program his VCR. But within a week I became addicted. The word processor has replaced the dog and the pencil as the writing man's best friends.

It was the airplane that set me free to follow my nose for news. I could roam the world from pole to pole, covering the news from a new dimension. My first attack of aviation itch came when a barnstormer landed in a pasture outside of Three Forks, Montana when I was still playing with bows and arrows. There was neither time nor money for flying until I hit Vancouver in 1932. I soon became a ramp rat, hanging around Dad Bacon's shop on Pearson Field, bumming rides. That lit the fire that has never burned out.

EDITOR'S NOTE: Richards "retired" in 1986 after 52 years of writing for The Oregonian, *but he still goes to the office every weekday morning and sometimes on weekends in pursuit of one more story. He does a little skiing and plays tennis three times a week. He quietly celebrated his 88th birthday at a tennis camp at Kona, Hawaii, February 14, 1996. He and Virginia belong to three ballroom dance clubs. They love the waltz, but can't resist anything with a good beat from mambo to Charleston and jitterbug to tango. "People who dance together, stay together." To prove it they celebrated their 60th wedding anniversary May 20, 1994 when Leverett was 86 and Virginia was 81. "Must be some mistake," Leverett will tell you. "We are just too young to be that old!"*

ACKNOWLEDGEMENTS

I owe thanks to a lot of people for their help. This book could not have been written without the foresight of my can-do wife, Virginia. My memory is fickle. But Virginia was smart enough to save my daily letters and carbon copies of stories from Greenland, the Antarctic, Europe and Vietnam as well as hundreds of pictures. It was Lieutenant Colonel Anis G. "Tommie" Thompson, press aide and advisor to Major General Chester E. McCarty, who was responsible for my tours of duty in the Antarctic and for many other assignments to the Canadian Arctic, Germany, Aviano (Italy), and to Libya (before Muamar Kadafy). Tommie, author of *The Greatest Airlift*, also contributed advice and encouragement.

And then there is *The Oregonian*. I married *The Oregonian* in 1932 — before I married Virginia. In those 63 years The Old Lady of Alder Street has become a part of me. Many of the stories in this book grew out of *Oregonian* assignments. Others arose from 26 years in the U.S. Air Force Reserve and tours of active duty at home and abroad, thanks to the moral and financial support of *The Oregonian*.

I owe William J. "Bill" Stewart, *Oregonian* reporter, editor and all around walking encyclopedia, for taking the time from his hectic schedule to read the manuscript and offer advice.

I will be forever grateful to Mary Rose, author of a half dozen books and publisher of a half dozen more, for encouraging me to record some of the history I have seen in the making and reading, rereading and editing the manuscript, suggesting changes and publishing the book.

SECTION I

Elephants Don't Snore

CHAPTER 1

OLE PETERSON

A sign at the front gate warned: "Privit property. No hunting; No shooting." On the front door was a crudely lettered sign: "No KORKS aloud."

Around the corner of the house came an apparition in rubber boots and tin pants pushing a wheelbarrow full of chicken feed. This had to be the legendary Ole Peterson!

From the day I went to work for *The Clark County Sun* in Vancouver, Washington, I began to hear tall tales about Ole Peterson, the wild man of legendary strength, a veritable Paul Bunyan or Sasquatch — the ape man of Mount Saint Helens. He was portrayed as an outrageous rebel, an eccentric recluse, a hermit who hated all humanity.

He lived in a shirt tail corner of Skamania County only 33 rugged air miles from Stevenson, but a 125-mile drive through Cowlitz and Clark counties to get there. His cabin was the last smoke on the trail up the Lewis River for decades. But by the time I met Ole, he lived in a two-story cabin of vertical siding, surrounded by a barn, chicken house, monument to Chic Sales, tool shed and of all things, a garage.

It was early spring and Ole had just shed the soggy, shapeless hat that he wore in the winter rains. He looked like a cross between Moses and an unmade bed. He peered out of a cumulus cloud of white hair with his beady eyes like some mischievous troll. His beard hung down to his belly and stuck out in all directions.

He still wore his logger's tin pants, worn out at the knees and thighs. They were starched with the winter's accumulation of grime, stiff enough to stand by themselves when he took them off. A cautious man, he wore both suspenders and a belt. An automatic in a shiny holster hung at his right hand.

The house was a boar's nest, clouded with cobwebs, cluttered with boots, groceries and piles of tobacco stems. (Ole raised his own tobacco.) A pot of beans seemed to be forever simmering on the old kitchen range, while socks, shirts and winter woollies hung up to dry overhead.

Before long he was flourishing a strange looking cane about three feet long which bent like rubber when he put any weight on it. He chuckled gleefully when asked the story behind the cane. Seems he made it from the penis of one of the bulls that he butchered for meat.

Ole never married, but he always enjoyed shocking "the hens that come up here to cluck over me." He did have eyes for a school teacher in Cougar, Washington once, and she seemed to have eyes for him. But she left when school closed for the summer, and Ole never heard from her again.

The legend of Ole Peterson, outrageous rebel, began during the depression of 1892 when as a young man in his mid-20s, Peterson lost his shirt and a stable full of stallions in Emmett County, Iowa. Grover Cleveland, a Democrat, was president, and an enraged Peterson vowed to take to the woods until the world came to its Republican senses.

4

Some detractors spread rumors insinuating that Ole was a horse thief running from the law. But no evidence was ever produced.

He headed west in 1893 and when he reached Woodland, Washington, he turned east and hiked up an old Indian trail alongside the Lewis River for 36 miles. Old timers swear that he carried a sheet metal stove on his back with a bag of spuds in the oven to keep it from bouncing.

He proved up his claim on an 80-acre tract of timberland, built a cabin by the side of the trail and settled down to watch the rest of the world go by. He kept his vow, coming out of the woods only once during the next 60 years — to attend his mother's funeral in Iowa in 1926.

"I liked to starved to death that first year," he recalled, "until the Cowelskie Indians showed me how to snag salmon in the riffles." With the aid of the Indians, who were his friends, Peterson explored the untracked wilderness that lay to the north and east of his Cougar Flats. On the old lava flows that towered above his hideaway he discovered one of the longest of several caves formed by lava flows several hundred years ago.

In the 1920s Ole installed ladders to provide easier access to the mile-long lava tube and made a few dollars guiding visitors through his cave. He discovered Cispus Pass, lowest pass through the Cascades, and led Northern Pacific railroad survey-ors to it in the late 1890s. He was rewarded with a lifetime rail-road pass, which he used only once — to get to Iowa in 1926.

Ole became a legend in his own time. Sometimes it was hard to tell legend from fact. But Ole swore that his battle with a cougar on the trail near the site of the present town of Cougar was gospel. "That cat was out of his mind with hunger or he wouldn't a been slinking out of the woods at me," he declared.

"I took up a club about two feet long and brandished it, beating the ground and growling just as loud as he did. He was an old one, with most of his teeth gone and skinny as a snake. I got so close that I could see his teeth before I let out a real Saturday night howl that scared him back into the brush."

And then, when the moon was ripe and Ole was inspired, he would tell another tale about his pet cougar whose right front leg was bitten off by a bear. So Ole fitted the cougar with a wooden leg and the cougar went back and beat that miserable bear to death with his wooden leg!

Each spring Peterson would plant beans and potatoes in the meadow alongside the creek and bring in a few head of stock, about an equal number of bulls. He never did know how much stock he had. The cattle roamed the woods and only came down for hay and oats in the winter.

Asked what he raised on his 80-acre timber claim, Peterson thought a moment, then said: "Hair mostly." Every winter he grew enough hair to stuff a mattress. By spring he had a beard so long he considered it a serious fire hazard for a man who smoked a pipe, which he did. So, as the winter wore on, he had to use a series of pipes, each with a longer stem than the last. Over the years, the Indians and the occasional loggers in the area knew it was spring when Peterson got out his old sheep shears and cut away the winter's underbrush, leaving a handle-bar mustache to tickle his nose all summer.

Ole, explorer, pioneer settler, and outrageous rebel, cultivated his image as a profane recluse, an eccentric character who wanted to be left alone. "But he really liked people," his friend and attorney D. Elwood Caples of Vancouver said. "Every hunter and fisherman who ventured up the Lewis River knew him as a friend. He would share his bread and beans with every passerby. Sometimes, if he liked you, he would offer you a shot of Old Atom Juice — a potent home brew that he kept in the spring 100 yards up the creek."

As the years went by, Peterson widened the old Indian trail to accommodate a horse and buggy. At the turn of the century he fell in love with an old Reo Racer, bought it and drove it up the rocky road to his hideaway. Later, he traded it for a 1911 Hupmobile, which was soon joined by a 1916 Baby Grand Chevrolet, a 1916 Liberty and later a Model RT Ford.

When "that blankey blank Delano" (Franklin Delano Roosevelt) aroused his ire, he put the old Hupmobile up on blocks in front of his garage where it sat to the bitter end. Peterson loudly professed to hate all Democrats. But he made an exception for Caples, who happened to be chairman of the Clark County Democratic Committee. "Caples is the only honest lawyer in the country," he declared.

Caples not only managed his business deals with timber buyers, but came to Ole's defense when a couple of ambitious revenue agents during the Prohibition era charged him with selling bootleg liquor.

"The judge in Skamania knew Ole," Caples said. "He knew Ole would share his liquid dynamite with special friends, but would never accept money. The judge dismissed the case and gave the agents a tongue lashing."

"I first met Ole in 1930 when I was a Boy Scout," Ken Teter, one of his closest friends, remembers. "I would get his permission to sleep in the haystack on our Scout trips." Teter and his wife, Eunice, took over the store at Cougar, two and one-half miles downriver from Peterson's hideout, in the spring of 1947 and operated it through 1950.

During the long winter months when the whole area was snowbound, Teter would hike up the highway loaded with supplies for Ole. An old photograph showed Ken Teter setting out with a bag of coffee beans in one hand, a full case of "Old Panters Milk" under his arm. Ole used to write Teter notes on his old Underwood that only a skilled cryptographer could decipher. Teter, who had an eye for history, saved a drawer full of them. Here's a sample:

> *"dear friend kenneth, the ry o grand is running low how about another case of ole hickrey? before the snakes git out, inclosed check for $42.50 bring it up the first chans you git the snakes may come out eney minith now, the bibel sas be prepared — hoping everything is loveley and the GOOS hangs high, ole."*

Ole had an almost fanatical fear of fire. It was a tragic irony that he finally fell victim to the foe he feared the most. He had seen a firestorm at its worst when the flames from the historic Yacolt Burn roared overhead in 1902, skipping his sheltered valley but burning hundreds of square miles of virgin timber all around and killing more than 30 settlers. He recalled that ash and embers rained out of the sky as the wind generated by the fire swept over his hidden home by the side of the trail.

Thick clouds of smoke blotted out the sky to the south that hot, dry summer. There was no radio or television to spread the news, but Ole knew something ominous was brewing. "I had some small piles of slashing out in the meadow that I wanted to burn," he said. "But when I lit a match the air seemed to catch fire. I got her out real quick and never monkeyed with no fire after that."

"Ole had 'No Smoking' signs posted all over," Teter remembers. "When he let me sleep in the barn, he made me empty my pockets of all matches — and he searched everyone else, too."

Despite all his precautions, fire broke out in his weather-beaten cabin about 3:30 p.m. May 4, 1953. By sheer coincidence, Georgia Neal was driving by in the school bus when she saw the flames. She ran into the cabin and shouted at Ole. He ran out of the burning cabin, but turned and ran back into the burning building, hoping to save some of his treasured possessions. He was badly burned before he could escape.

He was rushed to Memorial Hospital in Vancouver in a Forest Service truck where he died May 7 with a smile on his lips. "This is my first time in a hospital," he told Teter. "I'd a come here sooner if I had known they had such pretty nurses," he declared with a mischievous leer.

Peterson's two nieces, his only heirs, sold Ole's 80 acres to Northwest Power, a predecessor of Pacific Power & Light Co. which built Swift Dam and power canal on the site. Nothing remains to mark the spot except a lone apple tree hidden in an alder thicket near the banks of the power canal.

After Ole Peterson's death the Vancouver *Columbian* printed an editorial urging that a county park or picnic site be named in his memory. Thirty years later Ken Teter and Elwood Caples joined in an effort to persuade the Cowlitz County Public Utility District to name its powerhouse on the site in his honor. As this book goes to press all efforts to honor the legend of Ole Peterson have failed.

Ole's only monument — and a fitting one — is the mile-long lava cave that he discovered so long ago. Ole's Cave still appears on maps of the area, but the trail to the cave has been obliterated by the U.S. Forest Service to protect the rare bats which make their home there part of the time.

CHAPTER 2

OLD BETSY

I must have been a bothersome baby, a trial to my patient, forgiving mother.

I was brought up mostly in Montana and Colorado, both frontier states, pretty wild and free in those days. I ran around with a wild gang. In Three Forks, a railroad junction and not much else, we kids used to get together for gang fights on Saturday.

Nobody got seriously hurt, maybe a bloody nose here and there, or a black eye. Nobody would have thought of using knives or guns. We would throw rocks and kick up clouds of dirt to simulate cannons, but mainly it was like a scrum in rugby where we all rushed together flailing about and ending in a heap. I usually managed to wind up on the bottom. That was the safest place to be and yet gave you lots of room for brags after the war ended.

We used to play cowboys and Indians. Made crude bows and arrows. I used to pride myself on throwing a mean "tomahawk" — Dad's old hatchet intended for splitting wood. I remember hurling that heavy hatchet at the pole that supported mother's clothesline, with devastating results. Don't remember getting my pants warmed for that, but I probably did. Dad and Mother both believed that the seat of the pants was the seat of learning.

It was a couple of years later that I really gave everyone a scare, especially me. I was planning to go duck hunting with a couple of my buddies. We were sitting on the bed in an old porch converted into a bedroom. I knew the .12 gauge shotgun was unloaded. So I aimed it at the wall and squeezed the trigger to test the pull.

The gun erupted with the roar of a cannon, belching fire and smoke. The shot missed one of my buddies by about three feet, blasted a hole in the wall and knocked me sprawling and gasping with fright. I gave up the hunt. Mother never wielded the paddle, but I got it in the end from Dad on that occasion.

My maternal Grandfather Goss left the most lasting impression on me, however. Brother Frank and I had gone with Mother to visit her parents on the brink of the Royal Gorge of the Arkansas River out of Pueblo. We spent a lot of time with Grandpa Goss scrambling over rocks, through the scrub juniper and cactus hunting rabbits and skinning them out for the evening meal.

One day Frank had an inspiration. We would gather up some of the old magazines around the house and sell them door to door. Doors were a long way apart and we were a long way from home come supper time. Mother was really worried about us. Grandpa, a rough, tough prospector type, wasted no time grabbing a stick and popping Frank over his knee. Whereupon I broke the Code of the West:

"Hit him Grandpa," I cried, "It was his idea." That was a tactical error. Grandpa dropped Frank, grabbed me, bared the target and raised some welts that hurt me a lot more than they did him.

I remember mostly the days the sun shines. But I can still see the horse trotting slowly along pulling Grandpa's buggy as Mother drove to town with my little brother, Norman, who suffered from heart trouble. He died without a sound as he sat in Mother's lap long before we could reach the doctor in town.

One of the highlights of the year in Three Forks, Montana was the annual ice harvest. An ice box was an icebox in those days. The electric refrigerator had not reached the boondocks, if it had been invented at all. By late December or early January the ice in the pond outside the ice house had frozen three feet thick.

The icehouse crew would take long cross cut saws and cut the ice into cakes about three feet long and two feet wide. They would use long, sharp pike poles to push the cakes of ice along the channel that led to the long, wooden ramp leading into the ice house. Layer after layer would be laid down and packed in sawdust. The men would sink ice tongs into the cakes of ice and a team of horses would be used to pull the cakes up the ramp to the top of the ice house for the top layers.

Those were the fun days.

The ice house was not far from Kid Johnson's theatre. Kid Johnson was a professional lightweight boxer who retired to run the only movie house in Three Forks. I got a job sweeping out the place in return for free tickets. Used to invite girl friends to share balcony seats. To my shame I used to keep track of the number of kisses I could wangle. Sure didn't make any impression. Can't remember any of the girls, or any of the scores.

In the winter we wild ones had our own version of Russian roulette. It was played with a Flexible Flyer, the steerable sled that every kid got for Christmas sooner or later. You attached about 30 feet of rope to the steering bar, flipped the other end over the bumper of the nearest Model T and hitched a ride down the streets. When you chickened out you just let go of the rope and went slithering on down the street dodging cars and pedestrians. Flexible Flyers were not equipped with brakes.

I don't remember anyone getting hurt sled hitching, but I remember some hostile reactions from drivers and pedestrians.

Later we tried skijoring, hanging onto a rope pulled by a trotting horse, which was safer and more fun, but not as available.

The Fourth of July used to be the most exciting day of the year when I was a kid. It even had Christmas beat. Firecrackers began to pop all over town by July 2 and rose to a crescendo as the big day approached. By the dawn of the Fourth it did, indeed, come up like thunder.

Every red-blooded kid considered it his patriotic duty to amass a hoard of fireworks to be expended with ingenuity and flair. A small salute cracker made a convincing volcano when exploded in a mound of dirt. A tin can could amplify the roar of a firecracker into a real banger.

Today you can buy dynamite like potatoes, but you can't buy real, explosive, firecrackers any more. It's hard to remember the time when you could still buy cannon crackers big enough to break the neighbors' windows, or blow your head off if you got careless. We thought we were Big Time Operators when we could afford a few cannon crackers. I remember bragging to my dad about some of the cannon crackers I had set off in my time.

"Cannon firecrackers?" Dad asked, with a hint of scorn in his voice. "We celebrated the Fourth with REAL cannons when I was a kid! I never dared tell you kids this when you were young and impressionable. But now that you have reached the age of discretion...."

It took a little urging, but the story of Old Betsy, the Richards-Martel cannon, finally unfolded. It happened in Pueblo, Colorado, about the turn of the century. Pueblo was a quiet, peaceful town on the banks of the Arkansas River. The tallest building in town was the three-story Congress Hotel. Dad recalled:

"We got the idea from the cannon in the park, a trophy of the Spanish War. Every city park had one in those days. It was a muzzle loader, with a touch hole in the rear to light it off.

"So we coaxed the foreman at the railroad shops into drilling a $\frac{1}{4}$-inch hole the length of a tempered steel piston rod from a locomotive pump. We mounted it on a heavy plank.

"We bought two quarts of black powder from the hardware store and a supply of $\frac{1}{4}$-inch bolts, which we cut to fit the barrel of the gun.

"We didn't sleep much that night. We were too excited. By the dawn's early light we slipped out of town, across the Arkansas River and climbed the high bluff that overlooked the town. There we set up Old Betsy and drove stakes to brace her against the recoil.

"We weren't sure how much she would kick, but we knew there was no chance of hitting anything. It was at least a mile and half or two miles across the uninhabited flood plain and across the river to the sleeping city. Just as an added precaution we elevated the muzzle about 65 degrees to make sure our shots would fall harmlessly on the open prairie.

"So we charged the barrel about half full of black powder, tamped in some wadding and added a small piece of bolt. Then I stood at attention, held my breath and gave the order `Fire when ready, Gridley!'

" 'Aye, aye, sir, fire in the hole,' cannoneer Frank Martel responded. He stood back and reached out gingerly to touch his burning punk to the powder in the touch hole.

"There was a soul-satisfying roar. When the cloud of acrid smoke cleared, the cannon had pulled up its stakes and recoiled about three feet.

"We stood in silent awe for a moment, then staked Old Betsy down with longer stakes, poured in a bigger charge of powder, tamped in a bigger bolt and fired again and again. As the morning wore on, our artillery barked louder and louder. Old Betsy kicked back six feet and nearly turned a somersault. The cannonading ended only when the supply of powder came to an end.

"It was with pride in our hearts and a loud ringing in our ears that we marched triumphantly back to town, smudged with powder and grinning from ear to ear. It's a wonder our parents didn't suspect something, the way we whispered and snickered the rest of the day like a couple of conspirators.

"Dad was reading the morning paper at the breakfast table the morning of the fifth when I got a glimpse of the bold headlines on the front page. 'Mysterious Shots Shatter Windows of Congress Hotel. Guest narrowly escapes injury from shots hurtling through the walls. Police seek clues to mystery of steel pellets.'

"I froze, numb with fear, mumbled some excuse and ran over to Frank Martel's house. We panicked. We grabbed the cannon and buried it deep under a neighbor's barn. Old Betsy was the best kept secret of our young lives from that day forward."

My dad was a great story teller. I've always wondered if the cannon was ever found.

CHAPTER 3

WINTER DANGERLAND

Gusts of wind scoured the pavement, leaving barely enough for our skis as we shuffled up the steep grade through the Golden Gate from the Gardiner Entrance to Yellowstone Park weighted down with 50-pound packs. When we reached Swan Lake Flats at the 7,000-foot central plateau we encountered deep, soft snow. The wind was icy, but the snow was soft, even sticky in spots.

We were nearly exhausted. It was the shortest day of the year and night was falling fast. We were about to stop and build a snow cave to survive the night when we spotted an abandoned construction camp just off the road.

Maybe that should have been a warning of what lay ahead, but, with the arrogance of youth we plunged on into our great adventure.

Dad was running a lumber yard in Bozeman, Montana, in 1925, when I was a senior in high school. There I started palling around with four buddies. We called ourselves the Fearless Five. George Markin, tall, lean and wiry, was daring. We stood somewhat in awe of George. He would hop a freight car or ride the tender anywhere he wanted to go. He and I were on the wrestling team. Glenn Muchow was a big blond, athletic Adonis with a reputation as a lady killer. Julius "Butch" Heuschkel was the biggest, the tallest and the strongest of the bunch. His father, Mox, spoke simple English with a strong German accent. Butch, his father and I all worked at the local pea cannery. And then there was Frank Wisner. Older and wiser than the rest of the gang, he was quiet and reserved. We called him the Professor. He was often the voice of reason, tempering the impulsiveness of exuberant youth. Frank was 22; Butch was 20. The rest of us were 17.

I was the wild-eyed rebel of the bunch. I had hair like the Medusa, kinky and sticking out four inches in all directions. I wrestled in the 145-pound class and fancied myself a real frontiersman. Ha! What is that which cometh before a fall?

The Fearless Five had been skiing together for a year or so. We built a snug cabin on a shoulder of Mount Hyalite where we spent some cozy weekends. We would climb up laboriously on skis, then cut a small tree and straddle it for the straight schuss back down the steep trail. We didn't worry about environmental impact.

No one knew how to stop except to fall on your tailbone, or straddle a tree. We made a few winter trips of 20 miles or so, including a climb of Mount Hyalite. On one of our early trips we laid out all our blankets into one big bed on top the snow, built a big fire at the foot of the bed and went to sleep. We woke up with a howl as the heat melted the snow and the bed started to slide into the fire. Dumb, but we learned from experience.

George got the idea for a winter trip through Yellowstone National Park. He and Glenn had hiked through the park in the summer and figured it would be more fun on skis. He didn't have any trouble talking the rest of us into the idea. The problem would be to keep from freezing on the 7,000-foot high central plateau where temperatures sometimes dropped to 40 and 50 below zero.

But with the recklessness of youth we dismissed the prospect without a further thought. We figured maybe we could use some park service buildings along the way for shelter. The other problem was food for the 10 days we estimated it would take to traverse the park. You couldn't buy any dried food except prunes, raisins, powdered eggs and powdered milk. George also bought split peas and hominy and a five-pound sack of cracker meal for soup. He tried drying potatoes in the oven, but gave up.

I made my own skis, about 8 feet long and 3 inches wide, out of hickory, with the aid of the shop foreman at the Copeland Lumber Yard. We turned up the tips of the skis by steaming them over an old boiler and set the camber the same way. I melted beeswax to coat the bottoms of the skis. I made ski poles out of broomsticks with condensed milk cans on the bottom for baskets. Poles not only help you keep your balance, but the pole push just about doubles your glide. George also made a set of poles, as I remember. The rest of the guys did not use poles until later.

WE'RE OFF

On Sunday, December 20, 1925, we took the train to Livingston and spent an uncomfortable night sleeping on the floor of the depot waiting for the morning train up the spur line to Gardiner, the north gateway to the park. George and Glenn managed to climb aboard the tender behind the locomotive and got as far as Corwin Springs before the railroad bulls chased them off. "We were quite willing to pay for a seat the rest of the way," George admitted. "That coal car was getting pretty cold."

There were only a few patches of snow on the ground at Gardiner, not enough for skis. So we set out to hike the 10 miles or so from Gardiner uphill to Mammoth Hot Springs, park headquarters, carrying our skis, and 50-pound packs. This area is alive with deer, mountain sheep and elk in the summer, but we saw only one deer along the road and one on the grounds of the headquarters building. It was Monday, December 21. We hadn't bothered to let anyone know we were coming. The park, the nation's oldest and biggest, was closed to the public, locked in deep freeze for the winter. All roads were blocked by snow as blizzards raged and temperatures dropped to 50 below.

The bears, the squirrels and the big cats hibernated. The deer and the elk and most of the geese and ducks migrated to lower elevations. Only the shaggy bisons and a few hardy birds braved the winter winds. The half dozen rangers and caretakers who spent the winter at Old Faithful and the Grand Canyon of the Yellowstone might as well have been on the moon. They had no radios then and the phone lines were frequently knocked out by ice and winds. There was no way of getting in or out once winter clamped its icy jaws on the wilderness.

Anyone who proposed to waltz through the park in December should automatically have been considered an escapee from a funny farm. Nevertheless chief ranger Sam Woodring, who later became head of the National Park Service, invited us into his office and listened politely to our request for permission to take a 150-mile tour of the park. He didn't say yes and he didn't say no. But he didn't treat us like escapees from the local asylum either. After sizing up our equipment and credentials he asked us to come back next morning for his answer.

We wandered around the Mammoth Hot Springs area taking pictures with our $5 cameras, then ate supper around an open fire. It was only eight degrees Fahrenheit. I remember eating with my gloves on that evening.

We were up early, Tuesday, December 22, 1925. We ate breakfast, packed up and were waiting at Woodring's office when he arrived. Evidently he was convinced that we had the experience and the equipment to survive. He gave his permission and offered us the use of ranger stations and snowshoe cabins along our route. We were to call his office every night, supply all our own food, replace the wood we burned, and leave a fire ready to be lighted with a single match in case someone stumbled in out of the storm with only strength enough to strike a match. We were not to cross the Continental Divide or head for the Yellowstone Lake region.

We wasted no time in setting out to hike up the steep road through the Golden Gate to Swan Lake Flats. There we encountered blinding snow and wind. The snow was wet and sticky where it crossed thermal areas.

Breaking trail through the deeper and deeper snow began to sap our strength. We had planned to reach the ranger station at Norris Geyser Basin, 17 miles from Mammoth, for the night. But these were the shortest days of the year and night was falling fast. We faced the prospect of trying to build a snow cave in the dark when suddenly George, our point man, saw the outlines of an abandoned road construction camp. There we spent a warm and comfortable night recovering our strength.

We took our time getting started the next morning, Wednesday, December 23, but the road to Norris Geyser Basin was generally level and we arrived in the middle of the afternoon, enjoyed a leisurely walk through the thermal area, melted clear of snow, and spent a cozy night Thursday, December 24. We awoke to deep snow but balmy weather, with temperatures barely freezing.

We decided to take a side trip to Yellowstone's Grand Canyon, several miles to the south. We left our packs behind and hit a fast pace, pausing only to marvel at the beauty of the trees, laden with snow. The canyon was robed in ermine. The falls were sheathed in ice, but the swift river was still open, sending up clouds of steam.

There is no place like home for Christmas. And we thought long about our families that Christmas Eve. But Christmas at Canyon proved to be an unforgettable highlight of our young lives.

The ranger on duty and the caretaker of the lodge had listened to our nightly telephone reports to the chief ranger and knew we were coming. The ranger, whose name I don't remember, provided Glenn, Butch and Frank with ski poles made from broom handles, which proved a real boon on the rest of our trip. They insisted that we join them for an early Christmas dinner. We ate and talked until night fell, then strapped on our skis and raced back in our old tracks which had turned to ice as the temperature fell. That hearty meal was more than a pleasure, it was vital to our survival.

We were virtually out of food when we left Norris Basin. George, our chief cook, left the Canyon early and raced down the trail back to Norris where he baked five pies with the odds and ends we had left.

That was his Christmas present to the gang. We slept late, spent Friday, Christmas Day, resting and enjoying the geyser basin. At the old Norris Hotel we visited with the lone caretaker. His main job was to shovel the snow off the roof when it got deep enough to endanger the building, but it had been a mild winter so far and only a foot of snow had accumulated. Again none of the gang had sufficient sense of history to record the caretaker's name.

We were nearly out of food when George found a sack of potatoes in the ranger cabin. We filled up on mashed potatoes for Christmas dinner. This was the only time that we used any of the stock of food at a ranger station. But frozen spuds spoil when they thaw. They would have gone to waste if we had not used them. We had planned to buy some food when we reached West Yellowstone, the western exit from the park.

The next day, Saturday December 26, was an easy glide along the Gibbon River, with a stop for lunch at scalding hot Beryl Spring enroute to Madison Junction. The streams, all heated by hot springs, were open and steaming in the cold. The sun shone brightly for a few minutes during our lunch break.

Fortune smiled on us again Sunday, December 27, as we left our heavy packs behind and skied the 17 miles past several geyser basins and along the Firehole River to Old Faithful. At times the earth seemed to be on fire as steam rose in clouds that obscured the road. The steam coated the trees with frost, turning the whole scene into a true winter wonderland. As we approached Old Faithful, Ranger Charles Phillips and Mr. and Mrs. Bauer, the lodge caretakers, hiked out to meet us. They had invited us by telephone to join them for a post-Christmas dinner.

After gorging ourselves we bedded down in a cabin comfortably heated with steam piped from a nearby geyser. (Sadly this now is called Abuse Geyser. Tapping its steam altered its behavior. The Park Service learned its lesson, and no one is allowed to tamper with any of the geysers these days.) The next day, Monday, December 28, after a hearty breakfast, we said farewell to the Bauers and to Ranger Phillips, a cheerful, genial nature lover with a good sense of humor. Little did we realize that this farewell was forever.

Ranger Phillips and the Bauers, firm friends and nature lovers, spent the winters of 1925 and 1926 uneventfully. The winter of 1927 was waning. The songs of the first birds were heard in the land. And the first plants began to sprout in the geyser basins. Hungry for greens after the long winter, Phillips and the Bauers on April 11 sat down to a meal of what they thought was wild parsnip. They all went to bed that night feeling fine. But about 2 a.m. April 12 the Bauers became violently ill. It was not until late that evening that Bauer checked on Phillips and found him dead on the floor of his station. The "wild parsnip" turned out to be the deadly water hemlock for which there is no antidote.

It took weeks for park rangers to hike in to Old Faithful on snowshoes through deep snow, improvise a toboggan and drag the body the 30 miles out to West Yellowstone. News of the tragedy sobered The Fearless Five. We felt we had lost a friend. Little did we know how near we might have come to suffering the same fate!

ALL DOWNHILL

At the time we savored life. The weather was mild. Our tummies were full. We were full of vim and vigor. We took pictures of Old Faithful, Castle and Riverside geysers, then made fast time back to Madison Junction for another comfortable night. Tuesday, December 29, dawned bright and clear and with lightened packs we sped over the snow to West Yellowstone, arriving soon after noon.

We had reveled in the luck of the Irish up to this moment. Suddenly we ran out of luck. The store at West Yellowstone was closed. We could find no place to eat and no rations to buy. We could have found shelter for the night, but the sun shone down out of a clear, blue sky and we decided to start on down the unmarked trail that ran along the surveyed boundary of the park, discounting the fact that this was still one of the shortest days of the year. We thought we could reach a snowshoe cabin along the boundary before dark. Night fell quickly and so did the temperature.

We floundered in the bitter cold and the deep snow. We split up, why I don't know. George and Glenn stuck together. Butch and Frank Wisner and I stayed within sight or sound of each other. Stumbling in the dark before the moon rose, George fell over a 20-foot snow bank, landing almost in the Gallatin River which they had been following. George was numb with the cold. (We later learned it was 43 below.) He refused to get up.

"It felt so good just lying there in the snow, so warm and comfortable that I just wanted to lie there and go to sleep," Markin recalled. "I can understand why they say it is a pleasure to freeze to death."

Glenn recognized this as the final stages of hypothermia. He kicked and cursed George and finally made him mad enough to get up and chase his tormentor. "That's all that saved my life," George said later.

We never reached the snowshoe cabin. We all had lost feeling in our toes and fingers. and were nearly exhausted when we sighted a light in the trees down a steep slope off the trail. We hailed the cabin and the reluctant occupant let us in. He said his name was Johnston and that he was a trapper. We suspected that he was a bootlegger.

But he did observe the code of the West. He took us in, rubbed kerosene on our frostbitten feet and let us bed down on his bare concrete floor. I can still remember jerking awake with nightmares and agonizing cramps in my legs during the long night. All of us had frostbitten fingers and toes. When I got home the doctor treated my feet with picric acid. I suffered from the paralyzing pain of chilblains for years afterward. So did George and Butch. The next morning, Wednesday, December 30, we limped on down the boundary trail.

We passed the snowshoe cabin just before noon. We would have dropped in our tracks long before reaching it if we had not lucked out and found the trapper's cabin. We stubbornly continued to shuffle on down the boundary trail. Night fell and so did we. The moon was bright, but cast deceptive shadows. I remember falling down a 20-foot bank in the dark without ever seeing it. The rest of the gang had similar troubles. But we were still on our feet when we reached the Gallatin ranger station.

We built a fire and stayed over night. I don't remember eating anything, but we did split a loaf of bread when we left the trapper's cabin.

The next day, Thursday, December 31, we made it to Bennett's Camp, the first sign of civilization we had seen in 10 days. New Year's Day 1926, we reached Karst Kamp on the Gallatin River where we phoned for a car that took us home. We had covered 153 miles in 12 days. Park rangers said we were the first and only party to ski through the park in winter without outside aid.

Strangely, although the park teemed with bear, elk, deer and buffalo in summer, we didn't see an animal of any kind after we left Mammoth Hot Springs. We did see plenty of bear sign at one of the ranger cabins early in the trip. A bear, probably a grizzly, had broken into the larder, despite the steel bars on the windows, smashed shelves of canned goods and left his teeth marks on cans of peaches and other fruit. And at Old Faithful Lodge a restless bear, instead of hibernating as any self-respecting bear should do, had invaded the lodge, rolled a barrel of salt down five flights of stairs and torn up some furniture trying to break open the keg. In the intervening years, park bears have been taken off welfare and forced to forage for themselves.

ENCORE

We didn't realize how lucky we were or how close to disaster we had come until 50 years later, when we did it again.

After months of correspondence and a scouting trip in June to enlist the help of the park service, four of the Fearless Five retraced our old route through the park in 1975, 50 years later to the day.

The years had been kind to us, but they had also left some scars. Dr. Frank Wisner, still making house calls in San Diego at 72, was unable to make the trip because of an injury suffered in an auto accident. George, 70, retired after 40 years as a school teacher, contractor and rancher, also had suffered back injuries in an auto accident. He couldn't do any strenuous skiing, but he could wrestle a snowmobile. Julius "Butch" Heuschkel, 67, a consultant on steel and other metals, was diabetic and suffered from phlebitis in one leg. One of his doctors ordered him not to attempt skiing. The other one ordered him to walk three miles a day. So he compromised and skied 50 miles in three days. Glenn Muchow, 67, retired engineer for the Bureau of Land Management and a World War II veteran, had suffered a serious heart attack in 1960, but was fully recovered and active.

None of the guys had been on skis for 40 years except me. I

was 67, an ardent downhill and cross country skier, tennis player, hiker, climber and ballroom dancer. "Never look back," the poets warn. The grass is never as green as it was in your youth, nor the snow as white or the sun as bright. Nonsense. We found the miles had grown a little longer in those 50 years, the hills a little steeper, but the park was just as wild and beautiful as ever. The "vanishing wildlife" was vastly more abundant. Deer, elk, coyotes and mountain sheep still grazed on the lawns and ate the wash off the line as they had 50 years earlier at park headquarters. But where we had seen not another creature in the rest of the park in 1925, we found scores of elk, hundreds of bison and an abundance of geese, whistling swans and a couple of moose in 1975.

On the third day we encountered a new form of wildlife — hordes of wild-eyed snowmobilers who entered the park in force at West Yellowstone and shattered the silence for miles on end. Tourists used to think the rangers turned off the geysers when the first snow began to fly and everyone turned in for a long winter's nap. Now about 150 miles of road is packed and groomed for snowmobiles and snow coaches, open to travel from December 20 through May. A peak of 1,700 snowmobiles was counted through the gate at West Yellowstone in one day in 1974 and the flood of winter visitors is still increasing.

Temperatures were mild the second time around, ranging from 20 below to 25 above. George carried our sleeping bags, food and cooking gear on the snowmobile, leaving us with 15- to 20-pound packs. Lightweight state-of-the-art cross country skis made a world of difference. In case any of the older generation should suffer from tired blood, the party included an injection of young blood. Pat Markin, George's son, a biologist based in Hawaii, and our son Durkee Richards, a 3M Company scientist, each 35 and strong, experienced skiers, added the spice of youth to the expedition.

BY THE LIGHT OF THE MOON

Night still reigned over the desolate moonscape when we started across Swan Lake Flats from the head of the Golden Gate at 6:30 a.m., December 20. But the moon was just as bright and it felt just as cold as it did 50 years ago. As the sky began to glow with the promise of dawn a band of coyotes set up a mournful howl, at once welcoming and warning us. Then all was silent as the Sea of Tranquility on the far side of the moon. It was a magic moment. For a brief interval we seemed to be suspended in space, all alone in a cold, pale orbit around the moon.

It took two days to reach Norris ranger station in 1925; in 1975 we made the 17 miles in one long day. It was dark by the time we reached the cabin at Norris which the park rangers had given us permission to use. There was a moment of panic when the key to the lock wouldn't fit. We didn't even consider breaking in. It was too late to dig a snow cave and we had visions of shivering in a snowdrift all night. But a ranger on patrol by snowmobile came along at the crucial moment and opened the cabin for us.

The next day was a breeze, 14 miles, nearly all downhill, alongside the silent Gibbon River under sunny skies. We had hot soup, tea and chocolate for lunch, heated in the overflow from Beryl Spring, where we had lunched on canned beans 50 years before. The old Madison ranger station where we spent Christmas Day in 1925 was long gone, but we had dinner in a comfortable apartment used to house seasonal rangers. Ranger Roger Olson, on patrol, joined us for a steak dinner and tales of long ago. He had kept track of us by phone throughout our trip. The next day, December 22, our families arrived from Old Faithful by snow coach and joined us for a side trip to Yellowstone's Grand Canyon.

There was nothing left of the old lodge and ranger station where we had enjoyed a pre-Christmas feast long ago. Even the Grand Canyon itself was showing its age. Inspiration Point, which jutted far out into the canyon 50 years ago, was gone — blasted away after it was weakened by an earthquake in June 1975. At daybreak December 23 we set out in a light snowstorm on the 17-mile trip to Old Faithful.

We never saw a living thing along our route in 1925. In 1975 we shared the road with a herd of shaggy bison, amiable elk and a skein of geese. Scores of elk and hundreds of bison grazed the Lower Geyser Basin, which was melted nearly free of snow. By afternoon the soothing silence was shattered by swarms of snowmobiles buzzing by like angry hornets.

We found Old Faithful more old than faithful. In 1925 Ranger Philips told us the famous geyser erupted about every 55 minutes. Fifty years later the average interval between eruptions had increased to about 67 minutes. The interval increased by about five minutes after the major earthquake of August 17, 1959. George D. Marler, park geologist, said that geyserite (from mineralized water) deposited at or near the vent was slowly sealing off Old Faithful.

The world famous Old Faithful Inn, "the world's largest log cabin," stood unscathed by the storms of 72 winters. Like Tennyson's brook it will go on forever, if fire and earthquakes do not bring it down. It was built in 1903 and 1904. One wing was added in 1913 and another in 1928, bringing the total rooms available to 370. The sight of the old inn, closed for the winter, brought back memories of trips into the park with my dad after the tourist season ended. As manager of the Copeland Lumber yard at Bozeman, Dad made many a trip to the lodge to estimate lumber required for repairs. On one trip he ran into a bear hibernating under the lodge. Dad beat a hasty retreat. He told of one carpenter working on a lodge building who was cornered by a bear and had to kill the ursine prowler with an axe. "The rangers hauled him up before a board of inquiry as if he had killed a man," Dad recalled.

As we approached Old Faithful in the fading light of late afternoon our families skied out to meet us. We were so weary that we barely missed a stride to greet them in our haste to reach the end of the trail and a hot tub. Virginia, the light of my life, was joined by Mary Jeanne, Durkee's wife, and our grandsons, Bradley and Trevor. George was met by his wife Ann and Glenn by his wife Vi. Butch's wife was at home under a doctor's care.

It was a Christmas that will live in memory forever. We stayed in modest rooms without running water in the snow lodge behind Old Faithful Inn. Vi Muchow had brought a special tiny tree with Christmas lights as the centerpiece of a surprise party complete with cookies, candy, fruit cake and hand-wrought Christmas candle holders as gifts for each family. We had hamburgers for dinner then sat around and feasted on Christmas goodies while Christmas carols filled the air. Then the gang began to remember all the old songs, from "Springtime in the Rockies" to "Home on the Range" and, of course, "Clementine," while Bradley and Trevor played with their pet rocks. That was when pet rocks were all the rage and their maternal grandmother, Amanda Hopper, seeking some presents that were small enough to fit in a packsack and could not be broken, hit on the idea of pet rocks. She had polished and decorated them with her own hands. The pet rocks were a big hit with everyone except the manager of the snow lodge, who complained of the noisy pet rock races around the halls.

There's no place like home for Christmas. But Christmas is where the heart is. And our hearts were shared with our families and friends that second Christmas in Yellowstone.

CHAPTER 4

HANDSHAKE TREATY

"Let the White Man leave!"

A mellow autumn moon cast a faint glow over Cultus Creek Campground. Hundreds of campers crowded the shadows. Children scurried from campfire to campfire. There was good old mountain music. There was wrestling and dancing.

It was September 1932, the depth of the Great Depression. Thousands of men, women and children without jobs had taken to the Twin Buttes area of the Columbia National Forest to live off the land. Normally only a few hundred outdoor lovers would camp out for a week or so in the string of primitive camp grounds in the area. But by September the rangers awoke to find a city of 7,000 homeless and penniless men, women and children living in a half dozen campgrounds from Smoky Creek to the Twin Buttes station. The Yakama Indians were ready to go on the warpath to repel this invasion of their usual and accustomed hunting grounds.

J. R. Bruckart, supervisor of what was then the Columbia National Forest, and his executive, K. P. Cecil, decided to survey the situation for themselves. They invited me to go along. I think we all expected to see slovenly camps, an air of bitter despair, or resentment. Instead we found an air of camaraderie, of almost jaunty self-confidence. Some families had only shelters built of boughs. Some had built makeshift shelters of ragged blankets and canvas. A few had nothing but the stars for covering and a fire to warm them.

Prolonged rains had added to the misery of the campers and delayed the ripening of the huckleberries. But there was no sense of despair. Brokers on Wall Street may have been jumping out of windows, but these jobless were not hopeless.

With the return of warm weather, pa, ma and the kids were picking up to ten gallons of berries in a long day, flooding the market, driving the price down to a paltry 30 cents a gallon in the field.

As night fell, the campers gathered around a fire in a natural clearing at the Cultus Creek campground for an old-fashioned hoedown. A small wooden platform had been built. The "Howling Coyotes" unlimbered violin, guitar and wind instruments and sang western ballads and old favorite tunes. An amateur trio wailed lugubrious lyrics of cowboy lore. Two professional wrestlers, out of work, spread plywood on the ground and put on a match with lots of action and no winners.

Young twins staged a tap dance to roars of applause from the crowd of 400 or 500 in the shadows. A young lady put on an exhibition of acrobatics, and there was a singalong that made up in volume what it lacked in harmony.

Bruckart mounted the stage and told the crowd how much he appreciated their care with fire in the forest and their cooperation in maintaining clean campgrounds.

LAST BIG POWWOW

Next day Bruckart and his men held the last authentic pow-wow with the Yakama Indian council. The Indians had complained that the hordes of whites were crowding them out of their traditional hunting and berrying grounds. Willie Yallup, chief of the Yakama Nation, called for a formal powwow. Bruckart, forest supervisor, met the tribal council on the shores of Surprise Lakes in the shadow of 12,120-foot Mount Adams on Friday, September 2, 1932, in a scene reminiscent of the powwows of 100 years ago.

The huckleberry harvest had already started. To dry the berries the Indian women dug a ditch alongside a long, dead log. The trench was sloped to face the log. A slow-burning fire was built in the bottom of the trench. The berries were spread out on blankets or burlap facing the fire. The log reflected the heat onto the berries, which were soon dried. Mixed with pemmican they made a hearty dish for the long winter. Other women smoked salmon in the traditional manner, split open and impaled on stakes.

Three tepees were erected near the shores of Surprise Lake for the principal chiefs. Steam rose from a sweat lodge made of blankets stretched over a framework of willows in the brush nearby. Men, women and children stood silently in a wide circle around the site, watching intently.

Chief Yallup rose to his feet, clad in his ceremonial robes, erect as one of his native pine trees, his long grey braids hanging down to his waist. He spoke, through an interpreter, with solemn eloquence:

"This is my land," he said. "I own it. It has always been so. Time beyond time, long as the old men can remember, my young braves have come here to hunt the deer, the elk and the bear. My squaws have gathered the huckleberries.

"Now, in the last two years, whites, thick as the needles on the firs, have driven our squaws from the berry fields. Our young men, too, are arrested for hunting the deer. Yet our treaty, signed in 1855, gives us the right to hunt, fish and gather berries for all time in our usual and accustomed places.

"So let the white man leave. This is our land!"

Other tribal elders also rose to speak. Job Charlie, jolly sub chief, wrapped in a wrinkled overcoat, spoke through an interpreter, although he spoke English fluently.

"Squaws tell me about an old squaw picking berries near our camp. She had her basket behind her and put berries in there. Then she hear berries go tinkle, tinkle. She looked around and there was white woman holding her pail so squaw dropped berries in white woman's pail."

There were smiles and knowing nods around the circle of watchers. One old woman with white hair and cheeks blackened by many summer suns, stood and told how she used to skin out the bears that the braves shot in the berry fields. She demanded the right to hunt the bear like in the old days. "I need the bear grease for my belly," she declared, slapping herself in the belly for emphasis.

Supervisor Bruckart rose to his feet, saluted the circle of chiefs and spoke in measured tones, with time for his words to be interpreted. The Forestry chief met every complaint with sympathy and diplomacy. "My heart is with the Indians," he said. "This has indeed been the Indian's land from time beyond memory. The land has been the Indian's mother. The Indian

38

has protected the land and preserved it, just as the land has nourished the Indian.

"But then the white man came and the Indians had to share the country with them. I myself was placed here by the Great White Father to see that all people enjoyed the forest equally. I cannot exclude the white man from the berry fields or I would also have to exclude the Indians," he said.

"I have no power over the treaty," he explained. Recent rulings by the Washington State Supreme Court have virtually abrogated the treaty. The court ruling requires the Indians to have a license to hunt off their reservation.

"My heart is with the Indian," he said. "I will do everything I can for your people. But I have no power over the treaty." He advised the chiefs to talk to C. R. Whitlock, their Indian agent, and appeal to the courts.

"I have no power over the treaty," Bruckart repeated. "But I can and I will set aside an area including Surprise Lakes and Cold Springs for the exclusive use of the Indians during the huckleberry season."

His pronouncement was greeted with nods, smiles and pleased grunts from the chiefs and murmurs of approval from the tight circle of watchers.

Slowly Chief Yallup rose to his feet and said, "I have spoken to the end. Nothing is hidden in my heart. Your words give me happiness. You are my friend. Now all is well between my people and your people."

Signs were quickly posted reserving the area for the Indians. They were still there, 51 years later, in 1983 when Iris Billy of the Yakama Nation invited me to be the guest of the council of chiefs at a revival of their traditional feast of Thanksgiving and celebration of what the Indians mistakenly thought was the fiftieth anniversary of the handshake treaty.

Virginia's sister, Dorothy Harris, and her husband J. W., Virginia, and I arrived a day early and set up camp. I learned that I would be asked to speak before the council, so I made some hurried notes.

The ceremonies this time were held in a modern "longhouse" of poles and plastic built to hold about 100 celebrants and guests. Frederick Ike, chief of the Yakama council, sat on reed mats at the front of the area with seven sub chiefs and elders, three of them with traditional Indian hand held drums.

The ceremonies started with solemn speeches of welcome. Then I was introduced as the only surviving witness to that 1932 handshake treaty.

In the hyperbole expected on such occasions, I greeted the principal chiefs by name, Chief Fredy Ike, Chief Moses Dick and Chief Sam Billy: "Klawaha, in 50 years of reporting I have been to the ends of the earth and 75 nations in between. I have been bitten by a duck, kicked by a reindeer and mistaken for a penguin's egg (showing my chrome dome). I have hobnobbed with presidents and paupers, kings and commoners, movie stars and Mafia. But never have I been more honored than to be invited to speak to this distinguished council of the First Americans.

"It was less than 51 years ago that I witnessed the first pow-wow on this site. I had hair then, long and thick as the needles on the pine. But one of your young braves mistook me for a game warden, slipped up behind me and scalped me. (Hat off). Now I am known as the Bald Eagle."

That tickled the Indian sense of humor.

After preliminary religious ceremonies a few of the season's first huckleberries were served to guests and then to the hosts. The ankutty tillicum, the ancient people, would not touch the ripe huckleberries until they had first thanked their gods for the bounty of the earth.

The first salmon was treated with reverence and small pieces were shared with guests and then the hosts. The tyee (chief) or shaman (medicine man) pleaded with The Swimmer's spirit to return to his river world and tell his people how respectfully he was treated, lest the salmon become angry and refuse to return to the Indians' nets.

The young braves had been busy hunting deer while the game warden turned his back. One young Indian lad had killed his first deer, which hung from a tree near the cooking fires. Poaching was tolerated as long as the deer was used for religious purposes. Token bits of deer meat and elk meat were passed around with similar ceremony.

After everyone had feasted to the limit, Chief Ike proclaimed a potlatch. Valuable gifts, ranging from beaded bags to baskets woven of squaw grass or bear grass, moccasins and rare coins were passed out to distinguished guests. I still cherish the pair of soft, beaded deerskin gauntlets that I took home from that potlatch.

That oral treaty, sealed with a handshake, has been scrupulously observed ever since, while many a treaty, inscribed on parchment or deer hide, sealed with pomp and ceremony, has been broken or badly bent. In the summer of 1991, a fitting monument to nearly six decades of mutual trust and respect was unveiled on a site overlooking Surprise Lakes where the handshake treaty was first consummated.

The central carving on the massive cedar monument depicts the handshake that brought peace to the Indian hunting grounds. The Indians, now free to hunt without licenses for subsistence and religious purposes in their usual and accustomed haunts, shot three elk for the religious feast that followed the dedication. They served salmon freely netted in the nearby Columbia River. As the sun sank behind the Sawtooth Mountains in the west, the Indians gathered around their camp fires to greet the night with endless, animated stick games.

Editor's note:

The monument may be reached on paved logging roads by driving west out of Trout Lake on Forest Road 141 to the 88 road. Turn right (north) on Forest Road 88. Follow 88 to Forest Road 24, (about 17 miles); turn left (south) onto the 24 road and follow it about five miles to the monument at Surprise Lakes.

Huckleberries are found all along this route from early August to late September, varying in abundance from place to place and season to season. Deer and elk may be seen early in the morning or late in the evening. The latest information is available at the district ranger station about a quarter mile west of Trout Lake on the 141 road.

CHAPTER 5

SHEER TERROR

"Flying is hours of boredom, followed by moments of sheer terror."- Anonymous

YOU SHOULD HAVE CAUGHT FIRE!

It was the kind of a day that makes you feel glad to be alive.

Oregonian photographer Jim Vincent and I were just beginning to relax, cruising along at 9,000 feet in smooth air just north of 12,120-foot Mount Adams October 1, 1975 in #1774, a 260-horsepower, fuel-injected Beechcraft, when it happened. We were passing the one stretch of rugged terrain where there was no place to make an emergency landing. Suddenly the engine began to run violently rough, threatening to tear itself out of its mounts. I throttled back to idle and headed for Ephrata, Washington's busy airport about 20 miles away while I tuned the airport unicom frequency and declared an emergency. No one answered.

I could see light planes in the pattern shooting landings and continued to call as we limped closer, losing about 500 feet per minute. I was maneuvering to line up for our final approach when the engine finally quit altogether. Just as we crossed the fence ready to touch down, a Cessna 172 cut in front of us. I had to make a violent turn to avoid a collision. We managed to land across the runway and roll onto a taxiway without damage.

Jim Vincent has done a lot of flying for aerial pictures in his day. He's always been a nervous flier, alert to every vibration and every change in the song the engine sings. But when the chips were really down, he never jittered, never said a word.

The field mechanic opened the cowling and whistled loudly. "You guys should have caught fire," he said reassuringly. "You had a broken gas line spurting gas under high pressure onto your hot cylinders."

Our chances of surviving an engine fire in flight would have been close to nil. We have been living on borrowed time ever since.

Aircraft Specialties, the plane's owner in Vancouver, sent a mechanic who replaced the broken fuel line while we drove to Grand Coulee and back. We took the long way back to Vancouver, Washington, keeping emergency fields in sight all the way.

BARNYARD LANDING

Forced landings are as rare as eclipses of the sun in today's general aviation world. But they were as common as flat tires 50 years ago. Show me a man who has never had a forced landing and I will show you a liar, or a pilot who has never been out of the traffic pattern.

Actually I had my first emergency landing the first time I left the traffic pattern. I started flying November 23, 1938, in an old open cockpit Bird biplane owned by a club. I was tooling around the Charter Oak area, about 10 miles northeast of Pearson Field when suddenly I blew a spark plug right out of its socket at the top of the radial engine. The plane began to shake. I had visions of blowing the rest of the plugs in the five-cylinder Kinner engine. So I looked around and chose an open strip behind a barn.

I had to make a sharp turn just as I passed the barn, but I sat the old clunker in without damage. The mechanic, who would not want to be identified, (he had just given the plane a 25-hour check) came out, replaced the plug and flew the old Bird out of the field without bothering to notify the Federal Aviation Administration.

CPTP

Next time an engine quit in flight I was practicing spins above a hay field near Ontario, Idaho. The Air Corps was in desperate need of pilots, so I had volunteered for CPTP — Civilian Pilot Training Program.

I knew the wind direction and set up a glide to land into the gentle breeze. But as I got close to the ground the wind hit the hills and formed an eddy, giving me a light tail wind. I had to groundloop the Piper Cub to stop short of an irrigation ditch, breaking the wooden propeller. Instead of getting Hell from my tough flight instructor for breaking a prop I was commended for escaping with minor damage.

LOST OVER SAN FRANCISCO

Early in World War II I was stationed at Blythe, in the California desert, as a check pilot at a contract flight school. I had a dental emergency and took off at sunset in a big, awkward single-engine BT-13 headed for Mather Field, Sacramento, armed with the latest aeronautical charts, which weren't very late, as it turned out.

In those days you followed beams by ear — an A on the left and an N on the right. When the two blended into a steady tone you were on the beam. I was flying above a light overcast following the beam out of Fresno headed for Sacramento when I began to see pools of light that didn't look familiar. One was a bright light that looked like San Francisco. I figured I was lost. I wasn't sure if I had enough gas to reach Sacramento and make an instrument letdown.

For a few minutes I entertained the idea of bailing out. I wore a parachute just for such occasions and had long wanted to make a jump. The thought of the plane hitting a house down below crossed my mind. Then a really horrible thought struck me. "They'll make me pay for the airplane." It was that thought that killed the idea of bailing out.

I discarded the screwed up navigation chart and headed for the lights of Sacramento. It turned out that the north beam had been changed to lead to San Francisco instead of Sacramento, but we never received the new aeronautical chart at little old Blythe contract flight school.

LOST OVER THE ICE CAP

I was lost in a much more hostile part of the world back in 1952 when I was stationed in Greenland during the Korean crisis. We had no long range navigation beacons so we learned to tune in the carrier wave of the teletype that provided communications between Torbay and BW8. There was no way to positively identify it, but we were sure we had the right carrier wave until, as we got close we could no longer hear the carrier wave. We were too far out to lock onto the non-directional beacon or the GCA (ground controlled approach) at Sondrestrom Air Base halfway up the big island.

Then we got a lucky break. The clouds opened up long enough to reveal Sukortopen, a distinctive mound of snow and ice appropriately named sugar-topped. We called for a GCA and we quickly were on the ground. We stormed into the operations office and demanded to know what the heck had happened to the radio. The technician in charge admitted that he had taken the station off the air to make some adjustments without first checking to see if there was any inbound traffic depending on it. Fortunately for us the GCA operator was on duty and alert.

CHAPTER 6

TALK ABOUT THE WEATHER!

Everybody talks about the weather, but one spring day in 1947 we did something about it. We triggered the first fully documented manmade snow and rain storm.

"We" included *The Oregonian*, the U.S. Weather Bureau and Western Skyways, a Troutdale, Oregon aircraft company.

I got the idea from Vincent Schaefer, an alert, imaginative research scientist in Dr. Irving Langmuir's General Electric Laboratories in Massachusetts. Langmuir and Schaefer had precipitated snow from clouds in their laboratory, using powdered dry ice (frozen carbon dioxide at 110 below zero Fahrenheit) to supply submicroscopic crystals on which snow flakes could form. Schaefer then tried seeding a natural cloud with dry ice and reported a virga or veil of precipitation, which dissipated before it reached the ground. He had no convincing pictures to document his claim.

I persuaded Eckley S. Ellison, senior meteorologist of the U.S. Weather Bureau in Portland, to try our own cloud seeding experiment. Ellison, a World War I veteran, had developed the use of smoke pots to save orchards from frost in Florida. He had earned the rank of lieutenant colonel as an expert on smoke screens in World War II.

I sold the city editor, Malcolm Bauer, on the idea. I persuaded Ernie Helms, manager of Western Skyways aircraft sales and service at Troutdale airport, to provide aircraft for the venture. Then we waited impatiently for the right weather conditions to develop. We needed a day when towering cumulus clouds covered most of the sky without producing any rain.

Such a day dawned April 4, 1947. The sky was covered with cumulus clouds with tops at about 10,000 feet, but no rain was falling anywhere within 100 miles.

Colonel Ellison sounded the alarm. I think we all felt a little sheepish after thinking things over for a week. It sounded like a cockamamie scheme. We would all look pretty silly if nothing happened.

But the lure of adventure gripped us all. The task force assembled on Pearson Air Park in Vancouver. Ellison took off at 11:10 a.m., Friday April 4, 1947, in the back seat of a war surplus single-engined BT-13 with Ernie Helms at the controls. I took off in loose formation, with Hugh Ackroyd, top Portland aerial and news photographer, in the back seat.

Bob Tomlinson, Navy veteran and KGW'S star radio announcer; Owen Cramer and Howard E. Graham, meteorologists from the Portland Weather Bureau, climbed into a single-engined, four-place high winged Stinson 150 flown by Russell Means, Western Skyways instructor. They were to watch and photograph the experiment as qualified observers.

There was no radar, no air traffic control in those days. But we were all linked by a common radio frequency. Helms and Ellison simply climbed to 10,000 feet, the top of the clouds, at a point a mile or so east and south of Troutdale airport.

Ellison rolled back his canopy and tossed out a few handfuls of dry ice pellets. The observers in the Stinson flying below the clouds reported a dark virga or veil of precipitation falling out of the seeded cloud and extending in a line to the south.

Ackroyd and I stayed in formation with the lead BT13 as he headed further east. There, at about 10,200 feet, Ellison sowed the rest of his 17 pounds of seeds. The fluffy white cauliflower cloud tops seemed to boil a little, but nothing worth mentioning. For awhile we thought we had failed.

Then we dived down through a break in the clouds to the 2,000 foot level, about 800 feet above Crown Point, the famous gateway to the Columbia River Gorge. It was an exciting moment. Suddenly we were flying through huge snow flakes, enough to plaster the canopy and obscure our forward vision. Fat flakes whipped in through the open canopy and plastered Ackroyd's big aerial camera.

I confess to moments of exaltation, a feeling of power and glory. We, puny victims of nature's weather tricks, had tricked Mother Nature into spilling her guts!

The snow and rain fell in a major storm extending about 10 miles to the south, along the line of our seeding flight, dumping hundreds of tons of snow and rain on Larch Mountain, south and west of Crown Point, Ellison estimated. Streamers of snow trailed out of the clouds like bridal veils at some ethereal wedding. And all this from a mere 17 pounds of dry ice, which cost a few dollars.

Most of the snow melted and fell as rain. It was a comparatively warm day in April. The freezing level was 3,500 feet. There were no official weather reporting stations in the path of the storm. But scores of residents of the area called *The Oregonian* and the Weather Bureau to report the snow and rain. Mrs.

Orr of Route 1, Corbett, Oregon, who lived about 2.5 miles southeast of Crown Point, was one of the first to report snow reaching the ground.

"It was about noon when I noticed wet snow coming down in sort of balls rather than flakes," she told *The Oregonian.* "The flurry lasted for five or ten minutes, then turned to rain," she said.

Ellison and his fellow meteorologists certified officially that this was, indeed, the first major man-made snow and rainstorm on record. Ellison had become the first Weather Bureau official to make rain.

"There is no doubt that the dry ice precipitated the snowstorm," Ellison said. "These cumulus clouds had reached their maximum development without resulting in any shower activity anywhere in the area. A temperature inversion at 10,200 feet prevented natural shower development."

The story hit the headlines around the world and started a flurry of commercial cloud seeding operations by farmers, ski resorts and power companies who wanted to increase their snow and water supplies. Dry ice was used to dissipate the fog over the runways at Portland International Airport, Medford and other fields.

Generators were developed for use on the ground to send up plumes of submicroscopic silver iodide particles into the air. The particles provided nuclei to trigger formation of snowflakes, which fell as snow or rain. For years cloud seeding was pretty big business.

Cloud seeders became the target of lawsuits by farmers and others who blamed the cloud manipulators for floods and damaging snowstorms. The threat of suits discouraged public agencies like the power companies and ski resorts. Cloud seeders had trouble collecting for the snow they may have triggered. They had trouble proving which snowflakes were theirs and which were Mother Nature's.

So "weather modification" seems to have gradually faded away. Colonel Ellison wrote a full report on the experiment, complete with pictures and diagrams, endorsed by F. W. Reichelderfer, chief of the U.S. Weather Bureau. But when an administration hostile to cloud-seeding took over the Weather Bureau, Ellison's report vanished from the files. Ellison died in 1983, after 49 years of government service.

CHAPTER 7

PURPLE PEOPLE FROM PLUTO?

As I was going up the stair
I met a little man who wasn't there
He wasn't there again today
Oh, how I wish he 'd go away! - Anonymous.

That's the way it is with UFOS. After 44 years no one has captured one. But they refuse to go away.

I was working the night shift at *The Oregonian* newsroom June 24, 1947, the day that Kenneth Arnold, then 32, triggered the UFO avalanche. He reported seeing saucer-like objects so bright that they blinded him flying between Mount Rainier and Mount Adams at 1,200 miles an hour. He said first there was one undulating like a fish, then it split into three, then nine, then merged back into one and vanished.

He didn't report them to aeronautical radio stations at the time. But when he landed his single engine Callair in Pendleton, Oregon, the Associated Press put a bulletin on the wire. The story spread like wildfire.

The saucers' reported speed of 1,200 miles an hour was twice the official world's speed record of 647 miles an hour, recently set by a U.S. Air Force P80. Some "experts" speculated that Arnold had seen a secret new Army fighter plane. Others speculated that it was a mirage or optical illusion.

Other pilots were in the vicinity, including United Air Lines captain C. J. Smith who was flying a DC-3 over the route. But none of them saw the "saucers." Later, on July 8, Captain Smith reported that as he approached Boise, he saw flying saucers flying just off his left wing. He said first there was one, then five then they vanished suddenly. He said his copilot and stewardess Marty Morrow also saw it. The passengers all said they saw nothing.

Within a few days mass hysteria swept the country. Everyone from Seattle to Kansas City and Miami was seeing flying saucers. UFOs were reported skimming over Portland, Vancouver and Woodland. Every new UFO headline triggered a deluge of additional sightings. One Texas preacher declared this was a portent of the second coming of Christ. The Reverend Lester Carlson, La Grande Gospel pastor, issued a public statement declaring that the saucers signaled the end of the world.

On July 5 *Oregonian* reporter Paul Ewing took off from an Oregon City airstrip in a light plane flown by a private pilot to chase reported UFOs, but wound up "disc-gusted."

I'll reluctantly admit that I, too, briefly flew "UFO patrol." While on a night training flight as an Air Force Reserve pilot, in a C-46 twin-engine transport we responded to reports of a flying saucer over Portland, but found only a lighted weather balloon, released by the meteorologists to measure winds aloft.

For the next two years I chased down rumors of flying saucers throughout the area. By July 7, Air National Guard pilots at Portland Air Base, Boise, Idaho and Spokane were patrolling the skies for the elusive saucers, with negative results. Finally a national guard pilot died chasing a bright light in the sky. It was identified by control tower operators as the planet Venus.

Saucer believers found a piece of fused material which their experts identified as a piece of a spacecraft from another planet. It turned out to be a piece of slag from the Tacoma smelter.

Arnold later said he believed the objects he saw were living beings, with a round, pulsating heart in the middle of their backs. The last time I saw Arnold, years later, he came into The *Oregonian* newsroom and said he was searching for little green men from Mars. He said you find them in the shrubs at the edge of your garden.

Finally, in the late 1960s, the Air Force contracted with Edward Condon, a recognized authority on physics, to investigate the UFO phenomenon in Project Blue Book. After studying hundreds of reports the scientists explained all but a handful of incidents as natural phenomenon — lights of airplanes, helicopters, balloons, mirages and optical illusions. Physicists pointed out that nothing but a beam of light could dash across the sky at the speed of light and change course 90 or 180 degrees instantly as some UFOs were reported to do.

The fact that a handful could not be explained does not mean that they involve little purple people-eaters from Pluto. That was the conclusion of Robert J. Low, project coordinator, who later became assistant to the president of Portland State University.

Over the years UFOs faded out of the headlines, but surveys indicate that some 13 million Americans still believe in them and their alien passengers from outer space. Scores of believers still report being kidnapped by extraterrestrial beings.

One woman claimed that she was raped aboard a flying saucer and gave birth to a 42-pound dog child. Hundreds of books have been printed and scores of organizations issue newsletters and hold annual conventions on the latest developments in UFOs.

UFO sightings may go on forever. No convincing proof of the existence of creatures from outer space has yet been submitted.

But how do you prove that something isn't there if it isn't there?

CHAPTER 8

FOX ABLE 110

Flying the oceans today in single-seat fighters is strictly routine. But it was far from routine back in 1960 when I flew Mission Fox Able across the wide Atlantic. I was a pilot in the active Reserves writing a book on the Tactical Air Command.

It all began with a movement order from the "paper palace" [Pentagon] alerting the 309th Tactical Fighter Squadron of the 31st Wing, George Air Force Base, California, to take over the air defense commitment at Aviano, Italy, 7,650 statute miles away, on July 10, 1960. This was Fox Able 110 — the code name for "Fighters, Atlantic, the 110th crossing thereof."

The first leg of the flight brought us to England Air Force Base, Louisiana in three hours 10 minutes with plenty of time to hit the swimming pool to dodge the 93 degree heat.

Then the flight surgeon took over for the mandatory "crew conditioning" required to prepare pilots for nine hours or more of formation flying in a cockpit like a straitjacket without benefit of autopilot, navigator, radar or radio operator, or engineer. "Crew conditioning is a sort of charm school with pills and pistols added," the squadron cynic explained.

We were herded into the mess hall under guard and forced to eat choice steaks, cooked to order, with potatoes, carrots, peas, salad, bread but no butter, and a single glass of milk or fruit juice — no tea. This controlled meal provided 920 calories, with minimum bulk. We got the other 600 calories at breakfast.

At noon we got our final briefing on the mission. As we left we were handed two red capsules, "no-go" pills, secco barbital to induce sleep, and "go pills" — dexedrine, dextro amphetamine sulphate. "They do for the human machine what the afterburner does for the jet engine," Doc Lee, the flight surgeon, explained. I never use sleeping pills, but I took my pills as ordered and fell asleep before I could get my socks off. When the wakeup call came I was still bouncing off the walls.

Just climbing into the cockpit ten feet off the ground, clad like a knight of old in cumbersome armor and weighed down with all this gear is a major undertaking in the dark. Strapping on the airplane is serious business: 1) First the parachute, then the shoulder harness, then the seat belt was fastened with the lanyard in place. The lanyard will open the parachute at 15,000 feet after bailout. 2) Then the dinghy pack in the seat was secured to rings on the parachute. 3) Connect the pressure hose to the partial pressure suit. 4) Connect the oxygen hose to the parachute fitting and plug in your oxygen mask. 5) Plug in the earphones. Fit helmet mask and test for oxygen leaks. 6) Hook the lanyard to the D-ring of your parachute, to open your chute instantly if you have to bail out at low altitude on takeoff. 7) Pull the safety pins. These prevent you from accidentally blowing off the canopy and ejecting yourself onto the concrete while parked on the ramp if you happen to hit the "next-of-kin" button which activates the ejection seat.

Sharp at 2:15 a.m. we start engines. At 2:25 a.m. Colin Leader called, "Colin Alfa flight, check in."

"One-one, lanyard, dinghy."

"One-two, lanyard, dinghy."

Each in turn acknowledged the radio check. Each noted his lanyard was fastened to his D-ring for low-level bailout, and that the seat pack containing the dinghy was fastened to his parachute harness.

"Ground Control, Colin one-zero and flight of eight, taxi instructions." The eight ghostly figures, flashing silver in the mellow Louisiana moonlight, began bobbing eerily through the dark, red and green wing lights playing a crazy tune in the night.

Colin Leader pulled onto the runway. His chicks cuddled up close behind. In the bitter black of the night, off the end of the runway a helicopter orbited ominously. Its searchlight probed the ground with a bright finger of light, looking hopefully for any of our birds that might falter and fall in flames on takeoff. A blowout or flameout at that critical moment could roll an F-100 into a ball of flaming Hell. A team of men clad in heavy asbestos suits was on hand to pull us out of the fire if we fell in flames.

"If she coughs on takeoff, punch out. Don't wait for me or you'll be talking to yourself," my pilot, Archie Lorentzen, said on the hot mike in a last-minute briefing. "I'll blow the canopy. But you have to eject first in this buggy, else you may get my feet in your face. If she flames, watch the altimeter and the airspeed. I'll pull her up. When we quit climbing and the airspeed starts dying off, hit the next-of-kin-button. Punch out. Be sure your lanyard is fastened. That'll pull your ripcord the second your seat belt blasts loose. Don't wait. Grab the D-ring yourself, and kick free of the seat. You only need a hundred feet of altitude to get out, if you act fast."

The tower cut in: "Colin Alfa, cleared for takeoff."

Major Prevost's gray ghost and the lights of his wingman

started to roll slowly. Suddenly the quiet of the night was shattered by a double explosion, bright blue and yellow daggers of flame stabbed the dark as the two lead ships fired their afterburners. Shock diamonds, like hoops of blue flame within the cone of white flame, testified to the speed of the angry fire that shot out of their tails — faster than the speed of sound.

Eight ...nine ...ten seconds and Lorentzen released our brakes and abruptly we began to waddle slowly down the runway. There was a dull pow and we were kicked gently in the tail as our own afterburner lit off, shoving us ahead the way a man shoves a boy on a swing. Faster and faster we gathered speed through the muggy night, our wheels bumping over the joints in the runway like the wheels of a streamlined train picking up speed as it roars out of the yard. Then the bumps smoothed out as we took to the air, pursuing and pursued by torches flaming brightly in the night.

The drowsy Louisiana night was hideous with noise as the gaggle of metal monsters clawed their way into the sky, wave after wave, roaring as if the Devil were after them. You'd roar, too, if your tail was on fire, shooting a cone of white-hot flame 15 feet out behind. Stabbed in the pants by this dagger of flame, our 19-ton juggernaut gathered speed, accelerating faster and faster as its speed increased. A jet's power grows with its speed. In a matter of seconds our indicator showed that we had hit 350 knots, climbing all the while.

"AB out ... now," comes the command from Colin Leader. And we died in mid-air. We seemed to stop and back up as the massive thrust of the afterburner was cut off. The pillar of flame was gone. The muffled roar of the blast from Colin Leader, faintly audible even through our pressurized cockpit and foam rubber earphones, died out. The night was strangely quiet now.

As the lights faded and our eyes grew accustomed to the darkness, the silver form of the lead F-100s become faintly visible, like astral minnows swimming up the depths of the night into the bright moonlight above.

"HOLYS check," Colin Leader cuts in. That's "H" for hydraulic system. Is it working? "O" for oxygen. Is that fluorescent eye blinking reassuringly as you breathe, measuring the flow of oxygen? "L" is for lanyard. Is the lanyard disconnected from the D-ring of your parachute? If not, both you and your parachute could be torn apart if you had to eject suddenly at this speed. "Y" is for yaw damper. Is it turned on to automatically keep the aircraft on a straight course when rough air is encountered? Early F-100s were torn apart when the nose yawed too far to one side in high speed flight. "S" is for the gun sight. No need to turn it on for this flight.

Back to the beauty of the night. The tensions of takeoff were gone. The younger pilots were still working hard to get into formation and stay there in the black of the night. But they were relaxed now. Nothing soothes the anxious spirits of a pilot like the miracle of flight. The air is his element. Flying is his life.

Lieutenant Lorentzen was talking to himself again. Happy talk. "Hmmm… We've got hydraulic pressure. Circuit breaker is staying put. Nice. Fuel flowing, or is it? That right drop tank's not feeding."

"Check tanks," Colin Leader orders.

"One-three, drop tanks not feeding," Archie answers.

"Check your bleed air," Colin comes back.

"Roger. That's it. Bleed air valve open. Feeding now," Lorentzen replied.

Peace descended upon the Colin Alfa flight. It was a time of quiet; with nothing to do but keep the direction-finding radio tuned to the station ahead and watch the Tacan count off the miles as we swam through the velvet night. We were on airways, our eight-ship section flying as one, checking in over each station like a single airliner. We rose to 29,000 feet, our assigned altitude. It was Colin Leader's job to navigate and report in. But we were navigating, too. We would take the lead if Major Prevost had to abort. We double checked his navigation in case his radios failed.

We had left Jackson, Mississippi, behind and were closing on Tuscaloosa, Alabama. Birmingham was hard ahead, and we turned east to Augusta. The lights of Atlanta peeked through the clouds below — a pot full of diamonds spilled on velvet cloth. A few rubies and emeralds sparkled there, too.

The beauty of the night began fading slowly. The moon was growing old and pale. The sky was turning green in the east — and about time, too! It was 3:30 a.m. and black clouds were looming up ahead.

"Close up," Colin Leader orders. But his silver chicks had seen the black wall looming ahead and were already scurrying for cover close under his gray wings. He had the only paint job in the squadron — a light gray — which gave him a ghostly look in the greenish light of predawn. We penetrated the lazy cloud in a matter of minutes and were in the clear again. The sky had a copper glow in the north. That could not be east.

Now the tankers began calling. "Colin Alfa, this is Shirk one-zero. I have a target southwest at 140 miles. Squawk three."

Our IFF [Identification, Friend or Foe] was already broadcasting pattern number three, which should have been received on the KB50J tanker's radar screen.

"Strangle three and squawk two," Shirk one-zero commands." And we switched to transmit pattern two.

"Target confirmed. We are 140 miles northeast of you," Shirk reported. Then, we forgot the airways and started following "steers" from Shirk one-zero.

"Steer one-one-zero," Shirk responded.

"Who's playing games?" Major Prevost demanded. "We couldn't be that far off course."

"The tankers are making a wide turn in formation in their holding pattern, turning onto course for the refueling run," Shirk one-zero explained. Their position was changing rapidly, not ours. We stayed on course. We were 18 miles out... 15... 12.

"Dive brakes down ...now," Colin Leader ordered. And we started down at 3,000 feet per minute.

The sky was blushing a ruddy red. The sun was about to burst into flame at any minute.

"Bogeys at 12 o'clock level," Colin one-four reported.

There in the molten rays of the rising sun we dimly made out four flat worms swimming through the red hot lava of the sky like Manta rays in a red surf. Our flight was spread out a bit, still in formation. Each element of two picked its tanker. Then Major Prevost gave the order to change to tanker frequency. Each pair of jets could talk directly to its tanker, but to no one else.

The tankers' lights flashed dimly against the dawn. For night refueling the tankers were lit up like Broadway. Bright lights were directed at the hoses from the tail of the plane, while more lights picked out the hose reel pods. Red and green lights blinking like pinball machines on the reel pods told the fighter pilot when he was getting fuel and when he was not; when to stand by and when to back off. The tankers, illuminated this way, have been mistaken for flying saucers. The fighters, too, have bright lights that spotlight their probes during refueling. We were about to be parties to a minor miracle that was the secret of TAC's ability to race with giant strides around the world in any direction, gun in hand. It was called AAR (Air-to-Air Refueling.)

It is impossible, as any sane civilian pilot will tell you. It's like giving a transfusion in mid-air from a lumbering pelican to a fleet falcon, with your eyes shut. The fighter pilot's "needle" is behind his back where he can't see it.

Against the ruddy sky the tankers gradually took the shape of flying grasshoppers with their ovipositors thrust out far behind. Upon close inspection they assumed the appearance of medieval monsters with their entrails hanging out. But these were not pterodactyls. Those were not intestines. Those were long black hoses, 80 feet to be exact, trailing 67 feet behind. On the end was a tassel that looked like a feather duster. This was the drogue, a wire basket whose steel fingers opened up into a funnel shape held open by a ribbon of parachute silk on the ends of the fingers. But to the pilot of our two-place F100F they looked no bigger than a badminton bird.

He was now faced with the obviously impossible task of impaling this elusive bird on the end of the darning needle, called a probe, that sticks out of the right wing of the plane. It was so far behind the pilot that he could not see the probe he was trying to thrust into the drogue. This game of jet-propelled badminton played at 20,000 to 25,000 feet over the middle of the icy Atlantic Ocean while dodging thunderbumpers at 230 knots-indicated (265 MPH); would have been fun if the stakes had not been so high.

The first refueling was just off the Atlantic coast. The others would be near islands, in case of an emergency landing. The margins were necessarily narrow. The slightest bump set the hose to swinging violently. Even in fairly smooth air it could break a canopy if it hit the considerable expanse of plexiglass. That not only meant explosive decompression, with the sudden loss of cabin pressure, but possible loss of the oxygen mask as well.

If nothing worse, it means descending to lower altitude to keep warm and get sufficient oxygen to breathe. The lower the altitude the higher the fuel consumption, which meant that the crippled plane not only could not keep up with the rest of the flight, but might not be able to make land on the fuel aboard. The only solution was to land at the nearest island, or to turn back to the coast if there was enough fuel available.

Refueling at night or in severe turbulence is like bobbing for apples, blindfolded. The hose can whip around viciously, while at the same time the tanker and the jet are being booted about brutally in rough air.

The trick was to forget that silly bird bobbing about off your right wing and "fly" the pod on the tip of the tanker's wing which houses the hose reel. First, we would slow down to 230 knots (265 MPH), the tankers' maximum speed. Then we put down 15 degrees of flaps. Lorentzen put the flap switch down, counted to ten, then pulled the circuit breaker to stop the flaps at 15 degrees.

"Look at him. He's leering at me like a shark with a worm in his mouth." Lorentzen was talking to himself again. "See — that trap door for the hose is just like a shark. His mouth is sneering at me. I'll show him," Lorentzen muttered. "Little left rudder trim. Little left aileron. Now drive her right on in."

And he did. With a nudge of the throttle he socked the probe home into the bobbing drogue. The trick now was to fly tight formation within five to ten feet of that wing tip reel pod up ahead while the reel operator on the tanker poured fuel into our thirsty tanks.

"Valves open. Fuel coming aboard," Lorentzen reported.

"You've got 1,000 pounds," Shirk one-two reported. "Stand by."

We weren't going anywhere without fuel anyway. There was a two-minute pause while all eight planes in our flight got hooked up and took on 1,000 pounds of fuel to be sure everything was operating properly. Then Colin Leader gave the order to take fuel. The tankers started pouring the JP4, lifeblood of the jets, aboard at 53 pounds per square inch pressure, about 200 gallons per minute. As the added weight of the fuel poured aboard, Lorentzen poured on more and more throttle until his throttle was wide open. Even before that moment, however, Colin One-Four, on the right wing of our tanker, had reached full throttle and was starting to fall back, while the reel operator unrolled more and more hose.

"Toboggan, toboggan," Colin One-Four called out.

And the big tanker gently poked its nose down and began to go downhill. This not only increased speed, which gave the heavy jets more lift, but enabled them to tilt their noses downward to relieve the high angle of attack which verged on a stall. At this new speed and shallow angle of dive with full throttle, they were able to hang on and take the full load, 8,500 pounds of fuel, precalculated for this refueling.

"You've got 8,500 pounds. Fuel pressure off," Shirk One-Two informed his hungry customers.

Then came another intolerable wait while all the fighters got their full loads. Holding tight formation on the wing of the mother ship was harder now, with a heavier load and no margin of power to play with. Someone was having trouble. We could not tell who. His tanks weren't filling as they should. Finally the command came to "top tanks". We took on another 300 pounds of fuel, 8,800 pounds in all. Now everyone's tanks were full. We switched back to Colin Leader's frequency. He called for us to check in, asked for a fuel check and then gave the word.

"Colin Alfa flight, AB ...now."

At this speed and altitude the afterburner hit us hard, snapping our heads back against the head rests. In a matter of seconds our speed had built up from 230 to 390 knots climbing speed and then some.

"AB out ...now," came the word and we were back to normal power for the climb back to 31,000 feet.

We had finished refueling just about on schedule. We were allowed no more than five minutes to hook up and no more than 10 minutes total to take on our load of fuel and back off the tankers. If you couldn't get hooked up in five minutes, you would be too far from land and too low on fuel to return to Myrtle Beach, your alternate. Or if you hit "bingo" fuel any time before that deadline you had to break off and run for it. "Bingo fuel" is the minimum amount required to reach your alternate for a safe landing.

Our tankers had a "bingo", too. They had to turn around and get back into position to rendezvous with the second wave of eight F-100s at the same spot where they had picked us up. And they had to save enough fuel to give them the same load they had given us. They couldn't give us more without shorting the second flights and causing them to abort.

Now we were relaxed, floating along over the Atlantic like painted planes on a painted sky. Colin Leader was calling Picket Ship Consult, our next check point, and getting no answer.

Suddenly my head caught fire. And then the other end. Same thing was happening to Lorentzen and most of the other pilots.

The flight surgeons had warned us this would happen. It

always does with leather helmet liners after sitting stone still in a cramped cockpit for hours concentrating on flying formation, unable to stretch or fidget. It was purely a physiological phenomenon called "stagnant hypoxia." The weight of the brain bucket resting on the brain box cuts off circulation and induces a fiery sensation that feels as if your head had caught fire. The only solution is to rub the hot spot, restore circulation. The same thing happens on the other end. Your pants catch fire, rather suddenly. The solution is to fidget and shift about and rub your afterburner. It is simple enough if you're riding the mother-in-law seat in the back end of an F-100-F.

But how do the sprogs alone in the single cockpit of the F-100DS manage to massage their heads clockwise and their other ends counterclockwise while flying formation at 31,000 feet? They are keeping their ears on the radio and their eyes on the fuel flow. They don't. They squirm and twist as best they can until their fundaments gradually grow numb. Improved seats, helmets and auto pilots have pretty well eliminated the problem in today's state-of-the-art missile-packing fighters.

And so, nine hours and three refuelings later we landed at Aviano, Italy "without incident." The return trip to Charleston, South Carolina took 13 hours, grinding and bumping along in a C-124 at 8,000 feet. I thought the flight would never end.

CHAPTER 9

AIR BEAT

I was released from active duty in the Air Force in October 1945, but continued to fly in the Air Force Reserve squadron based at Portland Air Base. Flying was my life. We quickly incorporated the airplane as a major tool in covering the news in Oregon, one of the biggest states in the union — tenth biggest to be exact.

The airplane dramatically proved its value on June 24, 1959, when a B-52 crashed in the rugged desert near Burns, Oregon, killing all aboard. The Air Force urgently needed a bomber that could fly on the deck, under the enemy radar screen. The huge, ungainly bomber, designed for high altitude missions, had been flying low level tests over the high deserts of Oregon and Washington to see if it could survive the violent turbulence generated by the desert heat. It did not.

It would have taken over six hours to drive the 288 miles to Burns, and no telling how long to find the wreckage and walk in to the site. It was the *"Oregonian* air force" to the rescue.

Photographer Dave Falconer and I loaded an A.P. wirephoto machine and A.P. technician Duane Jones into the single-engine Beechcraft and made a beeline for Burns. We covered the 200 miles in an hour and 25 minutes.

As we approached Burns we lucked out. We sighted the scattered tatters of aluminum that marked the crash site. We landed on a nearby dry lake bed, dodging rocks not seen from the air, and hiked the 200 yards to the site. We got our pictures and took off for Burns. It was getting dark by the time we reached the uncontrolled airport. I made an approach to the unlighted runway and was about to set her down when I spotted a light plane standing on its nose in the middle of the runway. I pulled up and went around, landing short and taxiing around the disabled plane.

We hitched a ride into town with our gear, looked up the editor of the local weekly, *The Burns Times-Herald*. We developed and printed the pictures in his laboratory and put them on the wire in plenty of time for the third edition.

FLYING FOR NEWS

The Oregonian became one of the first, if not the first to use aircraft as a tool in covering the remote corners of the state. The airplane was made to meet *The Oregonian's* need to cover one of the largest, most rugged beats in the country. Oregon, 368 road miles from north to south and 389 road miles from east to west, barricaded behind five mountain ranges, was one of the least populated, least accessible states in the lower 48. In one 10-year period I logged more than 1,000 hours covering the far corners of the state — and incidentally, saving the paper thousands of dollars in travel expenses and overtime.

When the powers that be in 1985 discovered, to their surprise, that I had been on the payroll for 50 years, they threw a party — probably a subtle hint that time was running out. They probably thought they had fired me years ago.

In rebuttal to the eulogies, I orally handed publisher Fred Stickel a bill for $10,000 in back flight pay. That is only $10 an hour, a fraction of the going rate for commercial pilots. But Stickel knew, and I knew that I would rather fly than eat and would gladly have paid The Oregonian for the chance to fly.

TALL SHIP

In June 1972, the Japanese sent their sail training ship *Kaiwo Maru*, manned by cadets, to represent the Land of the Rising Sun at Portland's Rose Festival. The *Kaiwo Maru* wasn't much to look at as it motored up the Columbia River under power with its sails furled and its rigging flapping idly in the breeze.

Under full sail her cloud of billowing canvas rivalled nature's own clouds. Problem was she carried her full complement of canvas only on the high seas. That's where the city desk wanted pictures for first edition. So I checked out in a Cessna Skymaster with two 200-horsepower engines, one fore, the other aft. Jim Vincent volunteered to do the shooting. Andy Mershon, from the copy desk signed on as "jump master". We borrowed life jackets and life rafts because the Federal air regulations required them aboard planes flying out of sight of land — and because none of us could swim worth a darn.

The skipper of the *Kaiwo Maru* estimated his position would be 46 N. latitude; 126 and 22 seconds west longitude at 10 a.m. So we flew to Newport and headed out over the ocean, guided by the Newport VOR (visual omni range). Flying low above a thin undercast we soon lost the beam. (Ever notice how the engines go into automatic rough the minute you lose sight of land?)

Now we were flying by dead reckoning. But what if we

reached our estimated rendezvous point and could not spot the *Kaiwo Maru*? Would we turn north or south, right or left? If we guessed wrong we would be lost.

But I remembered a strategy used by navigator's flying drop missions to the South Pole in Operation Deep Freeze II. They plotted their courses a couple of degrees to the right of the target (all directions are north at the South Pole.) When their time ran out they turned left and followed the sun line to find the drop zone at the pole site.

We were relying on this technique when we dropped down through the low undercast and levelled off just above the waves. As we cleared the last of the clouds what should our wondering eyes behold but a great white cloud skimming over the waves with a bone in her teeth. We had scored a bullseye. We circled the tall ship while Vincent squinted through a side window in the cockpit no bigger than a pie plate, to shoot a couple of rolls of film. Then we headed for home in time to make first edition with some sensational shots.

It was not until we reached the city room that we learned the skipper of the *Kaiwo Maru* had transmitted a new estimated position after we took off. The corrected position was about 10 miles north of his first estimate, precisely where we had aimed.

TRAPPED ON HOODOO BUTTE

August 1967 was one of the worst seasons for forest fires in years. Hot weather and low humidity turned Oregon's forests into tinder, just waiting for lightning to strike. And strike it did. Monday, August 28, dry lightning bombarded Oregon's Southern Cascades. Early on Tuesday, August 29, the dispatcher for Region Six of the U.S. Forest Service in Portland reported more than 400 strikes.

That spelled disaster. So I asked for a photographer and reserved a high-winged Cessna 182 with a window that would open for aerial pictures. David Hume Kennerly, a new addition to the photo staff, met me at Pearson Air Park and we took off at 8 a.m.

The day was bright and clear in the wake of the night's lightning storm. Columns of smoke rose like signal fires as far as the eye could see. We headed for the Big Lake fire on the crest of the Cascades near Santiam Junction. Fat red flames boiled furiously around the base of the plume of smoke that rose like a volcanic eruption from the virgin forest.

I spotted a DC-3 loaded with smoke jumpers approaching the area and closed in for pictures of the jumpers leaping out of the open door. We were unable to keep up with the faster gooney bird, but got close enough for some spectacular pictures.

Then we returned to the Big Lake Airstrip fire. The airstrip showed on my aeronautical charts as open for use. From the air it looked clear of obstructions. I put down 20 degrees of flaps and started a slow approach. As I got down closer to the ground I could see some brush growing out of the runway surface. And at the far end of the field helicopters were landing and refueling.

We gave up on Big Lake, but the action on the ground was too good to miss. We spotted another airstrip in deep timber near the Santiam highway and circled to look it over. It was a one-way strip. We had to make a steep approach from the west and would have to take off to the west to avoid tall timber on the east end of the field. We set in a routine landing, hitched a ride in a pickup truck to the Big Lake airstrip and returned with some spectacular pictures of fires and fire fighters.

Two days later, Thursday, August 31, 1967, my logbooks show that Kennerley and I returned to the Santiam fires, which were still spreading out of control. We landed on the Santiam Junction airport, a 3,100-foot field owned and maintained by the state of Oregon. We bummed a ride to the HooDoo Bowl ski resort three miles to the southeast.

The air was full of smoke and the road was crowded with trucks, tankers, bulldozers and crew buses. Fire could be seen licking through the woods on the west side of the main ski hill and smoke indicated fire on all sides. We were told that a team of fire fighters was cut off at the top of the ski lift. So we climbed the hill alongside the chair lift to get in on the action. We were met by Ward Monroe, the fire boss in charge of a squad of fire fighters.

Kennerley wrote a book *The Shooter*, (C1973) with an exciting account of what followed:

> "The next five hours were touch and go. We might have died but for a large bed of lava that lay between us and the flames, preventing them from spreading any closer. "The fire surrounded us completely. I shot dozens of pictures as the tall trees crowned out with a loud roar. The smoke was so thick it was hard to breathe, and our eyes were burning almost as badly as the trees.
>
> "...Meanwhile, back at the bottom of the hill, word had reached other newsmen that a group of people were trapped at the top of the mountain. The photogs were all braced to cover the dramatic rescue of the trapped firemen on the flaming mountain top. The look on their faces when Lev and I, covered from head to toe in soot, emerged from the smoldering forest with the firemen made the whole trip worthwhile."

Memory is tricky and the notes in my logbook are sketchy, but that's not the way I remember it. It is true there were some downed logs smoldering alongside the wide, cleared ski runs. And Ward Monroe, the fire boss, did suggest that we all stick together until the smoke cleared a little, but I had a feeling, from a lot of past experience, that we could have jumped over a few logs and coasted down a ski run to the bottom at any time.

My recollection is not as dramatic as Kennerley's. Maybe that's why he wrote a book and I didn't — plus the fact that he won a Pulitzer Prize for his portfolio of pictures shot under fire in Vietnam in 1973.

KITTY O'NEIL

Kitty O'Neil, Hollywood stunt woman, was poised to set a new world speed record for land vehicles. O'Neil was born deaf, but she had built a reputation as an able and daring movie stunt artist. She had been trying out an especially designed rocket car on Alvord Dry Lake deep in the desert of southeastern Oregon. The old lake bed, as level and smooth as only nature can make it, had a reputation rivalling Bonneville Salt Flats in Utah for speed record attempts.

The city desk wanted to cover this bit of history. But it is a long 420 miles by road and the last 40 miles or so is only a gravel track across the desert. It would take 9 or 10 hours to get there by road. On December 7, 1976, it took Jim Vincent and me one hour and 45 minutes by air.

The only problem was to choose a landing spot, the whole lake bed, five miles by 10, is level as a pool table. We taxied back to the operations center in a mobile home where the rocket plane was being serviced, and sized up the scene.

Kitty O'Neil was obviously upset. She was complaining in a voice peculiar to those who have never heard the sound of a human voice. She was frustrated. She had been feeling out the controls of the flimsy looking little race car with its rocket engine and its bicycle wheels and picking up a little more speed with each run. But after surviving the dangerous tryouts she was being denied the fruits of her efforts. Some agent with an unlimited bank account and ego to match had turned up at the last minute and bought the right to break the world record — and Kitty's heart.

Suddenly our hot news story had turned to a mere sob story. The city desk decided it was a non-story.

We flew back to Burns, refueled and tried to get through the Columbia Gorge to Portland ahead of a storm front. We lost the race, landed at The Dalles and came whimpering home in a land vehicle with our tails between our legs. This was one of only three times in 35 years that we had been thwarted by weather or engine trouble on an assignment.

THE BLUE ROCK

Homer Groening was a man of many talents. He could hold his breath for more than six minutes. I have personally timed him while we shared the cockpit of a C-46, the last of the twin-engine tail draggers, on missions for the 403d (combat airlift) Air Force Reserve Squadron at Portland Air Base. He was a top pilot, a cartoonist with a weird sense of humor. And he played a hot game of pickup basketball at the YMCA every noon when sane people were eating lunch.

And finally, he was a movie maker of rare if not weird talents. He approached me, as a fellow free spirit, with a proposition. Make that a proposal. Homer had been commissioned by the U.S. Army Corps of Engineers in November 1980, to produce a documentary to show how the Willamette River had been restored to its pristine purity, once again the land of the salmon and the home of water sports.

There was to be nothing dull about this movie. Homer set up his camera with its long lenses in the rear seat of the Cessna 172 to shoot through the open window on the right. Day after day we took off just before sunrise when the light was magic and the morning mist hung low over rivers and lakes. We would dive down through the thin layer of fog, level off just above the black water, pick up speed and pull up through the fog layer, catching the first rays of the sun on the Willamette River and the pastoral countryside.

As the sun rose so did we, following the Santiam River to its source in the snowfields of Three Fingered Jack. Suddenly Homer would announce that the light had gone blah. The magic was gone. We would head for home. Next clear day we would take off at dawn to chase the Sandy River to its origin in the glaciers and snowfields of 11,239-foot Mount Hood. On a Saturday in May we shot a string of climbers in the Chute, nearing the top.

Another day we would fly over the bar where the Columbia River empties into the Pacific. We would skim low alongside fishing boats, crab boats and sports craft, then turn and head up river, zooming around heavily laden freighters, chubby and square, plowing their way up stream. Zipping under the Astoria bridge (no big deal, 125 feet of clearance), we would shoot the freighter fleet at anchor waiting for clearance.

Another day we ventured far inland to shoot the dams on the Columbia River, the powerhouses and the spider's web of power lines that radiated out to light the lamps of cities as far away as California. Just to add a final touch we circled the top of Mount Rainier, mother of Northwest mountains. We logged 25 hours before Homer was satisfied.

Homer was given free rein to edit and narrate the 45-minute film in his own distinctive style. That was in the contract. He entitled the film The Blue Rock — (that's the way the earth looks from space).

Environmentalists had never been cozy with the Corps of Engineers. But the Engineers entered The Blue Rock in an environmental film festival in Paris in 1986, where it won top honors. The Engineers entered a film every year. This was their only win.

ANTELOPE ORGY

Thirty years ago the Royal Order of the Antelope commanded the kind of respect usually reserved for the Elks Lodge or the American Legion. It was a secretive if not secret society that first commanded attention when organized in 1932 to work for the establishment of a 240,000-acre Hart Mountain Antelope Refuge, 27 miles from Lakeview in the southeastern corner of Oregon.

The members reached their goal in 1936 and are reported to have been celebrating outrageously ever since. Every year in the heat of July the Chief Whitetail, the Grand Herdsman and the Grand Jackass Buckaroo call their jackasses to the Blue Sky Hotel for a weekend of rowdy, uninhibited gambling, drinking and whoopee — for men only.

"No woman would want to be found within 100 miles of the Blue Sky Hotel," a former Keeper of the Tail declared. The celebration had the reputation of a Sagebrush Woodstock, without the women and the drugs, where he males let it all hang out. As if to emphasize the all-male character of the annual carousal, the center piece of the Blue Sky Hotel compound was reported to be a tall wooden Indian with an erect two-foot appendage attesting to his manhood.

Members came from all over Oregon. They ranged from cow pokes and mechanics to lawyers, merchants, chiefs (of police), journalists, business executives, state legislators, Oregon governors and, in 1947, U.S. Supreme Court Justice William O. Douglas himself. U.S. Senator Mark Hatfield and Representative Bob Smith, one-time representative from Bend, supported the Order in their day.

I was so intrigued by the air of mystery that cloaked the event and reports of the annual revelry that I jumped at the chance to fly a planeload of Antelopes to the annual orgy in July 1967.

The Blue Sky Hotel/Hart Mountain was more than 300 road miles away from Portland, a two-day drive by car. It was only 265 miles, two hours, by air. I checked the aerial charts, which at that time showed a 2,500-foot dirt landing strip at the 5,500-foot elevation. The U.S. Fish and Wildlife agents at Hart Mountain Refuge said the landing strip was in usable condition.

I rented a six-place 300-horsepower, low-winged Piper Comanche at Hillsboro Airport and took off for the 265-mile flight. I remember one of my Antelopes was Herb Lundy, editor of *The Oregonian's* editorial page, fisherman, hunter, outdoorsman and highly respected community leader. Jim Brown, *Oregonian* purchasing agent, was another. I neglected to log the names of the rest.

I found the narrow strip of gravel they called an airstrip, circled to look it over and decided to land uphill on a slight up grade. The strip looked mighty short. But the moment the Comanche touched down she sank down. And my heart sank with it. It was like landing on the soft gravel of one of those highway escape ramps for runaway trucks.

It was obvious we would never get off that landing strip with any kind of load. We were met by a fleet of dusty vehicles offering to ferry us to the Blue Sky Hotel. I stayed behind and took off empty downhill. I circled to the southeast and landed on Spanish Dry Lake about 15 miles away where I had at least two miles of hardpacked desert for takeoff.

With that load off my mind I hitched a ride to the Blue Sky Hotel. The scene was more like a hunting camp than an orgy. Grey-haired executives in blue jeans and cowboy boots were sitting around, consuming adult beverages and telling lies. The bar and the kitchen were the focal points of activity.

As the day wore on, high stakes gambling games sprouted up here and there. I saw a few campers who seemed unusually loud and happy, but no one who was really schnickered, rotten, or rolling much less anyone "on the turps," as the Aussies say, or "two shades off the horrors" (close to delirium tremens.) Of course, I am not an expert. I'm a tea totaler and was, therefore the designated driver for the weekend.

There among the stunted Ponderosa pines was, indeed, the anatomically advantaged tall wooden Indian. Old timers said that Indian George had been there as long as they could remember. There was a bulletin board with some official notices and a few centerfolds from *Playboy* and *Hustler*. If that was pornography, it could have been borrowed from many executive offices, or any construction site in the state.

There were some wild rites as a flock of new jackasses like me, were initiated into the Order of the Antelope. But these were nothing to compare with the initiation into the Order of the Eggman in the Canadian Royal Air Force. To qualify, the candidate had to put a whole hen's egg into his or her mouth, break the shell with his or her jaws and swallow the contents, shells and all, without spilling a drop. When I was stationed in Greenland in 1952 I saw a pretty, young secretary on an inspection team survive the rites and wash the contents down with a shot of raw Scotch.

It was the memory of those nights under the stars that is forever burned into my mind's eye, blocking out the dusty days. The stars were big and bright. They crowded the sky and seemed to reach down as if to touch the earth. It made you feel as if you could reach up, grab a handful of stars, and take them home in a jar.

The Blue Sky Hotel is as quiet as a graveyard these days. The landing strip is closed to the public. Aircraft are no longer permitted to take off from Spanish Lake. The Order of the Antelope is barred from the Hart Mountain Antelope Refuge which they initiated — in some ways a victim of its own success.

"New members just kept coming," Al McCready explained. McCready, retired managing editor of *The Oregonian* and a past Chief Whitetail, has been an active member since 1952.

One year 800 celebrants crowded the 10-acre camp site. "The chow line was so long it never ended," McCready said. "We had to limit our numbers to about 300."

In 1977 Gary Kline, a wildlife biologist, complained to his superiors about the Order of the Antelope and the Fish and Wildlife Service revoked the Order's permit to use the antelope refuge. But Oregon's Senator Mark O. Hatfield and Representative Al Ullman came to the rescue and the permit was reinstated.

The Order of the Antelope continued to flourish until July 1991, when a sneak attack by Paul Koberstein of The *Oregonian* nearly ended the annual blowouts. Koberstein and a photographer invited themselves to the 56th annual convention and reported seeing "members screaming obscenities, dropping their pants in public view, drinking and driving, scattering beer cans, gambling and drinking until they passed out." They quoted a biology professor from The Evergreen State College in Olympia as saying that he saw the genitals of an antelope tacked to a sign at the camp site.

McCready denied that the Order of the Antelope had anything to do with the barbaric display reported by the professor. "I have been going to the annual outings ever since 1952. I haven't missed one in the past 20 years. And I have never seen anything as disgusting as the professor reported. Neither has anyone else in the Order that I know of. The story gives a completely false impression of the event."

"Creative journalism," McCready called it, in the understatement of the day. McCready said that in the weeks that followed publication of the "expose" he was deluged with protests from members of the Order.

The Fish and Wildlife Service once again revoked the Order's permit to use the antelope refuge, effective in 1992.

But that didn't stop the Order of the Antelope. They promptly bought 80 acres of private land on Deer Creek, about three miles from the Blue Sky Hotel. "We miss the Blue Sky Hotel," McCready said, "but we have built new shelters at Deer Creek and we are adding more each year."

"We may have a few members who might be described as uncouth, but they all respect the environment, and all join in the fellowship of the weekend," said McCready. One man's orgy is another man's almost-religious, therapeutic retreat. "It is a great experience, a sort of renewal," McCready reminisced. "There's no place quite like it.

"And the Order of the Antelope has not forgotten its original purpose," McCready noted. Koberstein's story did acknowledge that every year members volunteer to help out on the range, spearheading projects that improve conditions for the antelope and the bighorn sheep that live on the range.

The Order has contributed money to build a new bath house at the hot springs on the Refuge. It has paid for summer scholarships to study antelope and in the early 1970s created a tax-exempt foundation that provides a scholarship at Oregon State University. In 1991 the order spent $10,000 to build a new sign at the entrance to the refuge.

MOMENT OF TRUTH

It was August 1977. The space shuttle was to be dropped from the skies over Edwards Dry Lake in its first free flight Friday August 12. It was the moment of truth for the whole multibillion dollar space program, the proof that the shuttle could actually orbit the earth and land like an airplane. Air Force Lieutenant Colonel Charles Gordon Fullerton, Oregon's own astronaut, would be at the controls.

On August 11 *Oregonian* photographer Dale Swanson and I flew the 754 miles nonstop down to Fox Field, next door to Edwards Air Force Base, in a single-engine Beechcraft in five hours and thirty minutes. (It would have taken two days by car.) We were up bright and early the next morning, camped in our rental car in the tules alongside the takeoff runway.

We were no sooner parked than we began to see a new breed of dinosaur with a snub nose, stubby wings and a runty tail stalking through the sagebrush as if about to attack. On closer inspection it proved to be the space shuttle *Enterprise* mounted on top of the modified Boeing 747 mother ship, towering 80 feet in the air.

"The scariest part of the whole project was the ride in a crane to the cockpit of the shuttle 80 feet in the air," Fullerton later confessed. Like the bumblebee, the combination obviously could never fly. But it did.

At 30,000 feet the space shuttle actually dropped the 747 as the mother ship pitched over to pick up 310 miles an hour airspeed. The shuttle, free of its bonds, popped up and away. The landing was a grease job. Had to be. There was no way this big powerless glider could go around.

Fullerton flew the 80-ton bird on the base leg while flight commander Jack Lousma made the landing. "It flew like a fighter plane," he said.

After the landing Fullerton took time out of all the official foofaraw to grant us a quick interview and photo opportunity. He confirmed reports that he saved the shuttle from disaster when he quickly solved a computer problem that left the craft helplessly out of control. It was this ability to solve complex problems under pressure that assured Fullerton of a place in the orbital flights to come.

Leading the cheers as Fullerton addressed the press conference were his wife Marie, son Andy, daughter Molly and his parents Charles and Grace Fullerton of Salem, Oregon. They had flown down the day before. It was typical of Gordon Fullerton that he took time out of last minute rehearsals for Friday's crucial flight to spend late afternoon and evening with his family.

"We are a very close family," Fullerton's mother said. "Gordon always finds time to keep in touch with us by phone. Our phone bill is something horrendous, but it is worth it."

And that was no PR. Gordon Fullerton lived for two things, his flying and his family. The first of these was his family, but in the pressure cooker atmosphere of the astronauts' training center at Houston, Texas, where he was honing his skills in preparation for the third orbital mission of the Space Transportation System (STS) in April 1982, it sometimes looked as if Fullerton had married the Air Force.

Instead, Fullerton was married to Marie Buettner, a talented blonde nurse whom he met at Edwards Air Force Base while in the test pilot school. The life of an astronaut's wife is not for sissies. Marie Fullerton's typical day began at the crack of dawn, driving 25 miles from their sprawling ranch house in Clear Lake City, a suburb of Houston, to Texas City where she worked as a surgical nurse. Fullerton left home at 7 a.m. for a long day of conferences and sessions in the space shuttle simulator working out solutions to possible emergencies that might be encountered on the upcoming flight.

Marie Fullerton put dinner in the oven, planning to serve at about 6 p.m. Six o'clock came and went. No word from the errant astronaut. "I never know when he will get away, but I know he will get here as soon as he can without jeopardizing his training," his wife said. She and Molly practiced duets on the piano to while away the time while Andy roamed the house restlessly.

It was 8 p.m. before Fullerton wandered in the back door. "I don't know how he keeps up the pace," Marie Fullerton said. "I fixed him a sandwich this morning, which he ate in the simulator. That's all he has had to eat all day. He never seems to get tired."

But the iron man does get hungry. He hugged his wife, daughter Molly, 8 (in 1982), and son Andy, 6, both adopted, then plopped down on the davenport with a plate of roast beef, mashed potatoes and gravy.

"Gordon will eat anything," his wife said. "But he never seems to gain a pound." He usually runs when he gets home at night and he plays tennis with Marie, an ardent tennis fan, whenever they find the time. Gordon remained a fit and trim 165 pounds.

Marie Fullerton is frankly, refreshingly patriotic. "I believe Gordon's part in this mission is important to the nation and to all mankind. I am only happy to be playing a supporting role," she said.

Marie Fullerton takes the dangers of space flight seriously. Who could forget the fire that killed Virgil Grissom, Edward H. White and Roger Chaffee in the *Apollo I* capsule January 27, 1967, or the narrow escape of the *Apollo 13* crew in 1970?

"But there are risks to anything you do in this life. If anything is going to happen to him I would rather see it happen while he was doing something he was excited about, something that is important to him."

His parents, too, are well aware of the dangers he faces. His father Charles gave Gordon his first airplane ride in a World War I Jenny. Gordon was determined from that day on to be a test pilot, although the title had not been coined yet. "I don't take the risks lightly," Charles Fullerton said. "But to see Gordon lift off from the Cape on his first space mission was the biggest thrill of my life."

The whole family watched Fullerton and Lousma blast off the pad at Cape Kennedy March 2, 1982. The mission was a joy ride for the first seven days. Then the weather socked in at Cape Kennedy. The order went out to prepare for an emergency landing at a desert landing strip on the White Sands Missile Range, an unpaved, unmanned runway of hard packed gypsum.

Dale Swanson and I flew the airlines to El Paso, rented a car and headed for the landing strip by the first light of dawn Tuesday, March 30. As we neared White Sands we could see clouds of gypsum sand boiling up out of the desert, obscuring the whole dry lake bed. It was the kind of desert storm that can sandblast the paint off exposed cars, or the skin off exposed flesh.

Reporters and cameramen, bundled up to the gills and breathing through makeshift masks, were huddled in and around vehicles and the 20-foot towers erected for the cameramen. A few hardy shooters, hooded and wrapped in towels, were standing by their cameras ready for action. You couldn't see more than 10 feet, when you could see at all. Gusts of wind wrecked several campers, blew a television network camera off its stand and sent a dozen spectators to the army medics for treatment of eyes irritated by the blowing sand.

The crew of the *Columbia* reported from orbit that the whole valley looked like a moving carpet of sand. Mission Control gave the shuttle a wave off.

How long would they be stranded in orbit? How long would

the supply of fuel and oxygen last?

NASA soon announced that the *Columbia* had saved enough fuel for another day in orbit. The landing was rescheduled for Wednesday March 31, 1982. The 40,000 spectators in the public viewing area five miles north of the landing strip went home, disappointed. Swanson spent most of the night cleaning up his camera equipment. The fine powder penetrated everywhere in spite of the plastic covers designed to protect it.

The delay gave the Fullerton family, Gordon Fullerton's prime support team, time to fly out for a ringside seat at the shuttle's historic first emergency landing.

Tuesday dawned bright and clear, marred only by vagrant breezes. On their 129th orbit of the earth the crew of the *Columbia* came coasting down the sky over Baja California at 13 times the speed of sound, seen only by high-powered NASA cameras.

At 9:03 a.m. a sudden double shock wave rattled the grandstand and scared the socks off the media crowd. The space ship could be seen swooping down out of the northwest.

Fullerton's family, watching from a special viewing site within a few hundred feet of the runway, led the cheers of jubilation and relief as the stubby space shuttle touched down at 9:05 a.m.

Lively Andy, dressed in red for the occasion, could be seen running foot races with his sister Molly while they waited for the landing.

After a short debriefing, Fullerton was driven to a makeshift reviewing stand for an official welcome. Andy was first to pop out of the vehicle and run to the VIP section where he sat fidgeting and building sand castles with his feet during the formal ceremonies.

When the scene was repeated a few hours later at Houston, Andy was the first to pop up on the stage and wave to the crowd. While waiting for the countdown at Cape Kennedy, Andy, full of spizzeringtum, literally started to climb one of the outside walls at the Fullerton's quarters.

Fullerton spent eight days in orbit, setting a new record, and ending with the shuttle's first emergency landing, unscathed. Then he started on one of NASA's compulsory lecture tours in June 1987 — only to be struck by lightning as he landed at Cleveland in his supersonic T-38 jet trainer. The blinding flash of lightning took a chunk out of the tail of the plane and melted the radio antenna. Once again Fullerton escaped unscathed.

LOGBOOK RECALL

Cryptic entries in my logbooks conjure up memories of years of aerial assignments, some challenging, some pure fun. These entries include ones like:

September 3, 1970 Flight to Sun River, Oregon with photographer Bob Ellis and two bicycles to cover the Carnival of Wheels.

April 2, 1971 To Kellogg, Idaho with Dave Falconer to cover the Kellog mine disaster — 90 miners trapped a mile under the ground. All died.

September 15, 1974 Flew to Burns, Oregon with Bob Ellis to cover a roundup of wild horses on the range. Two days round trip by car — 90 minutes each way by air.

April 5, 1976 To Pasco, Washington for reenactment of the 40th anniversary of the first air mail flight by Varney Airlines, later incorporated into United Airlines. Took off in formation with biplane for aerials, returned to *Oregonian* for first edition.

February 26, 1979 Flew photog to The Dalles, Oregon to cover total eclipse of the sun at Goldendale Observatory and flew film back to Portland for first edition.

August 5, 1979 Flew Mike Lloyd to Kinzua, Oregon to cover fire in big lumber mill. Landed up steep hill on mill airstrip. Took off opposite direction down hill. Airstrip like a saddle, hills both ends. One hour, fifteen minutes each way.

September 25, 1979 Flew to Tillamook, Oregon. Had to sneak through Columbia Gorge and down the coast under 700 foot ceiling to reach Tillamook. Slept in hangar.

September 26, 1979 Up at 2 a.m. ready to cover launch of Da Vinci balloon at 8:19 a.m. Took off through overcast at 9:30 a.m., climbed to 14,500 feet over Portland to get pix of balloon. Photog Dale Swanson started to feel lack of oxygen. So did I — felt mean. So we folded our wings and headed for Pearson Field.

And so on for 1,000 hours over 10 years.

CHAPTER 10

ELEPHANTS DON'T SNORE

It was midnight at the zoo when I pulled up to the gate high in Portland's West Hills. It was a bitter, black night. A chill wind sighed through the surrounding firs and seemed to scurry past the black hulk of the bear pits, which looked like catacombs in the faint glow of light from the penguin pool.

An owl hooted hoarsely. A muted growl from the cat house made my hackles rise. The monkeys chattered in fright.

Midnight at the zoo. What a setting for a murder — or the birth of an elephant.

It all started at 4:10 p.m. Thursday January 18, 1962, when Belle, the matron of Portland's passel of pregnant pachyderms, squatted and squealed loud and long. Matthew Maberry, zoo veterinarian, was sure she was in labor, about to give birth. It would be the first elephant conceived and born in captivity in the western hemisphere in 44 years, and the only one ever to survive to maturity.

Belle was supposed to be having a baby, but you would have thought she was having a party. The feed room was jammed with reporters, photographers and consultants standing around in tense, expectant groups. The lights were turned down low in the elephant parlor.

"Got to keep her calmed down," Doc explained tersely. "She's hurting." But the lights burned brightly in the back room where the bailed hay was piled almost to the ceiling. The coffee pot was boiling and a portable radio was broadcasting the latest "Belle-tins."

"How do you know she's pregnant?" the press kept asking Morgan Berry who owned Belle and Thonglaw, the ding dong daddy of the pachyderm family. Berry had loaned his elephants to the Portland Zoo because he knew and trusted director Jack Marks. He felt that Belle and her baby would have the best chance of surviving and thriving in Marks' hands.

"Belle mated with Thonglaw July 19, 1960, at Seattle's Woodland Park Zoo where I was giving rides," Berry said. "Trouble is, no one knows for sure what the gestation period is. The books say anywhere from 17 to 24 months. Belle's been on the launching pad now for 18 months."

The phone rang off the wall with tips and advice, including this rhyme copied from the wall of a zoo in Colombo, Ceylon:

> An elephant planning a blessed event
> Knows that 641 days will be spent
> Before she will know and can answer with joy
> The question: "Is it a girl or a boy?"

For the next four days and nights I slept with the elephants. Berry introduced me to Belle, and we quickly became friends. I would order "trunk up" in a voice of authority, and she would toss up her trunk and open her cavernous mouth for an apple or even a peppermint.

I found that the pencil was as mighty as the ankus — the "elephant hook" that elephant trainers use to push their "bulls" around. (All elephants are bulls to elephant men.) Belle would back up or move over upon command, reinforced by gentle pressure from the point of a pencil.

Belle, only 10, was every inch a lady. She was always gentle, well-behaved, affectionate and cooperative with her keepers. Her wildest enthusiasm was reserved for Morgan Berry, who had raised her from a baby.

Belle and Pet, seven, youngest of Berry's elephants, were inseparable. Berry pointed out that Belle had chosen Pet for her "auntie," another sign that she was elephanticipating. They walked trunk-in-trunk, ate side by side and slept side by side, endlessly caressing each other with their sensitive trunks.

"In the wild, every elephant chooses a female companion when she approaches the date of delivery," Berry said. "She knows instinctively that she has to have help to defend herself and her baby during her accouchement and to protect the baby for a year or two after birth."

Rosy, the zoo's first elephant, matriarch of the family, was a sweet, gentle beast, too. Her inseparable companion was Tuy Hoa (Tee Waa), eight years old, gentle, well-mannered, but a bit of a knot head.

Thonglaw, the bull of the herd, the biggest Asian elephant in the country, loved Berry and acknowledged Berry as boss of the herd — when he was in his right mind. Right now he was out of his mind. He hated everybody. He was in musth — a form of insanity peculiar to male elephants. When the musth glands in his head five inches behind his eyes, began to swell, oozing a yellow fluid, all bets were off. Thonglaw was a killer.

The huge bull would tremble like a big dog and rumble his affection when his master came to pet him in normal times. But he would kill anyone he could reach when in musth — including his beloved boss.

Thonglaw, the outlaw, had been lured into his isolation cell and would remain in solitary confinement until his meanness glands quit cutting up; then he was himself again. Meantime, he stood in the middle of his cell, glaring red-eyed at all comers, restlessly doing the twist, the double twist, as only an elephant can.

That completed the cast of characters, except for one — the Dirty Bird, an odious Abyssinian Ground Hornbill with a beak like a cast iron banana. He was lank, lean and mean. When the dignitaries of the press played cards on top of his cage, he would become obscenely annoyed and rasp his iron beak along the iron bars of his cage like a small boy running a piece of pipe along a picket fence. When this didn't get attention he would back off, fix you with a malevolent eye and begin attacking each bar individually with the point of his beak like a woodpecker in a petrified forest.

He had a cold in his head, which is why he was confined to the warmth of the feed room, plus the fact that his mate had kicked him out of their penthouse. She couldn't stand him either. The only way to shut him up was to usher him forcibly into a cardboard box inside his cage where he would fall fast asleep.

One thing you could say for the Dirty Bird. He didn't snore. Neither did the elephants. At least I never heard one snore in all the time I slept with the big beasts, and neither did Morgan Berry. Their breathing does become stentorian when they are fully relaxed. But they always sleep on their sides and carefully curl their delicate trunks up under their chins out of harm's way.

To snore you have to sleep on your back and no self-respecting adult elephant would be caught sleeping in such a ridiculous position, although Belle would roll onto her back and rest her feet on the wall occasionally like a playful dog.

When the four pregnant pachyderms were sprawled out in a disorderly row in the gloom of the elephant house, they loomed up in the dim light like a range of mountains with the heaves. Their great sides rose and fell ponderously, like the swells on some silent sea.

Belle breathed only eight times a minute once she was deep in sleep. As Belle's time grew near, she seemed restless and apprehensive. Berry would drag in a half-filled sack of oats and sleep on the floor just outside the bars of the elephant parlor within reach of Belle's inquisitive trunk.

"Belle doesn't know she is an elephant," Berry explained with an air of apology. "She thinks she is people. She was raised with the rest of the kids, like one of the family.

"She was only a month old when I found her in Bangkok, Thailand, in March 1952. She had been born in a jungle camp just outside Bangkok in February. I bought her in March, but it was June before I got her back home."

The Berry family lived in a towering old-fashioned two-story house in the Fremont district of Seattle. They had a big yard, carefully screened by tall trees, where Berry's ever-changing menagerie of wild animals, birds and reptiles could indulge in a little outdoor exercise. Nervous neighbors grew acclimated, if not accustomed, to the snarling of leopards, the screaming of cougars, the chatter of monkeys and the roar of lions.

Belle slept in the basement with Kenneth and Howard, Berry's other youngsters who made her a bed of hay in one corner of the big furnace room, fenced in by cots. It was their job to wake up every two hours, feed the wood furnace that kept the animals warm, and feed baby Belle.

Even the alarm clock wouldn't wake them sometimes. Belle would add her baby voice to the clamor, without success.

Finally she learned to clamber over the sleeping boys as they lay dead to the world on their cots. She would open the door, climb the narrow, cluttered stairs to the kitchen, and wander through the house until she found the master bedroom.

If the hungry baby's plaintive cries didn't wake the boss, she would tickle him under the chin with her dexterous trunk. Then the master would lie in bed and feed her balls of well-cooked rice, mixed with sugar, powdered milk and vitamins in a secret formula that Berry had developed with the aid of a Siamese elephant man. When she had eaten she would go back to bed with the rest of the kids.

Belle stood 35 inches high at the shoulder and weighed only 185 pounds when she came to live with the Berrys at four months of age — not much more than she weighed at birth. But she gained steadily on her special formula.

She had the run of the house from the day she arrived. She was housebroken from the first, never made a mess and never broke anything. "In fact, she was the best-behaved of any of the kids," Berry recalled. She craved affection, like any baby. Leave her alone for a minute and her little heart would break. Her pitiful cries would bring the family running." She had to be literally in touch with her family every second. She would stand and rub against Berry or the boys or the two Berry girls, Jane and Barbara by the hour, or follow them in their play, always close enough to reach out and cling to them with her tiny trunk.

Her favorite was Mrs. Berry. She would follow her mistress around the house as she swept and washed and ironed. "She followed so closely that she would step on the wife's heels and pull off her shoes," Berry said. "As she got bigger, if you stopped suddenly she would knock you down before she could put on the brakes.

"Baby elephants have to have affection or they will die," Berry declared. "You can give them all the food and vitamins in the world, but they won't live without something to cling to."

Callous animal dealers long ago learned from the natives that a young baby elephant can't be left alone or he will die of grief, despair and terror. It is common practice to give an orphaned elephant a quick substitute for his lost mother.

If his mother is killed in the wild, or dragged away, the bereaved baby will seize upon the nearest man and cling to him piteously. Sometimes the little orphan will fix his affections on a goat, a cow, or a camel. Even a chicken will give an elephant baby the living companionship his nature craves. It is not uncommon among native animal collectors to ship a chicken along with a baby elephant to comfort the hapless waif.

TLC was the secret of Morgan Berry's success with elephants. He "fathered and mothered" most of his babies. He rode the cargo plane that brought them back from Bangkok or Saigon. When the air got rough and the elephants trumpeted their alarm, Berry, who was always uneasy in an airplane, would clamber over the backs of the elephants and reassure them in confident tones.

Every evening Mrs. Berry used to take Belle and the other kids out for a walk. At first a wave of excitement preceded them, but the neighbors quickly got used to the sight of the little elephant shuffling earnestly along close on the heels of the kids. She had to hurry to keep up during those first months.

"The kids took her to school one day," Berry recalled. "But we had to call a halt to that. School was several blocks away, across a couple of busy streets. Traffic stopped for the kids and their elephant all right. That was just the trouble. Cars came to a screeching halt, creating a traffic jam as motorists stared in disbelief.

"We had a big, open Cadillac," Berry recalled. "Belle would follow the wife into the back seat. She would climb right up on the cushions and put her puny trunk around my wife's neck. Maybe you think that didn't drive a lot of spectators to swear off drinking."

Kenny, Berry's oldest son, never had a bicycle, but how many other kids in the block had an elephant to ride? This one would stand guard like a watch dog and stand up for her master if anyone gave him trouble. But elephants will be elephants, and that means big. Soon, when Belle stood five feet high at the shoulder and weighed a ton, she went to live with the rest of Berry's elephants in Seattle's Woodland Park Zoo.

Meantime, back in Portland, The City of Roses went crazy over the elephants. Radio stations issued hourly "Belle-tins" reporting Belle's every grunt and groan. Belle was deluged with gifts in a spontaneous baby shower that wouldn't quit. The Grandmother's Club brought diapers fit for an elephant, and safety pins to match. A Nut House sent two gunny sacks of peanuts, one tied with blue ribbons, one with pink. Elephants don't care much for peanuts, but their keepers did.

A florist sent blue boots fit for an elephant, filled with 300 red roses. Belle loved the thorny stems, but spat out the flowers. School children knitted a huge blanket for Belle's baby which covered half the wall of the elephant barn. Someone sent a gigantic nursing bottle with an elephant-sized nipple. The

Lions Club ladies designed two flags, 9 by 6 feet to fly from the highest flagpole, blue if a boy, pink if a girl.

The fever of elephanticipation spread universally. Three hundred fifty wealthy passengers on a sea safari around the world aboard the cruise ship *S. S. Breasi,* including a dozen from Portland, waited breathlessly for a daily wire from the zoo. Aboard ship king of the sea Neptune Rex, also infected with "Bellephantiasis," inaugurated the first of many betting pools on the weight of Belle's baby. Guesses ranged from 300 to 640 pounds.

Back at the elephant barn, Maberry mounted his stepladder and proceeded to perform a rite known as palpation. He reached up the birth canal until he could feel two big arteries which feed the fetus through the placenta.

"Belle's on the launching pad," Doc declared, as winter faded into spring. Electrocardiograms taken by Dr. James Metcalfe, associate professor of cardiology at the University of Oregon Medical School, showed Belle's heart beating a strong 38 to 40 thumps per minute and detected the baby's heartbeat a fainter 68 beats.

When does the countdown begin? None of the experts had answers. They did have apprehensions. All bullmen remembered the story of Angry Alice, the circus elephant that had four babies and tried to kill each one. She used each in turn for a football, kicking them violently around the elephant barn, crushing them under her two-ton body, trying to smash them with her head. None of her unwelcome offspring lived more than a few weeks in the face of this unnatural fury. That was 44 years before, and no elephant in the western hemisphere had delivered a baby since then. The shades of Angry Alice hung over the elephant barn like the Sword of Damocles as the coldest winter in years wore on.

Finally, at 7:30 p.m. Friday January 19, 1962, Maberry, Marks, and Miss Guinazzo, an interpreter, called Dr. Emmanuel Amoroso, West Indian professor of obstetrics at the Royal College of Veterinary Medicine in London, who had some experience in the elephant camps of the Indian jungles. It was 2 a.m. in London when the call finally went through. Dr. Amoroso came wide awake when Maberry said he had an elephant birth on his hands. The veterinarians held a long consultation. They agreed that Belle was about to blast off the launch pad.

Nobody asked Belle. She continued to look bored; so did the red-faced elephant watchers. Finally, Jack Marks turned out the lights and locked the door. "This is getting to be ridiculous," he said.

1. (Above) Glen Muchow, "Butch" Heuschkel and Frank Wisner, Yellowstone National Park, 1925. "We nearly froze to death." *Richards photo*

2. (Right) Ole Peterson, outrageous rebel, hermit of Mount Saint Helens with weird walking stick.
Richards photo

3. (Above) Meteorologist Eckley Ellison seeds clouds with dry ice. *Hugh Ackroyd photo*

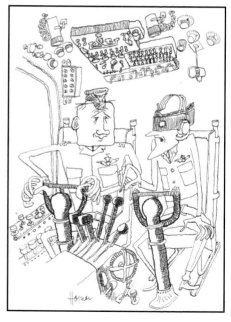

4. (Right) "You put your wheels down again. The throttles are over here." Artist Homer Groening's talents reflect the "wild blue yonder" with Richards.

5. (Right) First Lieutenant Richards, check pilot at primary training school, Blythe, California.

6. (Below) Captain Richards, B-29 commander and crew, 1945. "We never saw action."
US Air Force photos

7. (Above) Morgan Berry frolics with Belle, Thonglaw and Packy — a happy family in 1964.

8. (Right) Berry and Maberry watch day-old Packy tip the scale at 225 pounds. David Falconer photos

9. All eyeballs and appetite. Packy, born at 5:58 a.m. on April 14, 1962, the first born in 40 years. *Falconer photo*

10. (Right) Pilot Valery Chkalov hands over the barograph, proof of the nonstop record of the world's first transpolar flight: Moscow to Vancouver, U.S.A. 1937.
Richards photo

11. (Below) Max Conrad, "Born to Fly" and the author at Pearson Field, 1952.
Bob Ellis photo

12. (Left) A balmy midsummer day, -45 below, 90 degrees south, with a brisk 5 knot breeze at South Pole, December 1962. Richards photo

13. (Below) U.S. Antarctic base lies in the shadow of an active volcano, the 12,450 foot Mount Erebus.

14. (Left) Gus Shinn, pilot of the Que Sera Sera, *cooks lunch aboard an R4D at McMurdo Sound.*

U.S. Air Force photo

15. (Below) Daring Eskimo "grabbers" corner hostile musk oxen on Nunivak Island.

Richards photos

CHAPTER 11

IT'S A BOY!

I think that I shall never see
An elephant as big as she.
The reason for her hefty girth
Is her reluctance to give birth.
If it's longer, pray me tell —
Will they have to wring the Belle?
-from "Elephantasy" by Sally Ryan
AP writer with a passion for pachyderms

Matt Maberry was, indeed, seriously thinking of "wringing the Belle."

More than two months had crept laboriously by since Doc Maberry first punched the panic button and proclaimed Belle in labor.

The cheers of the zoo world had turned to jeers. "Isn't it rather unusual to allow a pregnant animal to suffer labor pains for two months or more?" George W. "Slim" Lewis, elephant man at Seattle's Woodland Park Zoo, coauthor of *The Elephant Tramp*, demanded in a sarcastic letter to the media.

Maberry was getting desperate. Belle had been on the launching pad for 135 days. The countdown had been on hold for 86 days. Something had to be done.

He was seriously considering performing a Caesarean section, or inducing labor with drugs. "Over my dead body," Morgan Berry, owner of the elephants, snapped. "Nobody is going to experiment on my babies. Belle's a natural mother. When her time comes she'll do what comes naturally."

And that's the way it was at 5:58 a.m. on Saturday, April 14, 1962. Only Jack Marks and Dick Getchell, night attendant, saw the whole historic event.

Marks called Berry in Seattle at about 11 p.m. the night before for the umpteenth time, to say Belle was really in labor this time.

"On Friday the thirteenth? You're kidding," Berry said. "You know how superstitious I am." And he rolled over and went back to sleep.

Maberry was asleep on top of the baled hay. Marks hollered. Maberry sat up with a start, cracking his head on a light shade. He slid down from his perch just in time to see Belle's baby drop onto the floor with an audible splash.

Belle whirled around and felt the little lump of helplessness with the tip of her trunk. Then she turned loose a trumpet blast "so loud you felt it rather than heard it" — a blast that was heard around the world.

I was at the top of the call list and arrived in time to see pandemonium breaking out in the pachyderm parlor. Tuy Hoa, Rosy and Pet, ears up and tails rigid, were all trying to force their way through the door at the same time to Belle's side, all trumpeting, squealing and rumbling in a full scale flap. It looked as if Tuy Hoa was trying to sit on Belle's baby while Pet knelt down and pressed her nose to the floor as if trying to get her trunk around the feebly kicking infant.

"Get 'em out of here," Marks barked, visions of Angry Alice racing through his head. Marks, Maberry, zoo foreman Bill Scott and Getchell grabbed elephant hooks and dived into the forest of elephant legs pushing and shoving and shouting commands.

It was Rosy who finally helped herd the excited midwives out of the parlor.

Marks was on the phone answering calls from New York, London and Miami and passing out cigars when he passed out, period. Scott and a reporter gave him first aid while guards called an ambulance. Wire services suspected the faint was a publicity stunt, but Marks was under heavy medication for arthritis and the strain of pushing the elephants around had been too much for him. He was out of the hospital in two hours and stopped by to check on "that little punk" on his way home.

The country's first homemade elephant looked like a homemade job that never quite got finished. His ears were too big, even for an elephant. His trunk was too small. Little Fuzzy Face had a beard like a rabbi and a big blue moustache. He had a crop of coal black hair standing straight up on his pumpkin head. In fact, he was as hairy as an ape. He was the color of an old overshoe, except for his blue-black head and face. His eyes were red-rimmed and looked bigger than his mother's. Only a mother could love such a homely lump of eyeballs and appetite.

It took him a while to figure out how to reach his mother's free-flowing breasts. His ridiculous little trunk got in the way. He tried kicking it out of the way. He stepped on it and pulled, to no avail. He finally flopped it to one side and connected with the lunch counter. For the next year life was one big milk shake for little Hose Nose.

He bounced the scales at 225 pounds, stood 35 inches at the shoulder, 38 inches at the highest point of his arched back, measured 46 inches around the chest, 53 around the belly and 19 inches in circumference at the hock. This proved the old Indian adage that "twice around the hock is the height of the elephant."

Packy was born 635 days after he was conceived, close to the 641 days named in the rhyme on the wall of the Colombo zoo.

Word of the birth spread like wildfire. Crowds jammed the zoo and lined up for a look at the new arrival. They added to the crowd of youngsters and parents who gathered for the annual Easter Egg Roll on the broad lawns outside the pachyderm palace. The director of the kiddy contest rapped on the parlor door and asked for a word with Dr. Maberry.

"How about letting Belle roll out the first egg?" he suggested.

"I'm afraid not," Maberry wearily replied. "Belle's rolled her egg for the day."

Circuses and animal dealers rushed to the zoo to bid for Belle and her baby. Animal dealers from California offered to meet any bid up to $50,000. An Eastern zoo director said they were worth $100,000.

Reports of the possible sale aroused a wave of indignation that broke over City Hall like the flood of 1894. Switchboards at the zoo, radio stations and newspapers lit up like Christmas trees. Angry citizens formed "Save Our Baby" committees.

Morgan Berry anguished over the offers. "That's a lot of money," he said. "And Lord knows I need it. But I promised Jack Marks that I would give him first refusal. This is the only place I know where they will get the TLC that makes them one big happy family."

"You can have them for $30,000," he told Ormond Bean, the city's zoo commissioner.

"Done," Bean said, although he didn't have the money or the authority to accept the offer.

Elephant fever swept the city like a gold rush. A "Ring the Belle" campaign was launched before the day was over. Service clubs "Rang the Bell for Belle." School children poured out their pennies. The Portland Zoological Society was on hand with a trunk and collected a trunk full of money so that "Belle won't have to pack her trunk and leave." *The Oregon Journal* ran its own contest. A record 22,300 visitors crowded the zoo in one day, Sunday April 22, 1962.

In less than two weeks the $30,000 had poured into the pachyderm pot, from an estimated 20,000 elephant lovers; $6,000 more rolled in later. Berry promptly made the city a May Day present of Thonglaw and Pet, to keep the family intact.

Packy's birth shook the world of zoos. Animal men from all over the world flocked to see the miracle baby. The International Society of Zoo and Aquarium Directors held their annual meeting in Portland and gave the zoo its highest award for the most memorable birth of the year.

Life magazine rated Packy's birth bigger news than the World's Fair, which was just opening in Seattle. *Life* gave Packy top billing in 11 pages of pictures and text. The World's Fair rated 9 pages. Seattle had its Space Needle, but Portland had its Packy and the TLC which made its zoo the pachyderm capital of the Western world. Portland's happy family of pachyderms produced more than 25 elephant babies in the next 30 years.

CHAPTER 12

REQUIEM FOR AN ELEPHANT MAN

The months following the birth of Packy were the happiest of Morgan Berry's life.

Berry had achieved his lifelong dream of a happy home for his favorite elephants where professional care and TLC set the stage for a successful breeding program. He bathed in reflected glory as Packy won acclaim from zoos and the public.

He lost no time buying 80 acres of logged off land on a high hill overlooking the Columbia River just off Interstate 5 between Woodland and Kalama, Washington. He moved his menagerie from Seattle's Woodland Park Zoo to Morgan Berry Hill, over Seattle's protests.

You could wake up in the morning on Morgan Berry Hill and expect to find a llama in the living room, a wild cat in the kitchen and an elephant eating off the fireplace hearth. That's what it was like to live with nine elephants, one baby cheetah, one juvenile African antelope (eland), one lovesick hippo plus two lonesome dromedary camels, five frisky horses, a compatible cow, three white fallow deer, and a llama that thought he was people.

Berry's farm, with its barns and big indoor arena caught the eye of Eloise Berchtold, a fearless blonde animal trainer with Ruduy's Circus. Berchtold, 35 at the time, was the only woman in the United States who trained her own animal acts. She was the only woman to mix bears, lions and tigers in a single act, and the only woman to train and work with male African elephants. She succeeded in training three young African elephants in an act that drew crowds wherever she went.

She and Berry formed a partnership that lasted for years. Berry helped Eloise load their nine elephants into one semi-trailer and ten bears, two tigers and four lions, plus her show equipment, into another semi truck. He took care of the elephants and helped with the other animals on tour. They were on the road for six to nine months out of the year.

Morgan was so busy that he let months go by before he found time to drop in on Thonglaw, his first love.

He was shocked and alarmed at what he saw. Thonglaw looked haggard and miserable. He was only 27, but looked 50. He had lost a ton of weight. He hobbled painfully when he moved at all. His left front leg was stiff, his right foot was infected and his toe nails had grown grotesquely from inactivity.

Berry cancelled his travels and began to commute 80 miles round trip every day to help Dr. Michael Schmidt, the zoo veterinarian, treat Thonglaw's feet. Thonglaw merely tolerated his keepers, but would let Berry, his beloved boss, trim his nails and treat minor problem without the use of a pain killer.

On Monday, November 25, 1974, Schmidt administered a small dose of acetylpromazine transquilizer to immobilize Thonglaw while he worked on the animal's sore and infected feet, with Berry's help. The treatment had been completed. Thonglaw regained his feet, flapped his ears and took a couple of steps.

Then he slumped to the floor, quit breathing and died, before anyone could make a move. Death was officially attributed to "an ideosyncratic reaction to the acetylpromazine," which had never been used on him before.

The loss of Thonglaw was like a death in the family to Berry. He went into shock. Sick with grief he drove the lonely 40 miles to his home on the hill to take care of the rest of his menagerie.

Thonglaw suffered the final indignity when someone stole one of his 40-pound tusks within hours of his death. The mystery of the missing ivory has never been solved.

He blamed himself for Thonglaw's untimely death. "I should have checked up on him sooner," he lamented. He never publicly criticized the animal's treatment in the zoo.

"But he never really forgave the zoo for the loss of what was probably the most valuable single elephant in the country — the only bull elephant with a 100 percent breeding record. He produced a healthy baby every time he mated," Maberry said. "It broke him up. He never got over the loss. Life seemed to lose its luster, you might say."

In 1978 Morgan sent Eloise Berchtold off alone. That was the last he saw of her. She was killed May 5, 1978 in the midst of a performance with Teak, her favorite elephant, in Rock Forest, Quebec. Berry was never sure exactly what happened. The police said that the elephant struck Berchtold with his trunk when she tripped over a tear in the canvas and fell flat.

Berry and bull men who knew her and knew Teak said her favorite elephant would never have harmed her intentionally. They agreed Teak might have been startled and lashed out by uncontrolled reflex action.

With Berchtold's death Berry's world began to fall apart. He was left all alone to feed, handle and doctor the whole miniature zoo. All the big cats were destroyed by the sheriff in the name of public safety as Berry tried to ease into retirement. Teak was shot by authorities in Canada.

Berry couldn't bear to part with his elephants, many of which he had raised from babies. He had three of his biggest bulls — Raunchy, Thai and Buddha — chained to trees on his farm Tuesday, June 27, 1979, just a year after Berchtold's death. Raunchy was a young bull. Buddha was a mature bull, Berry's favorite, the one he chose to lead his parades through the towns where they put on their animal acts. Thai was full of mischief, always making trouble. The rest of the elephants were in the barn.

Sharp at 9 p.m. Charles Wilson in nearby Woodland, called Berry on the phone. It was a nightly ritual the two old friends faithfully observed. This night Berry's phone rang and rang and rang. No answer. Wilson had an uneasy feeling. He called Joe Wodaege, Berry's next door neighbor and asked him to check on Berry.

The two men met at the Berry ranch and began to count trunks. They found Buddha and Raunchy chained to their trees, but one was missing. It was Thai, who was always either trying to tear down the barn or running away.

Wilson and Wodaege knew better than to try to look for the missing bull in the dark of the night, armed only with flashlights. Instead they notified Berry's son Kenneth, the elephant man in Seattle's Woodland Park Zoo. Then they called the sheriff's office.

In the first light of dawn Kenneth, Wilson and Wodaege found what looked like some old rags lying at Buddha's feet. It was all that was left of Morgan Berry, the man who lived and finally died for his elephants.

114

He had been trampled and crushed beyond recognition. "There wasn't enough left for an autopsy," Wodaege said.

Buddha lunged at the officers when they tried to retrieve Berry's body, as if trying to protect the remains of his old boss. Buddha, who loved Berry but hated Kenneth, was shot on Kenneth's orders.

Thai, the missing elephant that had escaped his chains, was shot with a tranquilizer gun after chasing a deputy sheriff down the lane off the farm. He was pardoned and wound up back in Portland's Washington Park Zoo where he still lived in 1996.

Nobody knows for sure what happened that night. There were no witnesses and elephants don't talk. Cowlitz County deputies were quoted as saying that Berry may have suffered a heart attack while working with the chained elephant. Others speculated that Buddha was in musth, a form of temporary insanity which periodically makes killers of male elephants.

"I don't think so," said Mathew Maberry, Berry's close friend and associate. "I think that when Thai got loose he picked a fight with Buddha. The two hated each other. I think Morgan heard the ruckus, dashed out to separate the two enemies and got caught in the middle of the fracas," Maberry said.

"Morgan was fearless," said Dr. Marlowe "Ditte" Dittebrandt, 84, one of Berry's closest friends and associates. "He acted as if he were immortal. It never occurred to him that any of his babies would ever hurt him."

Animal men said that you never own an elephant, he owns you. And Berry was, indeed, owned by his elephants.

Dr. Dittebrandt, a medical doctor as well as a veterinarian, probably knew Berry as well as anyone still living. When she retired from medical practice she volunteered as an unpaid assistant to Maberry when he was zoo veterinarian.

She had lived on Morgan Berry Hill for five years taking care of the farm, while Berry and Berchtold were on the road. She had fed and watered the animals and cleaned out the stables — which can be an elephantine job.

"I think Morgan had a death wish," Dittebrandt said. "I think all of those bulls were in musth. And he knew the odds. I don't buy the heart attack theory. He never had time for a heart attack.

"But he was popping all kinds of pills for his heart and other stuff. I'm not sure that he ever did go to a doctor. He was too stubborn. I know he had some deep scratches on his back from an argument with a leopard."

"I don't know how he got those scars," Maberry said. "But I remember one day when he came to pick up a pair of tigers and they got loose. Morgan ran after them, barehanded, and wrestled them to the ground.

"Morgan was a very complex man," Maberry said. "Two days before he died I dropped in to see him. He was playing the trumpet. He was a graduate of the Juliard School of Music and used to play the viola professionally, but he sure could play that trumpet.

"Suddenly he put down the trumpet and said, `For the first time I absolutely understand the meaning of music.'

"There's an old saying that when you absolutely understand something you are gone before you can communicate your revelation to anyone.

"And two days later he was gone.

"Morgan didn't feel good," Maberry concluded. "He was losing weight. He kept getting skinnier and skinnier. He wasn't doing well at all. He was at the end of his rope.

"On my last visit he turned to me and said, 'Some day they will find me out there among the elephants. And that's how I want it.'"

116

No monument nor so much as a plaque at Portland's zoo honors or even thanks Morgan Berry for putting Portland's zoo on the map as the elephant capital of the western hemisphere. But every April 14 when Packy adds another candle to his birthday cake, all true elephant lovers will remember Morgan Berry, the man who lived and died for his elephants.

SECTION II

To The Ends Of The Earth

CHAPTER 1

BIG, BAD BLOWTORCH MORGAN

It was said of Blowtorch Morgan that he used a blowtorch to shave and brush his teeth. He used it to open drums of gasoline, to cook his pemmican stew and light the big, black cigar which always stuck out of his frost-coated whiskers.

I never really met this Paul Bunyan of the Arctic face to face. He was lost and his cat train was broken down somewhere on the northeast coast of Greenland when I was flying copilot on a C-54 trying to drop supplies and spare parts to him. That was in April 1952. I was on active duty with the Air Force, based at Bluie West 1 (BW1), but on temporary duty to Thule, Greenland, the world's northernmost joint U.S.-Danish airbase. Thule was classified secret in those days. The only secret was why it was ever placed on the secret list.

The heat was on. Thule itself was still being built. In addition, a weather station and listening post to be operated by the Danes was being built with wartime urgency on the northeast coast, 740 miles across the ice cap, to guard the back door to the Arctic from the Russian threat. The effort was called the Parkway Project.

First we had to get to the dot on the map where the base was to be built. The C-47 (DC-3) on skis had delivered an advance party to select the site. Our four-engined DC-4s from BW1 were to deliver most of the construction material.

The only landmark on the white desert of ice and snow was the Kee Bird, a B-29 that had bellied in on a frozen lake 30 miles inland in 1947. (The fabled *Kee Bird* flew backwards because it didn't want to know where it was going, only where it had been, all the time wailing "Keerist but it's cold.")

The B-29 crew had flown from Fairbanks to the North Pole, then took up a wrong heading on the return flight and found themselves lost over the Greenland Ice Cap. They were about out of gas when they made a safe belly landing on the perpetually frozen lake.

Nature's own deep freeze protected it from rust, rot and corrosion. Seen from the air it looked like it was just waiting for a crew to take it off. A crew almost did, 43 years later in May 1995. After enduring insufferable hardships for three years while virtually rebuilding the plane, they were taxiing for takeoff when the plane caught fire and burned before their eyes.

The east coast of Greenland in the 1950s was about as inaccessible as any spot on earth outside the Antarctic. The east coast is blocked by land-fast ice for years at a time. The Army Transportation Corps had tried to cross the 740 miles of the ice cap by cat train — big D-8 caterpillar tractors pulling sleds as big as box cars. They nearly lost the whole train in the first nine miles.

The route had been carefully scouted by plane and helicopter with the aid of Paul Victor, Danish veteran who had spent of two years exploring the ice cap. There wasn't a sign of a crevasse as the cat train camped for the first night, full of confidence. Next morning, one of the cats pulled past the wannigan or bunkhouse in the heart of the camp area to refuel.

Ten feet from the wannigan the nose of the cat dropped 45 degrees, revealing a gaping hole 40 feet wide. They pulled that cat out of the crevasse, only to crash through more snow bridges every time they tried to move. At one time two of the three cats were stuck nose down in gaping holes. All were finally rescued and the big cats returned to base to regroup.

Next, a light-weight tracked snow vehicle called a weasel was sent ahead to find a safe route. A big D-8 cat followed the weasel's tracks over apparently solid snow and ice — only to plunge through a 40-foot snow bridge. Nerves on edge, the driver jumped and ran, leaving the cat quivering nose down at a 45 degree angle, resting on the wedge of hard packed snow at the lip of the crevasse. Put the cat in gear and the vibration would surely jar the snow loose from the ice and send the cat plunging out of sight. A similar accident recently had hurled one Dane and two French explorers into the depths of a crevasse, where they disappeared.

Then a reckless lad, his name lost to history, stepped forward and allowed as how he'd skin that cat out of there. He climbed through the back door of the cab and revved up the engine. He gave the signal to the second big cat tied to him by a 1.5 inch steel cable, and shoved the D-8 into reverse. There was a groaning of gears, a growling of steel treads on crunchy snow. As the tracks bit into the snow, the cat dropped down almost out of sight. The nose hung down so that the daring driver looked straight down into the green-black depths of the bottomless crevasse.

A cloud of fine ice particles rose up as the treads ground through the snow and bit into the ice. Man and machine seemed doomed. Then the cab came slowly into sight.

Shaken to the bone, the cat train commanders gave up and turned back. Now it was up to Blowtorch Morgan, with help from the air.

Blowtorch Morgan was a tough, profane dozer jockey from Oklahoma. He was part Eskimo, part polar bear, part Sasquatch, with the survival instincts of a sled dog. Whenever the Weather Bureau had an impossible mission in the Arctic, they called on Blowtorch. He had built runways to resupply most of the Weather Bureau's remote Arctic outposts, including Canada's Alert, the northern most weather station in the world.

He was reputed to be as mean as a junk yard dog when he was sober and even worse when he was drunk, which was most of the time. It was said when he couldn't find liquor he would squeeze alcohol out of the very rocks. He would distil white mule out of anything, with the aid of his blowtorch. The problem was to find a crew that would work with him. This time he was allowed to pick his own crew of fellow construction stiffs. He chose two hardbitten survivors named Pete Moore and Cecil "Buck" Courtney.

In April, when the first signs of spring were seen in the north, Morgan set out to round Pearyland, the northernmost tip of Greenland, on the sea ice, then to follow the shore ice down the east coast to the Nord Site.

When skies are clear over the Greenland Ice Cap you can see forever. You could see the tracks of a fox and follow them for miles. That's how we located Morgan's cat train.

But Morgan was hampered by fog and clouds that blended with the ice, and he was confused by the perpetual daylight. When we swooped low over his camp April 21 to drop supplies and repair parts, he was headed in the wrong direction.

His first question was, "What day is this?" We told him it was 4 a.m. his time, April 21. "Don't care about the date," he said. "What day is it?" We told him it was Monday and morning.

Then he was able to resume navigation. At the top of the world the summer sun rolls around the horizon endlessly. You can't tell whether it is morning or night. It is amazing that Morgan had gotten as far as he had — without a compass, without a reliable map and with icy fog frequently obscuring the low-lying ice islands in his path.

He used an old Boy Scout trick. He knew that the sun was in the west at 8 p.m. and in the east at 8 a.m. He could then interpolate for north and south. But after staying underway for up to 48 hours without a break, he lost track of time and didn't know morning from night. We later dropped him a compass.

Here, where the lines of longitude converge, we were turning back the clock every ten minutes as we crossed the lines of longitude. It was confusing even for flight crews with navigators to keep track of time. We left Morgan's cat train at 5:20 a.m., East Coast time, flew four hours back to Thule and landed at 5:10 a.m. We landed before we took off, but logged about nine hours in the process!

That April 21 air drop was a bit nerve-wracking. I handled the throttles to help Major Julian hold 120 miles an hour and 200 feet of altitude in order to see the camp through the low clouds. "We'll have to drop down lower," Major Julian told Morgan by radio.

"Come on down. Don't care how low you come," Blowtorch bellowed. "I need a haircut anyhow. Could use a shave, too.

"That's a good'n. Dropped her right alongside the camp," he came back after we ducked down below 100 feet for the next drop.

"Got to fire up my blowtorch and warm my hands now. Off the air for a minute," he roared.

The next drop included a "pink letter" from his wife. Morgan stopped to read it while we made the rest of the drops. "Makes me want to go to bed," he said, "but not here, of course."

Morgan finally reached the Nord site on April 24. He expected to clear the snow down to the ice and scrape out a runway within three or four days. But this site was unlike anything he had encountered in his years in the Arctic.

After a few hours sleep, he mounted his cat and started to move snow. This was not soft feathery snow typical of most of the Arctic. It proved to be granular snow so deep and heavy as to pile up ahead of Morgan's D-4 cat until it stalled or became impaled on one of the pinnacles of sea ice hidden under the deep snow. The weasel kept burning out transmissions.

There was nothing to do but wait for the spring sun to melt the snow to a manageable depth, while seven planes with their crews stood by to deliver their loads.

We had dropped Morgan and the stranded scientists an Atwell hut, shaped like a quonset hut, but made with double walls insulated against the cold, to serve as a temporary weather station. It became the base for the two Danish weathermen and two Danish scientists.

Early in June, Pete Moore, one of Morgan's helpers, complained of severe pain from an impacted wisdom tooth. About June 12, Dr. Dick, a Northeast Air Command surgeon from Torbay, flew into Nord and extracted the painful tooth, then decided to fly Moore out to avoid the danger of infection. Moore returned to the Nord site on the next ski landing.

Morgan and Cecil "Butch" Courtney moved in with the squeaky clean, patrician Danes, where they were confined for the next two months with nothing to do but eat, sleep and bitch. Morgan was a hero with a blowtorch, but an embarrassment, actually a menace, as an ambassador of goodwill. He nearly precipitated an international incident with Denmark, a proud nation which tended to resent the necessary presence of the Americans in Greenland.

Morgan was a hard working, hard driving, give-'em-Hell mechanic and navigator when faced with a challenge, but he had never been fully housebroken. He didn't believe in shaving or bathing or cleaning house. The Danes radioed their protests to their base commander in Narsarssuak, who relayed their demands to our base commander at Thule. So we sent Morgan a bottle of whiskey and a little tin bath tub.

"Take a bath? Not this pilgrim," Morgan growled. "Baths are for sissies and sick people. Eskimos don't take baths and look at them. Healthy as polar bears." Which was generally true. It wasn't possible to bathe in igloos in the winter. Eskimos scraped their skin with ivory scrapers. Morgan wouldn't think of scraping either. He just sacked out all day and all night.

Morgan's tough helpers didn't believe in baths, either. They sewed their longjohns on in the fall and peeled them off like mustard plasters only when the summer heat drove them to it. But they were housebroken, at least.

It got to the point where Morgan wouldn't even kick off the covers to answer the call of nature. When he rolled over and emptied his bladder on the red hot stove even his buddies threatened to kill him. The Danes demanded that he be removed immediately. Instead he was given a separate hut of his own until he finished bulldozing the runway on the landfast ice in July.

It was late August before Morgan's helpers, Courtney and

Moore, were flown out of the Nord site in one of our DC-4s. "Morgan got where none of us could stand him," Courtney said.

Coming from Courtney, that was a shocking pronouncement, for Courtney himself was about as dirty as a man can get. His beard was as long and dark as the Arctic night, untamed as the Canadian bush and almost as full of wildlife. His hair hung in hunks. His hands were so dirty I first thought that he was wearing gloves.

The Weather Bureau's cook, John, told us that when Courtney peeled off his underwear it was like peeling rubber off a tire. John said that he lifted the offending unmentionables gingerly with a stick and consigned them to the incinerator where they smoldered for hours.

Courtney and Moore left for Torbay on the next plane. Blowtorch Morgan, a bear of a man with a long scraggly beard, yellow teeth and frost scabs on his recently frozen cheeks, followed on the next plane to the Outside.

CHAPTER 2

POST CONDITION ONE

The order came over the public address system with a note of urgency. "Metro has posted wind warnings for 96 knots with higher gusts," the head shed reported.

Condition One shuts down the base. All but emergency personnel return to quarters or take shelter. All travel ceases, except for emergency vehicles.

The warning came too late. A minute earlier the wind had picked up a rock the size of a marble and rifled it through the window of the cubby hole that passed for my office in the headquarters building. I thought I had been shot.

I looked out the window in time to see one of our Newfies swept off her feet and slapped down on her face in front of headquarters. Some of the airmen drove her to the hospital in a heavy truck. Newfoundland supplied most of our secretaries and other civilian help at BW1 (Bluie West One) at the end of Tunugliarvik Fjord near the southern tip of Greenland. The Greenlanders called it Narsarsauq, meaning "grassy plain."

An enlisted man was knocked down and injured in front of the chapel. The OD (Officer of the Day) started out on his rounds of the base in his station wagon. The wind caught him as he passed the fire station and rolled him over and over eight times down the runway toward the fjord. The firemen finally drove one of their heavy trucks out to stop him. He landed on his wheels, shaken but not seriously injured.

A couple of hours earlier, when the wind was only gusting 45 or 50 miles an hour, the firemen had saved a C-47 (DC-3) by similar tactics. The Gooney Bird, flown by Major J. Aitken, Commander of the 86th jet fighter-interceptor squadron from Germany, took off from Keflavik, Iceland, and had passed the point of no return before our operations officer could warn him that BW1 was closed.

He came tooling up Tunugliarvik Fjord, under a low overcast in fairly smooth air. As he approached BW1 he encountered violent turbulence. The flight engineer, standing between the pilots in the cramped cockpit of the old C-47 was hurled against the top of the fuselage and came down in a heap on the floor.

The radio operator, who had left his post and was seated in the rear of the plane, was struck by a big box of supplies that broke loose, smashed against the top of the fuselage, came down and hit him. Everything that was loose — cargo, emergency supplies, rations and spare parts — was flying through the air in all directions.

Pilot and copilot together fought the controls to keep the plane under control as they got gear down and turned in for a landing. They hit the runway nose high for a three point landing. The wind caught them and tossed them 50 feet in the air. Everyone figured they were going to pour on the coal and go around for another attempt to land.

Instead they let the wobbly bird drop, hit the tarmac and bound skyward again and again. Finally the bouncing bird bounced off the runway and came to rest in a parking area. They had to keep it headed into the wind with half throttle until the ramp crew could tie the wings down to a couple of heavy tractors.

By 1 p.m. the wind was screaming down the runway with demoniacal fury. The Gooney bird lifted its tail and switched it around like a wild goose straining to get off the ground. The cables held and it came bouncing back to earth, rocking over onto first one wing tip and then another. Finally the propellers began to turn like windmills. The ground crew had to feather the props by hand to stop them from turning. Two of the mechanics were literally blown away from the plane. One finally crawled back on hands and knees. The other was picked up by a fire truck.

By this time the air was full of debris — lids off garbage cans, sheets of tin and plywood. Heavy four-by-four timbers shot through the air like javelins. A big steel tank about to be buried in the aviation fuel farm went bounding end over end down the runway like a drunken elephant into the fjord.

As the wind slacked off a little, I helped to load the women from headquarters into jeeps and drive them to their quarters. Greenland is all ice or rock, virtually no soil. Stop signs and guard posts around the base had to be stuck into oil drums filled with heavy rocks. Incredibly, the wind had blown down a dozen of them.

Velocities of 200 knots are said to have been registered on the ice cap high above the base. When that high pressure area begins to work its way down to sea level it generates a foehn wind. The air is warmed by compression at the rate of three degrees per 1,000 feet. The result is a warm wind — 20 or 30 degrees warmer than at its starting point on the ice cap.

It was fascinating to watch the foehn wind working its way

down off the cap, licking the snow off the hills as it came. As the higher temperatures reached the base in explosive bursts, blue water began to show in the fjord as cracks and rifts appeared in the ice.

This proved to be an ill wind that blew some good. The base had been frozen in for the winter by eight inches of ice, stranding Lieutenant Rhodes and a dozen men at BW3, the emergency base at the mouth of the fjord. Now we would be able to take the base tug down the fjord and rescue them — if we hurried. Salt water doesn't freeze at 32 degrees, but the water in the fjord, diluted by fresh water from the creeks, froze quickly.

The meteorologists reported the official peak velocity, recorded at 2:30 p.m., was 110 knots or 125 miles an hour. The highest ever recorded at the base was 118 knots or 136 miles an hour. The gusty winds sucked the roof off the weather office, opening up a two-inch crack that let rain pour in and ruin some of the meteorological charts. Evidently this was not the first time the wind had picked on the old weather shack. After some previous storm, steel cables had been installed to prevent the roof from taking flight.

BW1 resembled an old CCC (Civilian Conservation Corps) camp built astraddle a big creek that roared out from under a glacier at the head of the valley. That stream was full of arctic char, a bright salmon trout that would leap out of the water into your net if you weren't careful, my fishermen friends insisted. The base was surrounded by 736,000 square miles of ice and ice cap, the biggest ice cube in the world except for the Antarctic.

Walls of sheer granite rose 4,000 to 5,000 feet on three sides, Tunugliarvik fjord on the other.

The base was built in 1941 to help the Danes defend the island and to serve as the center pier of the aerial bridge across the North Atlantic over which 1,400 combat planes were ferried to the front lines in Europe during World War II. Again in 1952 during the Korean conflict it became a busy service station for jet fighters and light bombers, the life blood of the NATO air forces.

The base had a single runway 6,000 feet long. It was the only airport in the world ever blocked by icebergs. You had to come in low over the fjord and land uphill. Greenland's principal item of export is icebergs, lots of icebergs. Occasionally a big one would park itself at the end of the runway. The operations officer would have to send out NOTAMS (notices to airmen): "Runway blocked by icebergs."

This ice, squeezed out of the bottom of the ice cap from depths as great as 1,000 feet, was no ordinary ice. It was bright blue and compressed as hard as rock. It was the delight of the officer's club. Drop a chunk into a glass of liquor and it would explode. The scientists called it paleocrystic ice, possibly thousands of years old.

It was no place for sissies. You had to have 7,000 feet of ceiling to make an instrument approach to the base, letting down on the radio beam, using radar to help check your position. You had to land on the first pass, or else. There was no chance to go around. The hills climbed faster than our DC-3s or 4s.

It was 10 days before I got my first look at the ice cap. It looked innocent enough, like some great wedding cake stretching as far as the eye could see. But as we made the "milk run" to BW8, 300 miles north along the edge of the ice cap we began to see Canada and our northern states as they must have looked when they began to emerge from the last of the Ice Ages 6,000 to 10,000 years ago.

Greenland is, indeed, emerging from the Ice Ages. It has been for decades, if not centuries. It is 1,600 miles long, 600 miles wide and covered with ice up to 8,000 feet thick. If you picked it up and laid it down on the United States it would stretch from Mexico to Canada and from the Pacific Ocean to Salt Lake City.

Greenland is only about one-tenth the size of the Antarctic. If all the ice on Greenland were to melt it would raise the level of all the oceans by 25 feet and flood a lot of seaports around the world. And therein lies the reason for some of the scientific interest in this island where winter comes to spend the summer and stays all year.

Greenland is a banana belt compared to the Antarctic, but it still gets too cold for men and machines, as we found out on a flight to BW8 in mid-winter. The mercury hovered around zero at BW1, but when we landed at BW8 the tower was reporting 50 below. We didn't dare stop the engines or the oil would congeal so that we couldn't control the pitch of the propellers.

So the passengers had to step off the plane into the full blast of the props. The first one off was the chaplain and in two seconds his face was frozen. By this time the crew chief reported that oil had frozen in the oil coolers and broken the oil line to the engine. That grounded us for the next week. The temperature remained 50 below and colder. Aircraft flown by VIPs had priority on use of the hangar and the mechanics.

For seven days and seven nights we hung around the operations ready room wearing our gloves and parkas and playing table tennis, however clumsily. I put on everything I owned and went for a brisk walk off the base toward a big lake where I could hear booms like distant thunder as I got within a mile of the lake. The cannonading got louder as I reached the lake. The ice was as black as a coal mine at midnight. Great cracks, two and three feet wide were splitting the ice to a depth of 8 or 10 feet. How do fish survive conditions like that?

BW8 was the scene of another, startling, world class mystery on November 27, 1951, that literally shook the base to its foundations.

We had been grounded at BW8 waiting for the weather to clear at BW1 when a brilliant light lit up the dark of the night. It persisted for several seconds, long enough for Captain Ira E. Grounds, base operations officer, to get out of his closed jeep and look around in all directions.

Everybody on base was startled by the brilliance of the light. First it was blue, then it built up to a brilliant white then seemed to change into a bloody red along the horizon.

The air traffic controller on duty in the tower had time to jump at the flash, turn slowly around and look in a complete circle for the source of the light before it died out. He thought the sky lighted up with equal brilliance in all directions.

He noted the exact time on the log and turned to talk to the airman on duty. He — and every one else — was still speculating about the light five minutes later when an explosion shook the glass in the tower and jarred the building. Airmen walking down the road felt the ground shake. To me and others it felt like the concussion from a dynamite blast. It jarred windows around the base and shook the earth, not with the rolling motion of an earthquake, but with the jolt of an explosion.

The controller on duty in the tower got out his computer and estimated the explosion was about 70 miles away. (The speed of light is essentially instantaneous. The speed of sound, at the existing temperature was 12.5 miles a minute.) Captain Grounds thought the flash came from the northwest. A pilot flying down from Thule thought he saw a crater in the ice at about that location. So the next morning we took off for the estimated location of the explosion. We set up a search pattern and flew for three hours, but never saw any sign of a disturbance.

The incident was reported through Air Force channels and passed on to the Danes who checked with Godthaab, the capital, but the mystery remains unsolved to this day.

16. (Above) Snocat bulldozer is rigged for a drop to the South Pole.
Richards photo

17. (Above) Polar exploration has gone high tech with a C-130 but the dogs still play a vital role. U.S. Air Force photo RF4684-2

18. (Left) Air Force specialist rigs pole topped by glass ball for an air drop. Quonset hut over-flowing with sup-plies fills the fore-ground of Mount Erebus.
Richards photo

20. (Above) An engineer measures the thickness of a sagging ice runway in the Antarctic spring. Richards photo

20. *(Above) McMurdo Bay, 1955. Navy Neptune bomber refuels from icebreaker.* Official United States Navy photo

21. *(Above)* Que Sera Sera *makes the first landing at the South Pole, October 31, 1956. Note shadow of a C-124.* U.S. Air Force photo

22. (Left) Richards greets Jack Marks, hero of the Great Penquin Search, en route to the ice. *Frank Sterrett photo*

23. (Right) The Oregonian's *Aviation Editor in flight over the arctic aboard Scandinavian Airlines. Frequent fliers will note some modern changes: "Actually, few kings these days live as royally as the garden variety passenger on a first class airliner. Gracious ladies-in-waiting to whom service is a proud profession greet you at the door, take your hat, coat and shoes, slip comfortable slippers on your grateful feet, provide you with a mask, sleeping pills, toilet kit, electric razor, wash-and-dry cloth, and conversation in English, Norwegian, German, French or Danish."* Carl E. Vermilya photo, The Oregonian

24. *(Above) Adelies search for bare ground on which to lay their eggs.* Richards photo

25. *(Above) At Cape Royd fiesty Adelies fight to defend their nests from trespassers.* Richards photo

26. (Left) Vanport, Oregon, Memorial Day 1948.

Hugh Ackroyd photos

27. (Above) Richards landed the seaplane. He and Hugh Ackroyd were trying to save a litter of puppies.

28. *(Right) The Alaska Earthquake, March 1964: Smoke rises from burning oil tanks at Whittier, Alaska.* Richards photo

29. *(Below) Engineers land in "Pummy Pond" on Mount St. Helens, April 1981.* Richards photo

30. (Above) Thirty brave Oregonian *survivors who flew with Lev. His wife Virginia Richards stands next to him.* The Oregonian *photo*

31. (Below) A ride on Thonglaw was the highlight of a career.
Leonard Bacon photo

CHAPTER 3

FLYING GRANDFATHER

They say that there are no old, bold pilots. But there was one —Max Conrad, the evangelist of aviation of Winona, Minnesota, Switzerland and way points.

Max was born to fly. He logged more time on the base leg than some professional pilots log in a life time. He held more records for long distance flights and logged more flying time in the process than any pilot that ever lived.

In 50 years he logged more than 54,000 hours in the air — 10,000 more hours than any pilot before him, according to records of the Federal Aviation Administration. He had as many miraculous escapes from disaster as he had triumphs in his long, eventful life. The story of his life would fill a book with thrilling, inspiring stories of adventure, misadventure, success and despair. In later years we talked about co-authoring such a book, but years ago he had promised to work with another freelance writer. Max Conrad never broke a promise. No book was ever published so far as I can determine.

In February 1964, he was ferrying a single-engine Italian airplane across the Atlantic when his engine quit as he was leaving the south coast of Greenland, headed for Iceland. He coolly set in a forced landing near the terminus of a glacier on the southern tip of Greenland.

His chances of rescue were worse than the odds of winning the Irish Sweepstakes. Dozens of aircraft being ferried to the European Theatre during World War II had disappeared on this leg of their flight and never been found. The nearest rescue base was 100 miles away or more.

Conrad quickly broadcast a May Day (Help Me) call, giving his position. Only military and some airline pilots monitor this emergency frequency and then only sporadically. The odds of anyone hearing his May Day were remote even on busy airways. The crew of an Icelandic Airlines DC-4 just happened to hear Conrad's broadcast. Chances of rescue on this remote, uninhabited tip of the ice cap far off the steamer lanes were virtually nil.

A Danish government supply ship that cruises the coast twice a year just happened to be in the area. The Iceland pilot managed to make radio contact with the skipper of the vessel, who altered course to search for the downed flier. Conrad survived the crash and was able to dodge the gaping crevasses and reach the foot of the glacier before dark, where he was rescued by the crew of the Danish ship.

"It was a miracle," Conrad said later. "But this has happened to me all my life. I have repeatedly escaped disasters, survived tragedies and lucked out."

He made all but one of his records flying solo. He led a lonely life always on the wing. But he was never alone. "My fairy godmother makes all my flights with me," he explained. "I don't have to pay her anything — anything but homage," he said.

He was referring to the Virgin Mary, in whom he placed absolute trust. He insisted on the best of navigation aids and personally maintained his aircraft in top condition. He studied the weather and plotted his course with the greatest of care. Then he relaxed and left the rest to the Lord.

I first met Max one sunny day in July 1952, when I was on duty with the Air Force, stationed at BW1 (Bluie West One) near the southern tip of Greenland. The Danes called it Narsarssuakk. The base had been on alert for days waiting for two H19 helicopters making a highly-publicized, high priority effort to prove that helicopters had reached the stage of development where they could island hop across the Atlantic.

They had taken off in the face of nasty weather forecasts and then kept going under increasingly lower ceilings until they encountered fog and were forced to land on a small island just off the mouth of Tunugliarfik Fjord. When the skies cleared the next morning, July 22, before Air Rescue's B17 could reach them, they came tooling up the fjord and landed about 11:45 a.m.

About 7 p.m. a tiny, two-place high winged monoplane powered by a dinky 125-horsepowered engine slipped in unheralded and almost unnoticed. It landed and taxied to the flight line. The pilot tied down his plane; he closed his flight plan with base operations, and disappeared.

After a couple of hours had passed the security officer reported the missing pilot to our new young commanding officer who promptly went into orbit. He was in the process of organizing an all-out search when someone looked in the chapel.

There we found a tall, quiet, athletic figure of a man with a tinge of gray in his hair. This was Max Conrad. He explained that he had been climbing the hills that rise above the base. "I checked in with Base Ops and the Lord," he explained. "Then I needed to stretch my legs after the flight from Goose Bay (Labrador)."

This proved to be Conrad's life style. In college he was an all around athlete, but primarily a high jumper of Olympic caliber. All his life he kept himself in top physical condition. That's all that pulled him through some of his closest brushes with death, that and his abiding faith in the Lord.

Over the years we grew to be good friends. He spent the night with us whenever he got within striking distance on his frequent flights around the country. I admired his flying skills, his mechanical genius, and his total dedication to the sheer joy of flying. The humble pilot sailed serenely through some of the world's worst weather in a frail single-engine plane where pilots flying powerful four-engine planes hesitated to venture.

Conrad made his first flight across the Atlantic out of a kind of desperation. He had married Beatrice (Betty) Biesanz in 1931. They had 10 children. Then she moved to Switzerland with the children. Desperate to see his family, Max installed extra fuel tanks in his little Piper Pacer and took off.

Everything from officialdom to snow, ice, winds and finances conspired against him. By the time he landed at Goose Bay Canadian Air Force Base in Labrador, he was broke and his spirits were as low as the lowering clouds that blocked his way.

He stepped into Base Ops to close his flight plan, then thumbed a ride across the field to the chapel. This was always his second stop on any flight.

In the chapel he "had a little talk with the Lord." Lacking funds or transportation to the base transient housing across the field, he laid down on the floor in front of the altar and slept. In the morning he arose, refreshed, filed a flight plan to BW1, opened a 20-cent bottle of glycerine from a stateside drug store, smeared it on his propeller and the leading edge of his wings.

140

He calmly bored through heavy icing that had dragged down many a four-engine plane.

By 1952 Max was still speaking slowly with occasional hesitations. He was gradually recovering from the accident that almost cost his life.

He had soloed in an Eagle Rock open biplane in 1926. He established a flight school at Winona, and soon had all the students he could handle. He also flew charter flights and at one time ran a small airline with two aircraft. Fortune was smiling brightly on Max Conrad.

Then disaster struck. Fire destroyed his uninsured hangar and operations building. Mismanagement by an associate cost him his ferrying business. He lost his mind and nearly lost his life in a ground accident. He had seen a passenger step out of a light plane after a short flight and start to walk into the spinning prop. Without hesitation Conrad made a dive for the woman and snatched her out of harm's way, but in the process he was thrown into the propeller. The blade bit deep into his brain. He gradually recovered physically. His memory was gone; he couldn't talk. By grim concentration he recovered his speech. He began to recall incidents that had happened years ago. For years he had to struggle to remember recent events.

The Piper factory gave Max a single-engine, low-winged Comanche, selected at random from the production line. Painted on the side was Conrad's slogan, his mission in life: 110LF for "Let's Fly." He was off on a new career. On June 2, 1959, he established his first official long distance record in his flagship 110LF, flying from Casablanca, Morocco to Los Angeles: 7,668.48 miles in 58.6 hours. He took off with 520 gallons of fuel, bringing the gross weight of the plane up to 5,000 pounds. His useful load was equivalent to 20 passengers, each weighing 170 pounds, more than the capacity of most twin-engine commuter airliners. Yet he was able to lift the aircraft gently off the runway after a run of just 4,000 feet.

This was the first of more than a dozen official world records and other unofficial records that Conrad established in 45 years of almost constant flying. He established a ferry service and flew more than 200 aircraft across the Atlantic and to Africa, Arabia and way points.

He overhauled the engine on 110LF by himself and rigged his own fuel systems. He would wait for the coolest air conditions to give him maximum lift, use full power to ease his overloaded airplane off the runway, and then gradually ease the propeller back to 1500 RPMs. He was able to reduce fuel consumption to an amazing eight gallons an hour. Special hot spark plugs were required at this low RPM and a special synthetic oil.

To help him stay awake, Max ingested nothing but a sip of water every hour. He admitted that after two days and nights of maintaining a heading and altitude, monitoring his radios and carefully managing his complex array of fuel tanks, he sometimes became confused. While he didn't doze off, he would momentarily forget where he was, and what he was doing up there.

To while away the hours he composed poems which he later set to music. He had been a band leader in college and had an ear for music. He turned out two albums, neither of which became a best seller.

By 1961 he had acquired Piper's top of the line twin-engine Aztec. In March 1961, Max set a new class record for speed in circling the globe at the equator, solo. He flew 25,946.3 miles in 8 days, 18 hours and 36 minutes.

He had broken all the records in the book, except one — circling the globe from pole to pole. He was determined to add that solo record to his log books. By that time he had logged more than 53,000 hours without a major mishap.

He was forced to abort his first attempt to fly over both ends of the earth. Then in 1971 he tried again.

In January he succeeded in landing at the Scott-Amundsen scientific station at the geographic South Pole, 9,300 feet above sea level. After refueling he managed to get up enough speed over the rough surface of the snow to get off the runway. Then, unable to climb, he ran into ice fog, lost visibility and struck the snow with one propeller. He managed to nurse the overloaded plane into a climb, feathered the damaged propeller and returned for a landing.

Again he hit the snow, wrecking the plane, but escaping injury. He left the wrecked plane to be buried by the drifting snows of the polar plateau. Undaunted he returned to his familiar Comanche 110LF and continued his crusade for aviation.

On a ferry flight in 1967, Conrad saw the birth of a new volcano off the coast of Iceland. He had just taken off from Reykjavik Airport headed for England, when he saw the sea boiling violently directly ahead. He circled to get a better look, and he saw liquid lava rise out of the sea and form the start of a new island which the Icelanders call Sertse. He described the eruption to Reykjavik air traffic control as it happened.

Max launched Operation Inspiration, flying around the U.S., Canada and Mexico giving free rides to children. He explained how airplanes work, and promoted a new association of Flying Grandfathers to support aviation.

All his life he was in great demand as a speaker, especially to aviation enthusiasts like the 99s, an organization of women pilots, and dedicated pilots like the Columbia Aviation Country Club in Portland. He would start out slowly, as if groping for words, candidly blaming himself for whatever went wrong on his flights and giving credit for everything that went right to his "Fairy Godmother." Then as inspiration grew he spoke as if in a trance, as if he were describing the images of his life and his flights that crowded across the screen of his mind. His audiences listened with rapt attention. You could hear a dime drop.

He always arrived by air, usually unannounced. Then in March 1979, he showed up in a car — first time I ever saw him drive a car. He seemed his old self, composed, soft-spoken, but he must have had a premonition. He said he was looking up his 10 children, including a son in Portland who was an airplane pilot. He wanted to meet his 33 grandchildren. He said he just wanted "to distribute my belongings."

He had no real home and died at the home of a friend in New Jersey. He wrote his own epitaph in his "Flyer's Rosary" which he composed and set to music during one of his lonely flights beneath the stars.

> *By night on swift enchanted wings I fly.*
> *Bright stars above become my Rosary.*
> *Each star a lonely prayer which bids me try*
> *To live in faith and hope and charity.*

CHAPTER 4

NORTH POLE

It was during one of those long delays in the Parkway project in 1952 that I got my first chance to fly over the North Pole.

Captain Robert S. Lucy, of Riverside, California, was scheduled to fly a drop mission to Ice Island T-3 a couple hundred miles from the North Pole. He needed an extended crew for the long flight to comply with regulations limiting the number of hours that can be logged on a single flight. He needed "pushers" to help handle the drums of POL (petroleum, oil, lubricants), so I signed on with his crew.

Lieutenant Colonel Joe Fletcher had landed on the floating ice island about two weeks earlier to establish a weather station and listening post. The Russians already had one and possibly two stations near the pole, and we were urgently playing catch-up. Fletcher was stranded there, hurting for supplies. So we took off at 1200 hours (noon) April 29, Thule, Greenland time with a load of groceries, gasoline and instruments for Fletcher and his three-man crew.

Our navigator took us unerringly over endless ice floes to 88 degrees, 5 minutes north latitude; 160 west longitude, less that

120 miles from the pole, the last reported position of the drifting island. The ice island was white like the snow-covered ice that surrounded it. But we could plainly make out the outlines of the island, extending above the broken sea ice like a low-lying barge without a tug. It was almost as conspicuous as Portland's Swan Island, but bigger — about three by nine miles.

We opened the rear "pneumonia hole" admitting a gale of comparatively warm air — only 10 degrees below zero. Captain Lucy dropped down to about 300 feet above the ice and reduced speed to about 120 miles an hour. My job then was to help wrestle the 350-pound steel drums to the open door where the rest of the crew attached cargo parachutes and kicked the drums out the door. They wore safety harness. We pushers did not, but we stayed well clear of the open door.

To deliver the bread and canned milk in cardboard cartons we dropped on down to 50 feet above the ice and never mind the parachutes. The bread was frozen so hard nothing could dent it anyway. I was wringing wet with sweat when we finished the drop.

As we climbed away from the drop zone I got a good look at that tiny camp on the ice below. It consisted of a couple of double-walled tents pitched in the snow alongside a landing strip marked by brightly colored flags. I couldn't help wondering what it would be like to be stranded all alone on that hunk of drifting ice.

"It was no sweat, but no fun," Lucy said once we were settled down cruising on autopilot. "I was there just last week, " he said. I was flying copilot for Lieutenant Colonel Jack W. Streaton. We were grounded — or iced — for eight days."

The story starts early in April when the Navy tried to beat the Air Force to a landing at the North Pole. The Navy P2V Neptune bomber, equipped with skiis, sprang an oil leak and had to make an emergency landing on T-3 (now Fletcher's Ice Island).

Streaton and Lucy were dispatched to deliver an engine for the Navy Neptune. Colonel Fletcher got on the horn and told the pilot that the snow was packed hard enough for the C-54 to land on wheels. It wasn't. Streaton was skeptical, but made a pass at the runway, touched his wheels to the hard snow gingerly then poured on the power and went around. This time he touched down. The heavily-loaded C-54 broke through the icy crust and came to a sudden stop.

There it remained for eight days. A tiny D-2 Caterpillar bulldozer was flown in aboard a C-47 equipped with skiis. Big Fritz Ahl came along to operate it. Ahl was a little fellow, about five by five, about 250 pounds of muscle and mustache. He didn't exactly ride that little dozer. He sort of wore it like a vest. Rumor had it that when the little cat got stuck Big Fritz Ahl would get out and push. Thus, in a few days, he cleared a 900-foot runway down to the bare but bumpy ice.

Now 900 feet is nowhere near long enough takeoff roll for a DC-4, even at sea level in cold air. But Streaton was getting antsy after eight days on the ice with nothing to do. So, on April 27, he held the brakes, warmed up the engines, shoved the throttles to the firewall, then released the brakes. For about two seconds nothing happened. Then the frozen left brake let loose and the plane lurched to the right. The right brake loosened just in time for Streaton to straighten out the big bird and go lurching down the runway like a drunken goose.

Streaton pulled the nosewheel off the ice, but the plane didn't come with it. The snow bank at the end of the runway was looming large when the pilot hollered for flaps. The engineer slapped down the flaps, almost full, and the plane bounced into the air, shuddering and shaking on the verge of a stall.

"We figured we had cleared that snowbank at the end of the runway," Lucy recalled. "We gradually milked up the flaps, gained altitude and switched to aux (auxiliary fuel) tanks. We set cruising power and were sitting there fat, dumb and happy when the stuff hit the fan. All four engines conked out, like wow, dead in the air. We scrambled all over the cockpit, pushing and pulling valves and fuel pumps. We got the main tanks turned on and the old fans came to life with a roar.

"We finally figured out that the valves from the aux tanks to the mains had frozen during our R. & R. (rest and recreation) on T-3. All that bouncing down the runway had jarred the ice out of the valves and the aux tanks had drained into the mains, leaving us suddenly trying to feed out of empty tanks.

This supply drop was the crew's first flight to T-3 since their narrow escape. They learned they had been closer to disaster than they realized. After Fletcher retrieved his groceries he came on the air to tell Lucy how close they came to cracking up on that takeoff from T-3 two days before. "You guys didn't clear that snow bank at the end of the runway," Fletcher said. "You ploughed through it for more than 20 feet. Then you hit a pinnacle of hard ice that kicked you into the air at the last impossible moment."

There was a long, sober silence as Lucy pondered his close escape then: "Let's take a look at the Pole."

About 30 minutes later the navigator declared we were at 90 degrees north, navigator talk for the North Pole. There was nothing there but miles and miles of miles of ice, laced with blue lines like varicose veins where leads or cracks in the ice revealed the deep blue of the Arctic Ocean.

This was an historic occasion so we improvised a fitting ceremony. We made a flag from the top of an in-flight lunch box, using my fountain pen for the blue stripes, and red from the crew chief's pencil. It fluttered down so slowly that we might have landed back at Thule before our flag hit the ice.

We took off at 1200 hours (noon)) April 29 and reached the pole at 19:35 (7:35 p.m.). But, by the navigator's log today was tomorrow. It was 00:35, 35 minutes after midnight the morning of April 30 at the North Pole. We had turned our clocks ahead four hours as we skipped across the converging lines of longitude. We circled the pole once from east to west, turning the clock back 24 hours and adding a day to our lives.

Fletcher's Ice Island was discovered by navigators for the 54th Weather Reconnaissance Squadron from Fairbanks on one of their daily flights to the Pole. It was formed in one of the glaciers on the tip of Ellsmere Land, broke off and floated into the Arctic Ocean in one huge chunk, unlike the smaller icebergs calved by glaciers further south in Alaska.

Evidence of its origin was discovered by Dr. S. F. Crary, Harvard oceanologist, who found lakes of fresh water on the ice island, covered by eight feet of ice. He also found pockets of dirt picked up by the glacier as it gouged its way to the sea through the frozen tundra. Crary's instruments showed that the island rocked and rolled, tilting as much as five degrees as it forced its way through the surrounding sea ice.

Crary's studies revealed that the island did not move at all some days. Then it would suddenly move three or four miles in a day. Once, it scooted 18 miles in one day, moving at three miles an hour at times, forcing its way through the ice floes with a great groaning and cannonading that shook the island and startled the hitchikers on its broad back.

Crews of the B-29 weather planes continued to discover other, even bigger, islands on their daily "milk runs." On the return trip from the pole, sliding 806 miles down the parallels of longitude to our base, we passed the giant of the lot, 15 miles square, lying peacefully about 20 miles from the pole.

T-2, one of the biggest of the lot, was about 185 miles southeast of the pole, near 15 degrees west longitude and 87 north latitude. We looked for another big island reported near the pole, but the area was fogged in.

We landed back at Thule weary-eyed after 12 hours and 10 minutes of staring at bright sun reflected from the polar ice.

CHAPTER 5

ORDEAL ON ICE

During my long year of duty with the U.S. Air Force in Greenland in 1952 I had plenty of time to read. Among the fascinating, sometimes heart-rending documents were reports of tragic, prolonged ordeals suffered by the crews of lost aircraft in Greenland and the Canadian Arctic. These were classified at the time, later declassified. Following is the story of the most tragic and prolonged of all recorded rescues, as told in the first person by Captain Armand L. Monteverde and Private Alexander L. Tucciarone to a board of inquiry.

We were tooling along at 7,000 feet over the Greenland Ice Cap, searching for a lost C-53 when it happened. The horizon was obscured by blowing snow, but I figured I was holding at least 1,500 feet above the cap.

I was banking about 10 degrees to the left when there was a sudden jolt. My first thought was that a turbosupercharger had exploded. I was stunned when I hit the instrument panel, but recovered immediately. I thought, "My God! We're on fire." The air was filled with smoke.

I looked out the front window and saw one of the crew lying on the snow, covered with blood. It was Sergeant Paul Spina. "Got to save him from the fire," I thought. I dived out the side window into the blowing snow. That icy blast woke me out of my daze. I realized that this was no fire, just blowing snow.

I called for help to get Spina into what was left of the B-17 out of the wind. He had been thrown out of the plane when it broke in two just aft of the radio compartment. His hands were frozen before we could get him into the tail section. My gangling, good natured copilot, Lieutenant Harry E. Spencer, Dallas, Texas, showed up to help get Spina into the tail section where the crew made him as comfortable as possible.

Once everyone was packed into the cramped tail section, with a great show of confidence, I assured the miserable men that rescue could not be more than a couple of days away. "We couldn't have picked a better spot to belly her in," I told them. "We're only about 25 miles from the ice cap weather station where they have dog teams and motor sleds for rescue work. And just off the cap, down below, is the base at BE2 (Bluie East Two)."

Handsome, dark-haired Monteverde knew they were down on the Greenland Ice Cap, graveyard of many a military aircraft en route to Europe, where temperatures drop down to 85 below and winds of 170 miles an hour have been recorded.

Little did he know that their ordeal by ice would last nearly five months — the longest on record for the ice cap — all would suffer the prolonged agony of frostbite; one of the crew would lose his legs, another would lose his mind; two of the crew would lose their lives and three paramedics would die trying to rescue them.

The engineers found a tarpaulin in one of the lockers and managed to fasten it across the open end of the tail section to block out some of the howling wind and snow.

Once they were settled into the cramped quarters I said: "Listen up, guys. I'm a California kid. I've never seen snow close up. I don't know diddly squat about the Arctic. But I'm commander of this ark and I will take charge and do my best to get us out of here in one piece. That's the way it is in this man's air force. But we are all in this together. So if anybody has any bright ideas, let's hear them."

He called for an inventory of the emergency equipment aboard. The engineers found half a case of in-flight rations, but no sleeping bags, no heavy snowbunny boots, no heavy mitts, no primus stoves. No cold weather gear at all. So the crew cut up the parachutes aboard and wrapped themselves in the canopies.

"The first aid kits are marked for the tropics," Spence discovered. "Lots of suntan lotion, insect repellent, instructions for treatment of sunstroke, nothing we can use except jungle knives and mosquito netting, which we used later to strain the tea leaves out of our sugar.

It is not surprising that we were equipped more for the tropics than the Arctic. We were not based in Greenland. We were ferrying this bomber to Europe. We landed in BW1 to refuel and they ordered us to join the search for this missing C-53 cargo plane on November 9, 1942. I picked up four passengers to help my five-man crew look for the C-53, which was believed be down about 300 miles northeast of BW1 about 25 miles from BE2. And that's where we were searching on November 9, 1943, when we went down.

That first night was hell. We were huddled together, hugging each other, trying to keep each other warm, stomping our feet when we could. We never knew how cold it got. The outside air thermometer in the nose of the airplane had been knocked off in the crash. But it was cold enough to freeze Spina's hands and feet in the three minutes or so that it took to get him inside. I froze my hands and feet about the same time and before we got off the cap everyone had frostbitten hands and feet. We were a sorry lot of snowbunnies to be stranded on an ice cap.

Those were the cowboy days of aviation. Proper throttle jockeys all wore fancy street shoes or cowboy boots with their pinks and greens. We had nothing but fleece-lined flight boots over our oxfords to keep our feet warm. Those abominations cost a lot of good pilots a lot of toes, feet and legs — as we were to find out.

Lieutenant William F. O'Hara, our navigator, had got some snow in his boots while helping to move Spina. He didn't dump it out and didn't mention it until he noticed that he had no feeling in his feet. We got his boots off and his feet were frozen as hard as concrete. In my ignorance I made the common mistake of rubbing his frozen feet. When that didn't help I warmed his feet under my armpits until they began to soften up. Then they turned purple, green and black.

We also made the common mistake of eating snow. But by the second day we were desperately thirsty, the few gallons of water we carried was a block of ice and we had no means of melting snow. Some of the enlisted men wanted to build a fire with gasoline in the tail section. They complained that they were going to freeze to death if they didn't do something. I felt their misery, but a gasoline fire at that stage would have spelled disaster. The long range tanks in the fuselage had broken and spilled all over. We could still smell the fumes. I had to knock that idea in the head.

We figured our best hope for rescue was our radios, but they had been torn from their mountings in the crash and lay, a tangled mass of wires, in the snow. It looked like a hopeless mess, but Corporal Loren E. Howarth, one of the passengers we had picked up in BW1, was a radio operator and started working on the mess during our short winter daylight with the aid of Private Clarence Wedel and T/Sergeant Alfred Clinton Best.

154

The wind seemed to blow even harder that second day and we were confined to the tail. Lying there in the barren tail of that metal trap with nothing to do but think I began to listen to the wind shake the fuselage like a dog shaking a bone. Then, during lulls in the storm, I thought I could hear rivets popping as the tail section tore away from the main fuselage. It felt like some Edgar Alan Poe nightmare, but I would swear we were slowly, inch by inch, settling into a crevasse.

To keep my mind off the possibility and to keep up the spirits of the crew, I tried to get each one to tell something about his family, his ambitions, his life story, anything to keep their thoughts from the creaking and groaning.

Along toward dusk of that second day I got a look outside. My worst fears were confirmed. The gaping black maw of a crevasse could be seen opening up at the end of the tail section. I wondered how many of our crew had heard the rivets popping. O'Hara had. "Let's get the Hell out of here," he suggested as the horror of our predicament dawned on him. "We'll slide into that damned hole in the night."

"So where do we go? " I countered. "We wouldn't last an hour in the open in this storm. We haven't any tools to build a snow house — if any of us knew how. We have to stay where we are."

We thought we were the only two who felt the tail creaking and sagging, but we soon saw that everyone felt the same chill, but didn't want to alarm anyone else. So Howarth and Wedel, the army men we had picked up in the States, took parachute cord and secured the tail to the main fuselage. The cords looked kind of flimsy. We hoped that they would hold us if the tail started to give way.

But the creaking and the groaning continued. It was enough to drive a man mad — if we didn't have so many more immediate distractions.

I was in constant pain. My feet had been frosted and were in the painful stage of thawing out.

POPPING RIVETS

We had begun to think the wind would blow forever, but on the third day (November 12) the wind died down, gray skies gave way to blue. Spencer and O'Hara woke up early that morning. They eased their way out of the plane to avoid waking anyone.

"We set out to see if we could see any landmarks," O'Hara said. "The ice cap sparkled like diamonds. To the north we could see forever. To the south and east we thought we could see the ocean. That had to be Itateq Fjord where BE2 was located. Rescue was literally in sight. We would make it yet. Euphoria set in.

We set off toward the blue water, all excited. We had only taken a few steps when Spencer drawled: "That's blue water, sure enough, and close enough to..." Then he sort of caught his breath and faded out.

I turned around to see what had cut him off in mid sentence. And there wasn't any Spencer. I looked again and there was this black hole in the snow staring at me like some evil eye. I hollered, but there was no answer, no sound. For a moment I couldn't figure out what had happened.

"I shouted for help and Monteverde scrambled over everyone in the tail and ran out onto the ice to help," O'Hara said.

O'Hara was on his belly looking into that black hole in the rock-hard snow, when I got out of the tail. He hollered at Spencer and faintly, like an echo in a rain barrel, came an answering hail. As our eyes became accustomed to the dark of the crevasse we could just vaguely make him out.

He had been lucky enough to land on a block of ice wedged into the crevasse about 100 feet down and cushioned by hard snow. If he had not hit that block of ice he would have disappeared into the bottom as so many were to do before this ordeal was over. We shouted at him to hang on and assured him that he would be rescued in a matter of minutes. But we knew that this rescue wouldn't be easy.

We had ropes from the tie down kit, but they wouldn't reach Spencer. Howarth, Best and Wedel, the skilled mechanics, however, quickly knotted parachute shroud lines together to extend the rope which they lowered down to Spencer. He tied a bowline. around his waist and brought the rope up under his arms. It took every able-bodied man and some not so able-bodied to haul the 180-pound copilot the 100 feet up the crevasse. Spina was nursing a broken wrist which grounded him. Best, a BW1 radioman from Waco, Texas, had been sick and vomiting for the past two days, but he managed to help pull his weight on the rope. By the time Spencer reached the top, the line had cut deep into his body, partly cutting off his breathing. He was breathless, sick and about to faint. We had to lower him gently back into the crevasse, hoping he could find his perch on that block of ice again.

This time I sent for a parachute harness, the kind you wear for a chest pack. Spencer managed to get this on and fastened the line to the hooks designed to hold the chest pack. This worked fine — until we got him to the lip of the crevasse again. Then we couldn't get him up and over the lip. The thin rope cut deep into the snow at the lip of the crevasse. No one had the strength to lift him up out of the crevasse. We didn't know enough at that time to use an axe handle or something like that to run the rope over to prevent it from cutting into the snow.

Here the jungle emergency kits finally came in handy. We dug down from the top with one machete while Spencer dug up with another machete. We finally cut a trench through which we could drag him out, with the aid of the ship's ladder to help him over the lip of the crevasse. He lay there shaking from the cold and from the shock of his close encounter with death. Then reaction set in. Exhilarated, we danced around, hugging Spencer and slapping each other on the back, not making much sense. We had started as strangers. But we quickly became buddies. We had just seen how each of us depended on the other for sheer survival. Together we had cheated death.

It was a weary but wiser bunch of survivors that began to hobble back to the plane on frostbitten feet, carefully following our foot prints in the snow to avoid any more crevasses. Snow may fall as fluffy flakes or ice pellets on the ice cap, driven by the almost constant gales. But it quickly hardens enough to bridge the crevasses and hide them from view. As the snow accumulates, pressure turns it into hard blue ice

In the full glare of the morning sun we could see what the storm had hidden from us for three days. A jagged black hole was opening under the tail of the plane like the gates of Hell. The tail section was, indeed, beginning to sag into the crevasse. That would confirm the sound of popping rivets that Spencer and I thought that we had heard during those first three days and nights. The crevasse still had a ways to go before she would swallow our shelter in the tail section of the wrecked Flying Fortress. I could only hope we would be long gone by that time.

About 50 feet ahead of the nose another crevasse grinned at us with shark's teeth. It was becoming obvious that we were near the edge of the ice cap where the constantly moving ice broke into crevasses as it oozed over the edge of the plateau like a water fall. As I ducked into the shelter I mentally took stock of our situation. It wasn't good.

Spina, with his broken wrist, cuts and bruises, could only lie helplessly in his nest of parachute canopies. But he continued to make wisecracks to help the morale of the rest of the crew. Best, who had been hurled through the plexiglass in the nose of the bird, showed no external signs of cuts or bruises, but was weak and sick to his stomach much of the time. He also had dizzy spells and could not be trusted to wander around by himself. He seemed confused at times. We figured that he might be suffering from a concussion incurred when he was thrown head first through the plexiglass nose of the plane. O'Hara, always the quiet one, kept his fears to himself until it was too late. Finally one night he asked me if I thought there was anything wrong with his feet. I pulled off his fleece-lined GI overshoes and his stateside oxfords with misgivings.

His feet were frozen solid as ice. I slipped them under my shirt and held them against my stomach. There was nothing we could do for him but hope for a speedy rescue. He developed gangrene and his feet began to rot. The smell wasn't pleasant, but we all pretended not to notice.

The break in the storm gave us a chance to look for the two and a half boxes of rations that were lost when we crashed. But you can bet your life that we roped up this time. If anyone fell through a snow bridge hereafter we would have a rope on him.

We found most of the rations in the drifted snow close around the wrecked fortress. We dug out the box for the bomb sight and set it up under the wing as a makeshift stove for our first hot meal.

The clear weather brought even colder temperatures. Howarth suggested that we build a snow cave to keep warmer, and to escape the popping rivets in the tail section. Everyone was beginning to hear them and feel our shelter slipping by now. But we didn't have snow shovels or snow knives and none of us knew how to build a snow cave anyway. If we had even had an Arctic manual on board we might have figured out how to use the machetes from our tropical survival kits to build a snow cave.

I set up a routine to keep everyone busy and keep up morale. I designated a detail to brush the snow off the wings of the old bird to make it more visible from the air. And whenever the weather permitted I posted a lookout to watch for aircraft. He was armed with a Very pistol that could shoot a red flare high into the air, visible for miles.

But we all knew our last, best chance for rescue was our radios. We had been cranking the hand-powered Mae West radio whenever the wind died down enough to permit us to send up our antenna on a kite. The Mae West (because it was shaped somewhat like Mae West) continuously broadcast a string of SOS's when the wind died down so that we could send up our antenna on a kite.

Most of the time, however, the wind was strong enough to break the antenna wire. And we didn't have much hope of putting out a strong enough signal on ice without a proper ground. The plane's radios had been torn off the wall and smashed during the crash and plastered with snow. It looked like a hopeless task, but Howarth, the radioman we had picked up from the base at BW1 for an observer, volunteered to try and build a transmitter out of it.

The fortress, like most military aircraft, had a gasoline engine aboard to power a generator. The APU (auxiliary power unit), most often called a putt-putt, had been shattered by the crash. But Clarence Wedel, the army hitchhiker we picked up at Goose Bay, proved to be a genius as a mechanic. He got the APU going by the sixth day to charge the batteries, provide juice for some lights to break the black dark of the long winter nights, and operate the Aldis lamp, a powerful hand held lamp, which Howarth promptly used to thaw out the mass of wires in the radio. Salvaging the radio was a miserable job. Howarth had to work with bare hands for minutes at a time, then he would come inside and let us warm his hands. Life on the ice cap had its ups and downs, like an elevator. The eighth day was an up day. That was the day that Howarth got the radio transmitter operating. He had found a tech manual with diagrams which showed him how to connect up the set. Two days later he had the receiver operating. We were no longer lost in space. We had a life line to the outside world.

We contacted Bluie East and gave them our location on the west leg of their radio range. "We'll have a plane over your location in a couple of hours," the operations officer assured us. But nothing every happens on schedule in this land the Lord forgot.

Before dawn the ship began to shake, rattle and roll like a bone in the jaws of a mad dog. For five long days and nights, the wind raged. Between gusts we could hear the rivets pop as the tail gradually tore away from the forward part of the wreck. Those were real down days.

On the fifteenth day, November 24, the storm let up a little. The wind died down to a dull roar. Above the moaning of the wind I thought I heard an airplane. But we had been straining to hear that sweet sound for so long that I didn't believe my ears, until O'Hara reared up and said: "Listen! It's a C-54." We all dashed outside, stomping on O"Hara and Spina on our way out. Sure enough it was a DC-4 swooping low over the wreck, dropping sleeping bags, warm clothing, food and a precious Primus stove. Most of the stuff dropped by parachute was seized by the wind and whipped away.

We didn't dare run after it for fear of the crevasses. But the sleeping bags were dropped free fall, and fell within reach. We retrieved most of the rest of the stuff next day when the wind died down and we could rope up and search the area. There were some glitches. The cans of white gas for the Primus stove burst upon impact and spilled most of the contents. And the Primus stove wouldn't burn leaded aviation gasoline. We did manage to melt a little snow for precious water, however.

We could laugh at our troubles now. We had warm socks and mukluks for our frosted feet. We had longjohns and sleeping bags. It was possible to actually be comfortable at times. Food was plentiful. Bluie East said that dog teams and motor sleds from the Ice Cap Rescue Station were trying to reach us. And the Coast Guard Cutter *Northland* had moved up the east coast and anchored in the fjord near the base. She carried a single-engined Grumman flying boat also equipped with wheels. Operations said the Grumman would look us over on the first clear day. But we didn't see how she could help. No one had ever landed a flying boat on the ice so far as any of us knew. But on the next clear, bright day, November 29, there he was overhead.

The pilot, Lieutenant John A. Pritchard, Jr. and Radioman 1/C Benjamin A. Bottoms dropped a note asking if it were safe to land, gear down.

"Are those guys crazy?" O'Hara and I demanded in the same breath.

We both started frantically waving them off. "Impossible to land," we signalled in international code. But these Airdales wouldn't take no for an answer. To our dismay we saw them extending their landing gear, putting down wing flaps and lining up to land on the ice a half mile away.

We hollered like mad and waved frantically, but on they came. Snow flew, the motor roared. Then we couldn't hear anything more. The plane was hidden in a cloud of snow. We figured they had wound up in a ball and we would have two more cripples on our hands. Then the snow cloud drifted away and there sat the cocky little bird with its propeller ticking over at idle. Evidently the belly float stuck out far enough in front to prevent her from nosing over, even with gear down. But we weren't home safe yet. We watched tensely as we saw the pilot working his way through the mine field of crevasses, probing for snow bridges with a long pole. Once we saw him go down as a snow bridge gave way under him. But he saved him self with his long pole.

It took him about an hour and a half to negotiate the half mile. We clapped the Grumman pilot on the back with relief. But there was no time for talk. The short winter day was waning fast away. Bluie East down below the cap, was already in deep shadow. "I can take two men,'" Pritchard said.

For days I had been thinking who to send out on the first rescue effort. O'Hara and Spina were in the worst shape. But they couldn't walk the half mile to the plane, dodging crevasses and we couldn't carry them. I couldn't spare Best because he was a good cook and knew where all his makeshift pots and pans were. So I sent Private Alexander F. Tucciarone, a Brooklyn man, and S. Sergeant Lloyd Puryear, Camp Bellesville, Kansas, the other radioman from BW1, who had volunteered to ride with us as observer on our search for the missing C-53. Spencer went along with Pritchard to help get the Grumman off the ice. He rocked the wings to help break the hull loose from the snow while Pritchard gave her full throttle. She got off the ice without any problem, with the aid of a brisk breeze that sprang up at just the right time. It looked like things were finally going our way after 21 days of despair. Two of our guys were down off the ice cap. Seven more to go. Motor sleds and dog teams manned by trained survival experts were on the way. And the C-54 was overhead again dropping more supplies.

"We could be out of here by tomorrow," Spencer exulted!

THAT OTHERS MAY LIVE

As night fell we could see the lights of the sled party far across the ice fields to the north. They were pushing through the dark with the aid of flashlights. Periodically we fired our Very pistol to send up flares for their guidance. About midnight we could hear the purr of their motors rising and falling on the night air.

About a mile from our location they encountered the mine field of crevasses that had slowed up Pritchard. The rescuers left their heavy sleds with their whirring propellers while they put on skis, roped up, and felt their way through the crevasses, staking out a safe trail for the heavy motor sleds to follow. Every eye was on those bobbing lights as they drew closer until we could hear the swish of their skis. Finally they hailed us: "Hello the Fort!" and we hailed them back: "Boy are we glad to see you guys."

Lieutenant Max H. Demarest, experienced Greenland hand,

commander of the Ice Cap Rescue Station, headed the team. He took over, examined Spina's splints and dressings with a practiced eye and pronounced them well done. "That wrist will pass inspection by any sawbones," he declared — and so it did, months later when Spina was finally rescued.

He and Staff Sergeant Don T. Tetley of San Antonio Texas, his paramedic partner, examined everyone's frostbitten feet, exchanging banter and war news as they did so, and finally examined O'Hara's case of gangrene in silence.

Everyone was in a festive mood as we turned to for a chicken dinner. Then Demarest and Tetley put on their skis and started to retrace their ski tracks back through the crevasses to their sleds. There was no room for them in the fortress and they would be warm and comfortable in their tent and sleeping bags.

"See you guys in the morning," Demarest said as they waved good bye.

"Don't go away!" Tetley joked.

Not likely, I thought, but said nothing.

The paramedics had a date with us for breakfast and we were all up and out under clear, calm skies to watch them as they skimmed along under the thrust of their whirring propellers, each towing a sled, with Demarest in the lead, sticking close to the ski tracks they had made to mark a safe trail through the field of crevasses

As Demarest came within 100 yards of the B-17 he started to swing the cumbersome sled in a wide arc in order to turn the heavy rig around ready to head back with some of our cripples. As we watched in stunned silence the big sled reared up deliberately, in slow motion, like some clumsy killer whale and dived steeply beneath the sparkling crust of the ice cap, dragging its sled with it.

The growl of the motor faded away. An ugly silence settled over the scene, broken by choked cries from the fortress crew and Tetley's hoarse, despairing shouts as he killed his engine, tied a safety rope around his waist, grabbed a coil of rope and ran toward the black chasm in the snow.

He could just barely make out the motor sled and its tow about 150 feet down, way out of our reach. There was no sign of life. I joined Tetley at the crevasse but agreed that nothing could be done. The jaws of the ice cap had opened and claimed another victim.

Tetley spoke a few words to comfort the soul of Demarest. "He died 'That Others Might Live,'" Tetley concluded, in the words of the Rescue Service motto.

As if to add hope in the midst of horror, the Grumman popped up almost unnoticed while we concentrated on the loss of Demarest.

The Grumman scooted in to a landing at the usual place. I sent Howarth running to tell the Grumman crew that Demarest was lost down the crevasse and to ask for help. He was to warn Pritchard and Bottoms that fog was threatening to sock in around the cutter *Northland* and leave him with no place to land.

We didn't see Pritchard take off with Howarth aboard, but he flew over and rocked his wings purposefully then made a beeline for the cutter.

When the Grumman failed to return with rope ladders or any other rescue gear, we didn't think too much of it. But when we made radio contact with the *Northland* they were asking us if their plane had got off the ice cap. It had never reached the cutter. It had crashed on the ice cap, killing all aboard. It was weeks before the wreckage was found.

Suddenly the toll of lives lost to the ice cap in a single day was up to four — four good men on what started out to be our brightest hour. There were no praying men among us, but Tetley spoke a few words to comfort the soul of Demarest. We added the names of Howarth, Pritchard and Bottoms. Then we all joined in the Lord's Prayer.

NO MORE SWORD OF DAMOCLES

We figured that Tetley could ferry us all back to the ice cap station in a single day on the remaining motor sled, once we got a break in the weather. He had only been assigned to the ice cap station for a month, but he had the instincts and training of a survivor. He took one look at the tail of the wrecked bomber drooping ominously into that growing crevasse and said: "How would you guys like to get out of this ice box? You know you picked the coldest spot you could find in this tin bucket when you have the best insulation in the world right under your feet."

He had brought a shovel and showed us how to dig a snow cave under the wing of the plane. He made a snow knife out of the top on the bombsight case to cut snow blocks to build a wall to protect the cave from the abrasive wind. The result was a snuggery about four feet high, with the underside of the wing for a roof.

There we could stretch out our sleeping bags in some comfort. Tetley also had a Primus stove and white gas in his sled, which made cooking a pleasure and even brought some warmth to the snow cave. Wedel ran a wire from the generator and installed one of the cabin lights for a final touch of comfort and cheer.

Just escaping the constant threat of falling into the crevasse which hung over our heads took the biggest load off our minds. No more creaking and popping rivets to give us nightmares. We felt liberated.

The storm whined on for seven days and seven nights. On December 7, 1942, the anniversary of the bombing of Pearl Harbor, the sun rose in a cloudless sky again. We packed O'Hara into a sleeping bag and lashed him on the sled. He was a sick man, dying by inches as gangrene crept up his ankles to his calves. He had to have medical attention quickly if he were to survive.

I sent Spencer to help handle the sled and to help navigate. Wedel, of Canton, Kansas, the army hitchhiker we had picked up at Goose Bay, went along primarily as a mechanic to help with the engine. He was a good mechanic, hard working, always eager to help, quick to respond to any orders.

The sled party got a cheery sendoff.

"No snaprolls with that rig, now," I warned.

"We'll straighten up and fly right," Tetley promised. "Got to get you out of here, too, for your birthday, sir," he said.

My birthday was two days away, the 9th of December, and the boys had promised me a party.

SLED PARTY

Spencer, unafraid despite his close encounter with crevasses, went ahead on snowshoes to test for snow bridges as he followed the trail mapped out by Demarest and Tetley a week ago. Wedel ran behind most of the time.

They were out of the known crevasse area in a few minutes

and past the point where Tetley and Demarest had camped on the way into the crash site. They stopped to take a breather while Tetley got his bearings. The route lay through a shallow dip and then up a fairly steep rise.

"Everybody get aboard," Tetley said. "We'll have to get a run at it to make it up that rise."

Spencer came back, shed his snow shoes and climbed aboard. Wedel came puffing up from behind and made for the side of the sled, pulling on his heavy mitts and talking to himself as he came.

"Boy, can I use a breath ..."

His voice trailed off into a choked cry. O'Hara felt Wedel grab at his sleeping bag with his clumsy mitts. He felt hands clutch frantically at his leg. Then there was nothing. Just another black hole in the ice.

The three remaining men uttered half-strangled cries, which were drowned out in the scream of the motor as Tetley rammed on full throttle to clear the flimsy snow bridge.

Then he cut off the power, tied a rope around his waist, anchored it to the sled and crawled on his belly to the edge of the hole where Wedel had stood full of life and energy a moment ago. Now there was nothing, nothing but endless, echoing ice as far down as Tetley's straining eyes could see.

The relentless ice cap had claimed its fifth victim in a single week. And that was not to be the end of the story.

The three survivors, shaken by the sudden loss of Wedel, stood around cursing the ice cap and staring at that black hole. It was Tetley who finally made the inevitable decision. The Ice Cap never gives up its victims. There was nothing left to do, but to save those who could still be saved.

"Okay, Lieutenant" said Tetley. "There's nothing we can do,

absolutely nothing. We got to make tracks if we're going to get O'Hara to the station before dark."

They bowed their heads awhile in silent prayer for the lost Wedel. Then Tetley grimly gunned the motor again and they were off as fast as the heavy sled would go through the soft, drifted snow. Time was running out on them. It was almost dark and the weather was deteriorating rapidly.

They made another couple of miles through the gathering storm and the increasing cold. Then the motor coughed and quit. Tetley found a leak in the fuel line and tried to fix it, without much luck. Twice he got the engine started and make a little more progress, then she cut out for good. The oil lines had frozen solid in the prolonged and increasing cold.

They were marooned, three lonely men stranded in an endless sea of snow and ice.

"We'll make camp here," Tetley said calmly.

He quickly pitched a trail tent for Spencer and O'Hara and dug a hole in the snow for himself. Tetley, tired and at ease in the Arctic, slept soundly. So did cheerful and easy going. Spencer. They could afford to wait for a motor sled or a dog team to come out from the ice cap station while aircraft dropped them more survival gear and all the food they needed.

But O'Hara knew that for him time was running out. Always quiet, he said nothing now, just clamped his jaw tighter and hung on. But he died a little every day as the gangrene crept up his legs.

The rescue fortress soon found the sled party and dropped supplies and gear, all they needed. Tetley, full of deliberate cheer, spent days vainly trying to fix the motor sled, with Spencer's help. But the oil was frozen solid. Blizzards drifted over the useless sled until it couldn't even be found.

Their situation was grim, but tall, tough Tetley kept Spencer and O'Hara busy, partly just to keep their minds off their plight. Together he and Spencer built a two-story "Hotel de Frostbite" where they could actually stand up, the better to nurse bedridden O'Hara.

Back at the crash site Monteverde, Spina and Best were up early under clear skies straining to hear the roar of Tetley's motor sled. They looked and listened all that sunny December 7 without sight nor sound of the rescue sled. Then the wind and the snow came out of the north again and the world shrank to the walls of their snow cave.

Monteverde's birthday, December 9, came and went and still the storm raged over them. Gradually it dawned on them that the sled was not coming back to get them. They were caught fast in the womb of winter in a land locked tight in the embrace of the Ice Age.

As the days dragged on, Monteverde kept everyone busy digging their snow cave deeper and wider and installing snow benches along the sides. Best, still suffering headaches and nausea, seemed to take heart helping to improve their quarters.

Sometimes, like the night of January 2, 1943, it seemed as if the very ice cap was writhing under the maniacal fury of the wind. We had never heard such furious gusts before. It was certainly gusting over 100 knots.

I snuggled down and slept peacefully. But I woke up in the night to find my sleeping bag almost buried in snow. Striking a match I found the cave almost filled with fine snow sifting like dust through the wall of snow blocks. We tried stuffing the cracks with parachute silk, but the snow continued to sift through cracks so fine that we couldn't see them. We were being buried alive in a smother of icy white powder.

I finally roused Spina and Best and we moved our bags into the entrance tunnel where we huddled together for warmth. We were all silently resigned to perishing in this tomb under the snow that night.

But the next day dawned clear and cold. We dug our way out and tried to patch up the north wall of our snow cave. But the snow was like talcum powder, too cold to work with. So we cut blocks from old, hard snow and built a new wall from the inside.

When Wedel left on the motor sled, we soon lost the bright light that cheered us through the long winter days and nights in our cave under the wing of the B-17. The little gas engine that powered the generator didn't like us. It wouldn't work for anyone but Wedel. That also shut off our radio, our last link with the outside world. We couldn't even talk to "Pappy" Turner, pilot of the faithful four-engined guardian angel that kept us supplied with food. Our walkie-talkie was on the wrong frequency.

To add to our misery we ran out of fuel for the Primus stove. That meant no water as well as no hot food. In desperation, Spencer and Best tried burning leaded aviation gasoline. This stuff not only filled the cave with sticky black soot, but gave off invisible, deadly carbon monoxide.

I finally had to get tough with the guys. "You're just breeding yourselves a funeral with this red gas," I told them. "There'll be no more of this crap and that's an order."

The rescue boys did drop a note telling us that dog teams were on their way. That really raised the morale of the boys. But by that time we had begun to doubt anything they told us.

And, sure enough, latter they told us that the dog teams had been caught in a storm and some of them had frozen to death before they could get back to the station.

For three weeks — 21 days, 504 long, dreary hours Pappy Turner and his flying grocery store couldn't reach us. Either the wind howled over the cap, or the base was socked in or both — 21 of the longest days of my life. We ran out of heat and fresh food. At one time we were down so low on food that I had to ration us to a single cookie a day.

We had a stock of emergency C rations, but they were frozen so hard we couldn't get them out of the can. We had to tuck the cans under our armpits or in our crotches for eight hours to thaw them out enough to dig the rations out of the can. Of course, in the dark, we spilled enough to contribute to some ripe odors in our sleeping bags.

The vacated tail section of our wrecked plane continued to sink slowly into the ever-widening crevasse that had threatened us for nearly two months. But who cared?

We were safe in our cave under the wing — or so we thought — until I began to have an uneasy feeling that the ice cap itself was moving under me when I lay quiet at night. I kept my feeling to myself — until Spencer asked me one night if I felt anything. He was feeling it too.

The ice was indeed moving. We could never be sure if or when a crevasse would open under our ice cave.

It was enough to drive a man mad. And we soon realized that that was happening to Best. He would sit up, wide eyed and talk a blue streak. Finally he began to attack Spencer and me. He seemed to think we were after him. It took all our strength to control him at times. We had to lie across the tunnel entrance at night to keep him from crawling out and falling into a crevasse or wandering off to freeze to death.

Back at the sled camp, O'Hara, too, was fighting for his sanity, as well as for his life. The gangrene continued to creep up his legs. He became sick and unable to stomach the constant diet of concentrated emergency rations. He wrestled and threshed about in his delirium. "We had to nurse him constantly, afraid every day would be his last. He survived on sheer grit," Tetley recalled.

This was their darkest hour. They had been trapped on the ice cap for three months. Six men had lost their lives. Best had lost his mind. O'Hara was losing his legs.

Then the weather broke briefly. Pappy Turner came over and dropped a new walkie-talkie. He said the plight of the six loneliest men on earth had finally reached the Pentagon itself. Colonel Bernt Balchen had been assigned to get us out. Balchen was a name to conjure with. He had been a pilot on Admiral Richard E. Byrd's Little America expedition in the Antarctic in 1929. He was also the top expert in Arctic operations. We figured, with Balchen in charge, he would finally get this show on the road.

A bush plane had been chartered from Canada, we were told, but had gone down en route to Greenland. A C-47 on skis had been ordered to the ice cap, but had been unable to get there. Coast Guard cutters couldn't get through the ice. The only hope now was Catalina flying boats. They had the range for the job and could probably land on the cap. The question was whether they could get off again. Balchen was going to try. Hope ran high, until February 6, 1943, when our B-17 guardian angel came overhead and reported that the Brass had changed their minds. They didn't think the Catalinas had a chance after all.

"Couldn't Sergeant Tetley fix the sled and rescue himself if they dropped him a few spare parts?"

Tetley breathed fire, mixed with ripe, red GI oaths.

"Fix it, Hell! We've dug down 20 feet and can't even find it. Why don't you guys just drop us some guns so we can shoot ourselves and end our misery."

Tetley and Spencer tried to keep this latest turn of event from O'Hara. That would be all it would take to snap the thin thread of hope by which he clung to life. But that retort finally stung the Brass into action.

After months of frostbite, misery and failed attempts, the rescue was an anticlimax, a piece of cake. On February 7 the B-17 was overhead early, escorted by two Catalinas. "We couldn't believe our eyes when one of the flying boats peeled off, approached and touched down easily 100 yards from our camp," Tetley said. "A couple of paramedics came over to prepare O'Hara for evacuation. We all got aboard and, after a couple of tries we took off. An hour later we were touching down on the landing strip at Bluie East 2.

Spencer the lean, easy going Texan, stepped stiffly out of the Catalina, stopped to stare at a bare rock, the first he had seen in nearly three months, then stooped down to pat it reverently.

"As he hunkered down, his pants split wide open, to the uproarious amusement of the base personnel who turned out to greet us. Spencer had gained so much weight during his 90-day ordeal that he could barely button his pants."

Now it was three down and three to go, three finally freed from the ice cap and three still in deep freeze.

It was some days before word of the rescue of the sled party reached the wreck of the B-17. Spina and Best were elated at the news. They figured they were next, and soon. I didn't want to dampen their spirits, but I knew our rescue — from the midst of the crevasses — would not be so simple. The news seemed to put the final touch to Best's recovery. He no longer had to be restrained. The best medicine had been some mail for him included in one of the drops. He was the only one on the ice to get any mail during our almost five months on the ice.

It was two more months before the fortress party smelled rescue. During that time we were fairly comfortable. Spina's frostbitten feet got better. So did mine. We would get Spina out for a little exercise, but once your feet have been frostbitten they hurt terribly when they get cold. So Spina would take a little walk, then dive into his sleeping bag and groan with pain until he got warm again.

I had the same problems. Both my hands and feet had been frostbitten and ached miserably when they got cold. For a long time I avoided walking unless absolutely necessary.

Most of the time we were well supplied with food. We lived pretty high on the hog. They would drop us chicken and pork chops already fried. To pass the time we even made fudge one night. We joked about being unable to find any place to cool it off so it would harden. We made ice cream, too, out of malt powder and powdered chocolate.

The long days and longer nights bled by slowly for nearly two months before the most powerful nation in the world, with all its resources, was finally ready to pluck the last of the survivors off the ice cap.

The rescue effort started March 17 when a PBY flying boat landed at the old sled camp carrying Colonel Balchen, a team of sled dogs and three old Arctic hands — Captain Strong, Sergeant Healy and Sergeant Doleman. Healy and Doleman, like Balchen, had served with Admiral Byrd at Little America in the Antarctic. On the 18th they started working their way over the sharp-edged sastrugi snow drifts to the crash site.

They reached us late that night. We felt like crying from joy.

These experts took over like a mother takes over an abandoned baby. We all sort of went limp and let them take care of us. We had been fighting for ourselves so long that we were ready to give up. They tucked us into bed and played nursemaid.

They set up an overnight camp for themselves. Next morning they came over early and gave us warm reindeer parkas and we started out. We all walked as far as we could. It took the full strength of the dogs just to drag the empty sled over those sharp edged sastrugi.

But Best started falling down and both Spina and I were too weak to walk for more than maybe a mile. About three miles out they set up a tent for Doleman, Best and me. Spina went on with Captain Strong and Sergeant Healy to another tent pitched a couple of miles further towards the old sled camp.

They broke through another hidden crevasse on the way, but they were roped up and Captain Strong was able to pull Healy out. Healy came back for us and the dog team and we finally reached the sled camp about dusk.

There were 12 in the party by that time and we had snow shovels so we dug a really palatial snow cave which we called the Imperial Hotel. We could stand up in one gallery and we laid out our sleeping bags in another gallery. It looked like it was all downhill from there.

But the ice cap wasn't through with us yet.

We had several days of good weather, before another storm blew up. It was during this interval that we took care of one piece of unfinished business. The B-17 was equipped with a Norden bombsight which was top secret. It was signed out to me. Under the circumstances I figured it was my responsibility to dispose of it where no enemy agent could ever get his hands on it. I asked Healy to throw it into the deepest crevasse in sight, while Captain Strong and I witnessed the last rites for this awkward chunk of iron that I had worried about for more than four months.

For a few days it was so cold and windy that we had to bring the dogs in with us. One dog stayed outside and froze a foot. It was another three weeks, 21 days, before the PBY was able to come back for us, on April 5. Once again we thought we had it made. We loaded everyone and the dogs on the flying boat and the pilots gave her the gun. We got under way, but not fast enough to generate any lift.

We stopped and unloaded Colonel Balchen, Captain Strong, Doleman, and Healy. We were going to leave them at the sled camp to lighten the load while we tried again to take off. We tried two more takeoff runs with full power. The right engine got hot, melted the cowling and burned a fuel pressure line.

We finally had to shut down the engines and wait for a head wind to help us get off the cap. The next day April 6, 1944 about noon we got our wind. The Navy pilots cranked up the engines. It took all of us to rock the wings to break the hull loose from the ice. Then the pilots started taxiing in a circle. We would run in and jump for the ladder on the blister, one at a time. Navy Chief Larsen, a tall, lanky guy, would reach out and haul us aboard.

We headed into the wind and made two attempts to take off, without success. The engines were about to catch fire they were so hot. Again it looked like we would spend the rest of our lives on the cap.

But the pilots decided there was nothing for it but to try one more time before the engines burned up. This time the pilot jerked the big patrol bomber off the ice in a stall and managed to hold her there while she picked up flying speed.

Once over the edge of the cap we dived for the runway at Bluie East 2. We were almost out of fuel. So the pilots decided to land gear up on the asphalt runway. If the landing gear had been extended it might have created so much drag that we couldn't have made it to the airport.

We touched down in a shower of sparks, skidded the length of the asphalt runway and almost hit a parked B-17s. We crawled out of the blister and took our first wobbly steps on solid earth as if we had just been born again after 147 days — just four days short of five months — in the womb of the ice cap.

We each gave thanks in our own way for our deliverance, but could not forget the price we had paid — five brave men lost — Corporal Loren Howarth and Private Clarence Wedel from the B-17; Lieutenant M. Demarest, from the Rescue Station; Lieutenant John A. Pritchard and Radioman 1C Benjamin A. Bottoms from the Coast Guard cutter — and the crew of the lost C-53, which started the whole chain of events.

No trace of the C-53 transport was ever found. It is ironical that the longest rescue on record on the ice cap was preceded by one of the shortest rescues on record. Two B-17 bombers and six P-38 fighters made forced landings on the ice cap July 15, 1942, within sight of the spot where Monteverde's B-17 crashed Novemebr 9, 1942. No one was injured and all were rescued within 48 hours.

CHAPTER 6

TRIUMPH OF THE HUMAN SPIRIT

Light rain fell from a lowering sky that sunless Sunday, June 20, 1937. Even the seagulls were grounded. Then out of the mists appeared a strange looking red airplane with long tapered wings like a sailplane. It circled Vancouver's Pearson Field once, then dropped down below the towers on the Interstate Bridge and approached from the west and set in a three-point landing on the sod airstrip. It rolled to a stop, turned and taxied back to the flight line near the white house that served as headquarters for the 421st Observation Squadron.

On the side of the long, slender fuselage was a slogan in an alien script, ("Route of Stalin"). On the top and bottom of the wings huge letters spelled URSS, NO 25. Out of the cockpit crawled three strangers, speaking a strange language. They looked like brown bears in their heavy fur flight suits.

They had just made history. They were the first ever to fly over the North Pole, challenging the unknown hazards of the Arctic. They had taken off from Schelkovo airport in the suburbs of Moscow and flown nonstop over the North Pole, logging 6,081 statute miles (5,288 nautical miles) in 63 hours and 16 minutes. (The straight line distance was 6,081 miles. Actually the crew had flown hundreds more miles when forced far off course.)

The Russians proclaimed the flight a triumph of the Communist system. Vancouver's Mayor Bryce Seidl years later more accurately proclaimed their feat "a triumph of the human spirit."

First out of the cockpit was Valeri Pavlovich Chkalov, 30, pilot in command; then Georgi Filipovich Baidukov, 33, and navigator Alexander Belyakov, 40. By the purest serendipity they were met by the only man within miles who could speak Russian. He was George Kozmetsky, who happened to be attending a Citizens Military Training Camp (CMTC) on the base.

Charles Alexander, corporal of the guard, who had been listening to news of the flight on the radio, grabbed the phone and called the quarters of Brigadier General George C. Marshall, base commander. "It's that Russian airplane, Sir," he said.

The general jumped into his car with the officer of the day and his chauffeur drove them straight across the parade grounds through the nine-hole golf course at top speed to greet the Russian fliers, while friendly guards and early spectators welcomed the weary crew on the flight line.

One of the apocryphal stories that persisted for years was the claim that General Marshall met the fliers in his pajamas, but Alexander swears that the general, an early riser, was in full and proper uniform. "I saw him in uniform," Alexander declared.

The Russians were reluctant to leave their plane, afraid that souvenir hunters would tear it apart. But Marshall set their minds at ease. He ordered a 24-hour guard to make sure that no one touched the plane. Reassured, the weary crew piled into Marshall's car and drove to the commander's spacious house. There they were welcomed by Katharine Marshall, the general's wife. They had breakfast in the tub and turned in for a few hours of sleep.

Within an hour, about 75 reporters, radio broadcasters and newsreel photographers had converged on General Marshall's home. Most of them had been waiting for the Russian fliers to land at Swan Island in downtown Portland. Mrs. Marshall herded us all into the library and appeased us with tea and cookies until Alexander A. Troyanovsky, U.S.S.R. ambassador, arrived from San Francisco where he had been awaiting the arrival of the ANT-25.

The fliers tried on some of General Marshall's clothes, but nothing fit. So Marshall called the Meier and Frank Department Store in Portland and asked them to send a selection of 20 suits, 20 pairs of shoes, plus socks, shirts, ties and underwear, and a tailor to help the base tailor fit the visiting heroes.

I also remember Marshall sneaking the pilots out of the back door and down to Jim Padden's retail clothing store on Vancouver's Main Street where they shopped for raincoats like kids visiting Santa's workshop. Padden and his salesman, James O'Banion, remember being called at home and asked to come down and open up the store to help outfit the fliers. "They pulled out American money and tried to pay for the clothes," O'Banion recalled.

When they finally made their appearance on the porch of Marshall's house they were neatly dressed in suits and ties. Troyanovsky translated and seemed to have briefed Chkalov on what to say. Freely translated, Chkalov said: "We come to extend the hand of friendship from the Russian people to the people of the United States. Russia's Volga River and your great Columbia River flow into a common ocean. We are one people. We share the same world as our rivers share the same ocean," he said.

Years later, in 1983, Vancouver activist Robert J. Morrison and his sister, Marie Ellen Eterno, published a book claiming the flight of the ANT-25 was a hoax. They claimed that the aircraft was dismantled and brought to Sitka, Alaska, by boat, where it was reassembled and took off from Sitka to Vancouver.

The story was absurd on the face of it. There wasn't a level spot anywhere near Sitka big enough for a helicopter, much less an airplane, to take off.

I saw proof that the Russians had indeed made the flight non-stop. I watched later that June day in 1937 as Chkalov pulled out a throwing knife from his flight suit and broke the seal on a compartment under the left wing which housed one of the three barographs installed and sealed by representatives of the Federation Aeronautique Internationalle (FAI) in Moscow.

A barograph is an instrument, designed specifically to record aviation records. It continuously and automatically records time and barometric pressure (altitude). Two more barographs were removed from the underside of the aircraft and the tail. One of them had malfunctioned, but the other two were working.

I took pictures showing Chkalov removing the barographs and handing them to Harry Coffey, president of the Oregon Aero Club. Coffey delivered them to Washington, D.C., where officials of the FAI broke the seals and examined the records. They proved that the ANT-25 had made its flight without a stop. The FAI then officially certified the record.

Coffey and other members of the official board appointed by Marshall also broke the seals on the fuel and oil tanks and certified that a little less than 11 gallons of fuel remained, enough to operate the engine for about 15 minutes.

Monday the troops stationed at Vancouver Barracks held a parade and review and fired a 15-gun salute for the Heroes of the Soviets. They were honored by a brief parade in downtown Portland. Then they boarded a United Air Lines DC-3 with Troyanovsky and flew to San Francisco, the first stop on a triumphant tour of the country.

THE REST OF THE STORY

There was no chance to talk to the fliers at any length during their brief stay in Vancouver. Chkalov never returned to the scene of his triumph. He crashed and was killed December 15, 1938, while testing a new fighter plane. But Baidukov returned to Vancouver a few times over the years. He recounted with great animation some of the hazards that almost downed the valiant plane and crew.

Baidukov, who said he was "too old to fly" any more, (85 in 1992) still did so at every opportunity. When he returned to Vancouver for the 55th anniversary of the transpolar flight, in 1992, he was offered a ride in a twin-engine Cessna. He immediately took the pilot's seat and made the takeoff and landing, with minor assistance from the plane's owner. "He kept trying to climb into the overcast," the plane's owner recalled.

The epic story of the flight was told in authoritative detail by Baidukov in a book entitled Russian Lindbergh, translated by Peter Belov and extensively edited by Von Hardesty of the Smithsonian Institution's Air and Space department in 1991. Baidukov died in late December 1994. Awarded Hero of the Soviet Union in 1937 for his transpolar feat, he was buried with full military honors in a prestigious cemetery outside of Moscow on New Year's Eve.

In brief, Baidukov said the takeoff was hairy. They used every foot of the runway and staggered into the air on a takeoff reminiscent of Lindbergh's last gasp takeoff from Roosevelt Field 10 years earlier, at 7:52 a.m. May 20, 1927. It was

Lindbergh's flight that inspired the Russian drive to set new records for polar flight.

The flight of the ANT-25 (named for the designer and builder, Antonovich Tupolev) was routine for the first nine hours. Then they encountered heavy icing. The plane began to vibrate violently as ice built up on the wings and propeller blades. "Icing seized us by the jugular in a death grip," Baidukov said, with a flair for the dramatic.

They survived this encounter, but after passing the North Pole 24 hours into the flight, they encountered high clouds and icing that repeatedly threatened to drag them down. They ran out of oxygen. Their radios went dead for 22 hours, robbing them of weather reports. Finally they turned west and dropped down to lower altitudes. Baidukov was the only pilot who could fly through clouds and darkness on the ANT-25's meagre instruments. Chkalov, a fighter pilot, could only fly VFR — by visual reference to the horizon. Baidukov was at the controls when he started losing altitude. The water-cooled engine was out of water and starting to heat up.

"Water! I need water or we are going to burn up," Baidukov shouted. Chkalov and Belykov tried the spare water container. It was empty. So was the drinking water tank. "Suddenly I remembered the balloons," Baidukov said. "Our scientists had provided us with balloons for our urine, which they would use in research projects," Baidukov said.

Chkalov scrambled back to the tail section and retrieved the balloons They contained the only liquid left which was not frozen. The contents were dumped into the tank and pumped into the radiator. Science was cheated of a considerable volume of specimens. But the day was saved and the donors lived to supply more specimens.

Baidukov said that he had flown on instruments through rain clouds almost to Eugene, Oregon, when Belykov passed a note saying that we were almost out of gas. They decided to turn back to Portland. They broke out of the overcast at about 150 feet above the ground and had to dodge tall downtown buildings en route to Portland's Swan Island airport. They saw crowds gathered at Swan Island and decided to land at Vancouver where the military could protect the airplane.

Baidukov said that the ANT-25, empty of all its fuel, floated like a glider when he was on his final approach to land at Pearson Field. Incredible as it sounds to pilots, Baidukov said that he actually turned off the ignition switch to kill the engine when it looked as if they would overshoot the field. They had wing flaps to increase the drag on the 110-foot wings and steepen their glide without increasing their airspeed. But they had no brakes. They had been removed to reduce weight.

Theodora "Teddy" Morrow, (70 in 1987) will never forget the Russian fliers. "They scared hell out of me," she said. "I was called in to General Marshall's house that morning to help out when the fliers were invited to the general's quarters for breakfast and a place to clean up. I went up to their upstairs bedroom, along with two other women, to pick up their clothes to be washed. They grabbed us and tried to get us into bed," she said. "I got out of there and never went back" she declared. "I was only 21 and I had been raised pretty strictly," she said.

Heart of the problem was the language barrier. The Russians spoke no English and no one on the scene at the time understood Russian. The Russian fliers, groggy from three days without sleep, exuberant over their feat of skill and endurance and feeling the effects of the brandy they were drinking, evidently thought that they were being supplied with women to go with the wine.

Morrow was employed as a maid in the home of Lieutenant Colonel James Marmon, base finance officer, and his wife Pearl. Her brother, Air Corps Captain Clayton Earl Hughes, had just won his wings and she was expecting him to land at Pearson Field that soggy Sunday.

"I heard a plane overhead and stepped out on the porch to look. I saw this big red plane. It didn't look like anything I had ever seen before, so I got permission to run down past the old mule barns to the airstrip to take a look," she said. "I saw it come in from the west, low and slow. It was way below the towers on the Interstate Bridge," she recalled. "It landed and taxied up to the squadron headquarters. I got there before the guards did, but when I saw it wasn't my brother I went back to the colonel's house." It was late afternoon before the weather improved and her brother landed in a low-winged single-engined A-20 and took her for a ride. That wild ride with her brother, her first ever, outshone any memories of the Russians.

Morrow said that the maids asked the Russian fliers to pass out their clothes so that they could be cleaned. "But they refused to give up their underwear," Morrow said. "We never did find out why." The mystery of the missing undies was not solved until 50 years later when Mary Kline, now Mary Rose, then director of Clark County museums, went to Moscow in February to help make arrangements for the celebration on the 50th anniversary of the Russian landing.

"We were entertained at Igor Chkalov's home one evening where General Baidukov was a guest and I asked him if the story was true," Kline said.

"There was a long pause while my question was explained by our interpreter, then Baidukov sheepishly admitted the story was true. He explained that the crew wore special silk underwear under their heavy wool and fur pants for the long cold flight. He said it was the finest underwear that they had ever seen, and they weren't about to part with it."

Baidukov said when he stepped out of the ANT-25 that soggy Sunday he was carrying a small satchel containing his shaving kit. He was stopped by guards when they heard a suspicious ticking like the timer of a bomb. He finally persuaded them to let him open the bag. He showed them a big alarm clock still ticking away after nearly three days in the air.

He said they were puzzled when told they would be meeting General Marshall. "We were sure the Americans had generals, but we weren't sure if they had officers with the rank of marshal, so we treated him as a general."

One mystery still remains unsolved. When the maids cleaned up the room occupied by the Russian fliers they found a wad of American $100 bills. Some of the bills had blown out the window and were scattered on the lawn. Presumably the Russians expected to pay their own way across the country and back home. But they found themselves guests of the generous Americans, at least in the hospitable West.

A few days later the Russians sent Vassily Berdnick, aviation engineer, to supervise dismantling of the airplane. When he went to hire carpenters to build the crates for the wings and fuselage he got a dose of culture shock. He discovered that he had to hire carpenters through the labor union hiring hall. "What's a union?" he asked his interpreter. This proletarian from the land of the proletarians had never heard of a workers' union.

A few days after the flight which put Vancouver in the headlines, Henry Rasmussen, Vancouver merchant and member of the city's aviation committee, proposed erecting a monument to the courageous crew of the ANT-25. He enlisted the aid of a Portland sculptor, who produced a plaster model of a monument, featuring a gull-like plane soaring over the North Pole. But enthusiasm faded under the chilling effect of the Cold War and the model vanished.

The idea was reborn one day in May 1974 when Richard Bowne, executive of the Clark County Public Utility District, and Peter Belov, a Portland area consultant who spoke fluent Russian, visited the Soviet trawler *Posyet* in Portland's harbor. Bowne and Belov took the ship's officers to see the spot where the ANT-25 had landed. They apologized for the lack of a monument.

Bowne immediately enlisted the aid of 15 major corporations and 91 smaller business firms. The state highway department contributed a site overlooking Pearson Field. The Russians contributed bronze plaques, and the distinctive monument was built. Baidukov, Belykov and about 50 VIPs and members of the Russian media, flew over the North Pole from Moscow in an IL-62, Russia's most modern jetliner, to help unveil the monument — only monument in the United States to a Russian achievement, on June 20, 1975. The whole project was completed in record time without a cent of government money.

Dave James, then a reporter for the *Seattle Times*, and I were the only survivors of the press corps that covered the original landing. I just happened to see the plane while taking my father and mother for a Sunday drive.

I wrote the commemorative program for the dedication of the monument to the 1937 Soviet Transpolar Flight. Virginia and I were invited to ride the Russians' IL-62 jetliner to San Francisco for a banquet.

I was the only survivor of the media to cover the 55th anniversary of the transpolar flight June 20, 1992, when another delegation flew over the North Pole to Vancouver to rededicate the monument. The flight crew of that IL-62 got lost over the pole, just as the crew of the ANT-25 had done in 1937, and nearly ran out of fuel.

CHAPTER 7

OPERATION OVIBOS

Our fleet of 10 snowmobiles bounded over the frozen snow-drifts like speed boats jumping waves on a frozen sea. Frozen mists obscured the horizon, frozen clouds obscured the sky. As we skimmed across the endless expanse of Nunivak Island it soon became obvious that the world was, indeed, flat and we were about to fall off the edge.

It was 10 degrees below zero and a 20-knot wind gave us a chill factor of about 53 below. Exposed flesh froze in seconds as the black scabs on the faces of our Eskimo cowboys testified.

Operation Ovibos was finally underway. Our mission: to capture the wild musk ox (Ovibos) that wintered at Ingrijoak on the southern tip of the island.

It all started when I flew into Fairbanks several times to cover construction of the Alaska oil pipeline. While waiting for a plane one day I got a look at the musk ox farm operated by the University of Alaska. I was active in the Portland Zoological Society then. The directors quickly agreed that if Fairbanks — where temperatures reach 100 in the summer — could maintain a herd of these relics of the Ice Age, so could we.

The U.S. Fish and Wildlife Service issued the necessary permit with alacrity. They were faced with a surplus of musk oxen. Every year they had to capture 40 or 50 musk oxen to reduce the Nunivak herd and transplant them to northern Alaska where they once had flourished. They offered to let us join their crew of experienced musk ox handlers.

We hired two Eskimos with snowmobiles — at $100 a day — to help capture the musk oxen for the zoo and Wes Peterson, zoo foreman, and I were on our way. We each checked a bag of arctic gear. Peterson's heavy clothing never reached Bethel. But we couldn't wait for it. We boarded a light twin-engined plane for the 140-mile flight direct to Nunivak, about 150 miles north of the Pribolof Islands. Wes was later able to borrow a snowmobile suit and heavy mitts.

Nunivak, the Forgotten Island, sits like a giant wedding cake 65 miles long, 55 miles wide in the Bering Sea. There is not a tree on the island, and in winter, not a speck of moss, a willow or any green thing to relieve the monotony of the barren plain. The only living things on this desolate island are the approximately 200 Eskimos who live in the village of Mekoryuk on the north shore of Shoal Bay, a few Arctic foxes, lemmings, reindeer — and 600 or so wild musk oxen which winter on the western and southern tips of the island where some browse can be found on the windswept tops of the sand dune.

We flew above a broken layer of clouds by dead reckoning — no help from radio aids to navigation — but hit the big island right on the nose. We landed on the village airstrip on packed snow about a half mile out of Mekoryuk. The arrival of the mail plane was a big event, like the weekly stagecoach to Tombstone, and half the village turned out to greet the few passengers. We were met by Richard Davis, U.S. Fish and Wildlife

Service Eskimo manager, and by Mayor Uyothitch, an unpronounceable name. We called him "Jack" for short.

They put us up in a house usually rented to hunters and other rare visitors while they made preparations for the annual hunt. It was heated by a single space heater, which ran out of oil one night. Call 9-1-1 and half a dozen Eskimos saddle up a snowmobile and sled and hike out to the fuel dump at the edge of town, dig a barrel of oil out of the snow, haul it up to the house and hoist it into place. Life was like that in Mekoryuk in 1977.

One of the elders of the island as well as the mayor, recalled that to cross the frozen tundra to Ingrijoak with a team of 20 dogs, once took all day. "Sometimes we had to dig a hole in the snow and sleep all night," he said. Operation Ovibos' motorized cowboys made the 60 miles or so in five hours with one brief stop at a major check point to heat a cup of tea.

We skirted highlands at the center of the island, which have their own special moonscape with grotesquely shaped hills rising from the central plateau, including Nunivak's own Crater Lake — Nunuaksjiak Crater — filled with a frozen lake. You might as well be on the moon as the Nunivak Ice Cap. You are utterly on your own. If you get in trouble there is no radio, no helicopter, no airplane standing by for the rescue duty, not even any contact with the village, much less the outside world.

Even Eskimos born and reared on Nunivak can get lost in blizzards or whiteouts on this enigmatic isle, so our snowmobiles followed close in the tracks of veterans like Uyothitch and Davis. But once on the downslope, with the shelter cabin in sight across frozen Duchitluk Bay, the Eskimo cowboys spurred their snorting nags and raced for the tiny log structure that stands on a rise overlooking the bay.

Topping the rise we were startled to see a big bull musk ox, the patriarch of the island, guarding the entrance to the cabin. He made a magnificent picture. His shaggy hair trailed in the snow. His horns were cracked and worn. His beard was hoary with age. He was lord of all he surveyed and proved determined to remain king of the mound. Snowmobiles dashed at him from all sides like a swarm of angry hornets. The Eskimos shouted, beat pots and pans, threw chunks of snow at him and finally charged at him, swinging a two-by-four. Old Ovibos just lowered his head, snorted and staged a lightning charge at his tormentors, but quickly stopped and re-treated to his chosen guard post. He had evidently been attracted to the spot by a bale of hay left from a previous roundup.

So the expedition paused for a brief lunch of hot coffee, dried dog salmon, seal oil and agoutak, a mixture of dried salmon berries and black berries of some kind mixed with lard or seal oil. Tasted good.

"Maybe the old bull will move on if we leave him alone," Davis suggested. Then they were off to start the roundup while the sun was still up. Returning about six p.m. they found their venerable bull still standing his ground. "We will have to get rid of him before someone gets hurt," Davis told his crew of daring bulldoggers.

No one had ever tackled a bull musk ox as big and stubborn as old Ovibos. In fact, it had taken the Eskimo cowboys quite awhile to get up nerve enough to tackle a 225-pound two-year old bull to serve as leader for the bands of females being transplanted to the mainland, according to Chris Dau, Wildlife representative from Bethel and the only "kusha" or white man involved in the official roundup. (Peterson and I were technically guests.)

But two daring young Eskimos grabbed a rope net and ran for the bull, tossing the net over his horns before he could decide which one to charge. Four more husky Eskimos jumped on the bull, toppling him to the ground. They tied his legs and managed to wrestle the 900-pound patriarch onto a sled. It took two snowmobiles and a lot of manpower to get the sled started across the bay, where he was released in his home hills.

The sun sank in an elongated ball behind the hills and the mercury dropped with it — to 25 below. We had a hot and hearty meal and got ready for the night. There was room in the cabin for only eight men. So Wes Peterson volunteered to sleep with some of the Eskimos in the snow under a tent cover alongside the log cabin in a heavy down sleeping bag.

"I was plenty warm," Peterson insisted, "except for my feet, but that snow was sure lumpy."

My sleeping bag was frozen to the wall of the cabin when I woke up the next morning, but heat from the crowded bodies in the cabin kept it more than comfortably warm. The day dawned cold and clear without a breath of wind. But the mercury rose with the sun to about 15 degrees above zero — perfect weather for a roundup.

This roundup was like a scene from the Old West — with certain dangerous differences. Musk oxen have no natural enemies on this remote island: no wolves, no bears, no dogs, no hunters. Left alone they are naturally amiable. But when chased, they instinctively turn and present a solid front to their tormentors.

One two-year old bull, chased by snowmobiles, turned and attacked one of the machines. The snowmobile was badly dented, but the rider escaped injury by diving onto the snow. Unable to bulldog the young bull, the Eskimo "grabbers" as they call themselves, used a rope net to snug him by the horns and throw him to the snow.

Another defiant bull backed up against a hill protecting a single yearling calf, holding off three mounted grabbers. An Eskimo cowboy with a lariat finally climbed the hill and swung a loop over the brave bull's head.

When caught in the open, musk oxen form a hollow square, with the mature bulls and cows protecting the young like the wagon trains.

When man or wolves attacked this Roman wall, individual bulls would dart out a few yards, head down and use their horns on the enemy, then quickly back into the defensive phalanx again. During the roundup one band of musk oxen backed up against a steep cliff, presenting a solid front, studded with sharp horns.

It was exciting stuff. I got a few feet of film showing some of the action, which now rests in the zoo archives, as well as scores of color slides.

The Eskimos, using cowboy tactics, would manage to stampede the tight-packed band from their defensive position. Once they had the musk oxen on the run they would dart in and split off the bulls and mature cows until they singled out a younger calf or yearling. Then with a flying leap, they would bulldog them to the snow and hold on until help arrived to hogtie the kicking captive.

Peterson, foreman of the Washington Park Zoo, who had never driven a snowmobile before, kept up with the pack and helped bulldog and hogtie his share of the yearlings. All the while Peterson kept an eye out for a healthy, rugged young bull and two young female yearlings, marked for the Portland zoo.

The bull we named Oomingmak, the Eskimo name for musk ox. One female we named Mekoryuk, the name of the only settlement on the island. The other we called Ingrijoak, the name of the cove where the musk oxen spent the winter.

It took three or four men to hoist the kicking calves onto a sled. The musk ox is docile and amiable by nature and never attacks unless threatened. Once captured the young ovibos bawled like any infant in distress, then seemed to relax and accept his fate placidly.

The trip back to Mekoryuk, dragging 37 musk oxen on sleds, was long and slow. The musk oxen were placed in a wire pen near the airstrip where they munched contentedly on Matanuska hay while waiting five days for a special C-82 "cattle car" to show up. But they continued instinctively to "circle the wagons" when anyone approached too close. They were in their glory when mother nature pulled an April Fool trick on us. A howling blizzard with temperatures down to zero and winds up to 40 knots blocked the airstrip with five-foot snow drifts. It took the whole village working two days to clear the strip.

The storm literally buried the sleeping musk oxen. Nature has given them a two-inch thick layer of qiviut next to their skins — finer than any cashmere. Over that they have a thick layer of course hair 10 to 12 inches long. In the field we found the carcasses of some of the musk oxen that die every winter. The hair, even on immature animals, was so thick I couldn't thrust my fingers through it to the hide. We found a skull with horns growing out of a horny plate or boss four inches thick. Bull musk oxen, like mountain sheep during the rutting season, clash head-on only to stagger back and clash again and again until the weaker one gives up.

The highly prized qiviut, like marine ivory, is reserved for the use of the natives only. The women spin it into yarn and use it to knit scarves and gloves. I bought a pair of qiviut gloves from an Eskimo woman for $75.

Sunday April 4, the C-82, dubbed Noah's Ark, picked up 34 selected musk oxen for release 550 miles further north. The next day, the C-82 picked up Peterson and his prized musk oxen and flew them to Anchorage where they transferred to a jetliner direct to Portland, landing on the hottest April 5 in Portland's history. The relics of the Ice Age took the change from 30 below to 77 above with equanimity.

It would be nice to conclude that they lived happily ever after in their own special compound, designed to resemble their native island. But the herd bull Oomingmak died in 1990 of complications of old age. He sired a calf before he died but Mekoryuk died trying to give birth. Ingrijoak was still living in 1996, the matriarch of the herd.

Editor's Note: None of the animals was injured or suffered as a result of their capture and subsequent transport to the Washington Park Zoo.

WILD AND FREE

My fascination with musk oxen started when I was stationed at BW1 — Bluie West One — at the southern tip of Greenland. I made a flight with the Air Rescue B-17 crew to the east coast to check on a small Danish outpost north up the coast. As we turned inland we spotted a band of a dozen musk oxen. They first formed their hollow square, then turned and galloped off at their own deliberate speed as we dived on them. They would turn individually and face us in defiance, wild and free, lords of all they surveyed.

Musk oxen, true relics of the Ice Ages, once roamed Arctic

Alaska, Canada and Greenland in abundance. Their only foes were wolves and an occasional polar bear. Their instinctive response, developed by evolution over the centuries, was to form a hollow square, which worked against their natural enemies. But it proved fatal against Eskimos even when they were armed only with spears or bows and arrows. Eskimo hunters had to kill every musk ox in the band before they could claim any of their kills. After centuries of unrestricted hunting, the Alaska herds had dwindled to near extinction. The last band of 13 musk oxen was reported killed by Eskimos about 150 years ago.

In 1931 the government bought 34 musk ox calves from Greenland and held them at Fairbanks until 1935 when the remaining 31 were moved to Nunivak Island in the Bering Sea. There, in the absence of all predators, they grew to a herd of 750 by 1968. That was more than the island could support and 150 of them died during the next winter.

The U.S. Wildlife Service immediately began transplanting the excess animals to their former habitats on the mainland where they were soon thriving. About 400 had been transplanted by 1977, including a controversial shipment of 41 to Siberia in 1976. The Alaska Department of Fish and Game, which shares jurisdiction over the musk oxen, protested the State Department's decision to ship the animals to Siberia and sent two state patrolmen to prevent the shipment. Washington overruled Juneau, however, and the animals were flown aboard Russian planes from Bethel to the Taymir Peninsula in Siberia and to one of Russia's Arctic Islands about the size of Nunivak. The Nunivak Eskimos strongly protested the shipment. "Why should we share our musk oxen with the Russians?" Uyothitch demanded. "We know what they would do to us if they got the chance."

The Nunivak herd still is the most productive of all, game

managers say. They expect to continue transplanting about 40 or 50 animals every spring until the number is reduced to about 550.

The transplanting program, coupled with the instinct of the musk oxen to drive off mature bulls when they could no longer lead the herd, resulted in an excess of over-age bulls and threatened to deplete the limited supply of browse and contribute nothing to the herd. The answer was to open Nunivak to limited hunting in 1974. In 1977, 40 permits were issued for bulls and five for cows. Game tags even then cost $1,000; native guides $2,000. Add the cost of transportation, board and room and the total has been high enough to discourage all but the most dedicated and opulent hunters. Only 31 trophies had been taken on Nunivak by the first week in April, end of the spring season, in 1977. The money from hunters was a major boost to the limited economy of the island and the meat was a welcome addition to their limited diet.

INUPIAT AND THE BIONIC WOMAN

Mekoryuk has one foot in the Ice Age, the other foot in the TV Age. It was the last village in Alaska of Eskimos, governed by Eskimos for Eskimos.

No kusha lives here, according to Uyothitch. Kushat, plural form of the word, literally means "you can't understand them when they talk to each other; you don't know what kind of people they are, and you don't know if they are friendly or killers," the mayor explained. Russians are called kushapiks and the Eskimos don't trust them. A 10-man squad of Eskimo Guards, a unit of the Alaska National Guard, periodically patrolled the island and checked out any sign of intruders. Guards say that during World War II signs of Russian scouts were discovered.

Some of the mamas and papas — the 'Old Ones,' spoke only Eskimo. They lived by the old legends. One elder, who spoke no English, showed us a carving of the walrus man, a favorite figure in Eskimo myths and legends. Legend has it that walrus man came ashore as a walrus who turned into a man. But to this Eskimo elder, this was no myth.

"I myself saw this walrus emerge from the sea on the south-west side of the island and turn into a man," he said through an interpreter.

"Once about 1,000 Inupiats (Eskimos) lived on this island," Uyothitch said. "In those days we lived in sod houses, partly underground. Now we live in wooden houses most of which the government built. The old sod houses were warmer in winter and cooler in summer. We cooked and heated with seal oil lamps, so everything was covered with soot. Today we use fuel oil, which is cleaner, but costs a lot of money, nearly $1 a gallon.

"We used to travel by dog sled, which was slower than snow-mobiles — but you can't eat your snowmobile if it breaks down in a blizzard."

The village also boasted a partial sewer and water system, 10 miles of summer road, a satellite radio telephone served eight hours a day, a nurses aide station and a school with 5 teachers and 47 students. The *North Star* U.S. Coast Guard cutter barges in heavy cargo once a year. Intermittent air service is available during the winter, weather permitting.

The Eskimos have stepped out of the Stone Age into the mechanical age in one generation. But in the transition the population has dwindled to 194, about 35 families, according to the postmistress. More and more of the young people fly to the mainland during the summer to work in the canneries and gradually move to Bethel or Anchorage, where most of them quickly succumb to alcohol, the scourge of the natives.

The village elders strictly enforce their rules against any form of alcohol on Nunivak Island, but they can't control the younger men once they leave the island. When I stopped in Bethel on the return from Nunivak one of the best young grabbers from the musk oxen hunt was on the plane. He headed for the bar and was ready to pass out before I had dinner.

Eskimos on Nunivak Island still hunt seal and walrus for fresh meat. In summer they catch dog salmon and grayling in the many streams and dry them for winter use. The women gather salmon berries and "black berries," something like huckleberries, which they dry and preserve in lard or seal oil for winter use. They raise no crops of any kind during the short summer. All vegetables are flown in. The cooperative store also carried canned goods and other staples.

Processing of reindeer is the only industry, aside from the occasional hunter. A herd of reindeer was transplanted to the island and quickly grew to a peak of 20,000 but the herd has since dwindled to about 2,500, Chris Dau, U.S. Fish and Wildlife biologist, responsible for the National Game Reserve, explained. The Eskimos, who own the herd, shoot the young, prime animals for meat throughout the year. In summer they send out herders on foot to round up the reindeer for slaughter in the village processing plant and sell the meat and hides to other villages.

"We used to have Eskimo dances once in awhile, movies just about every night," Moomikadlik (Chester Wesley), 25, one of the younger generation, recalled. Then, on January 1,

1977, culture shock struck Nunivak. Suddenly TV antennas sprouted from every roof. The state had launched a special satellite to serve the natives in the north.

"There used to be nothing to do in winter but hunt a few seal or carve a little ivory," Mayor Uyothitch recalled. "Now when TV comes on the air at 5 p.m., everyone rushes home and sits glued to the tube. Even the mamas and papas (the Old Ones) own TV sets," said Moomikadlik. "They don't understand English, but they get a kick out of it anyway."

Universal favorite in 1977 was the network news, live. High on the Mekoryuk hit parade was *Hawaii Five-O, the Bionic Woman, Charlie's Angels, I Dream of Jeannie, Baretta, Sonny and Cher,* and *Sanford and Son*. To these primitive Eskimos what they saw on television was for real. Father and mother sat wide-eyed in horror as they watched monsters from Space 1999. The little kids clung tightly their mothers in abject terror.

The villagers said they didn't approve of sex on TV, but they generally seemed to think that violence was acceptable in such shows as *Hawaii Five-O*. This was a conservative, Christian village, with an active Protestant church and strong patriotic attitudes. Many of the younger men said that they were planning to join the army to learn trades, or possibly to make the military a career. They never approved of the shipment of 41 musk oxen from the island to Communist Siberia in 1976.

"We should repopulate our own land first," said one of the elders. "What did the Russians ever do for us? Look what they would do to us if they got the chance."

CHAPTER 8

MISSION IMPOSSIBLE

Nature locked this frozen land away in deep freeze a million years ago and threw away the key.

More impossible missions have been accomplished in the name of science than the world will ever know. The most impossible mission on earth in recent history was Operation Deep Freeze — the conquest of the Antarctic during the International Geophysical Year (IGY) 1956. Scores of lives would be lost, and I would be there to see history in the making.

I was on the Air Force payroll as a news writer, but also wrote releases for the Navy PIO (public information officer) and helped arrange flights and interviews for the press corps. I also volunteered to keep records and write letters of commendation for the Air Force commander on the project and took pictures which were released by the Air Force. In my spare time I wrote a series of articles for *The Oregonian*. But when Rolla J. "Bud" Crick, crack reporter for the rival *Oregon Journal*, showed up in 1957 my role was reversed. My job was to help him cover the Deep Freeze story.

The Antarctic adventure started on a note of foreboding. Enroute to Christchurch, New Zealand, with an Air Force crew we heard that Operation Deep Freeze II had claimed its first victims. Max R. Keil, bulldozer operator from Joseph, Oregon, had crashed through a snow bridge into a deep crevasse while clearing a trail for a cat train on the Ross Ice Shelf in 1955, during Deep Freeze I. Four men had been killed October 18, 1956, when their Navy P2V Neptune crashed while trying to land on that same ice shelf in Deep Freeze II.

The Antarctic was and still is the grimmest, most remote and inaccessible spot on earth, guarded by 2,500 miles of vicious ocean currents, wild winds, and the earth's biggest ice bergs. Biggest on record was 96 miles long and 22 miles wide, about the size of Long Island. It broke off the Ross Ice Shelf at the Bay of Whales October 1987. The tabular berg, designated "B-9" by the scientists, pirouetted and do-si-doed just offshore for two years. Then it began to drift counter clockwise, hugging the shore until 1990 when it broke into three pieces.

Nature locked this frozen land away in deep freeze a million years ago and threw away the key. It is the highest continent on earth — and the coldest. The lowest temperature on record before 1956 was the 96 below zero Fahrenheit recorded at Verkohansk and Omykon in Siberia. That's a heat wave compared to the 113 and 127 below zero later recorded on the South Polar Plateau. Special thermometers filled with alcohol were required. Mercury would freeze at those temperatures. The Antarctic Ocean is rich in marine life but nothing lives on the land or ice of the continent itself.

Ninety percent of the world's ice, locked up in the Antarctic, hangs like the Sword of Damocles over the world. If all this ice were to melt — and some scientists think it is melting — the level of the world's oceans would rise 300 feet. New coast lines would be formed. The world's great port cities would be drowned out, and millions of lives would be disrupted.

In 1955 during Operation Deep Freeze I, the Navy sent a task force of ships and ice breakers to establish a beach head, scratch out a runway on the floating sea ice shelf and lay down a supply of fuel at McMurdo Sound. The Navy had twin-engine R4Ds (same as civilian DC-3s) equipped with skis that could land work crews and scientists at the South Pole and four-engine R5Ds (DC-4s) on wheels pressed into service to land on the ice shelf with materials and supplies.

But only the Air Force's C-124 Globemasters had the range and power to cross the Antarctic Ocean and climb to the South Pole to drop the bulldozers, snocats, prefabricated buildings and supplies of oil required to build and maintain the scientific station at the geographic South Pole. The Globemaster, biggest transport plane in the world at the time, looked like a cast iron cloud. Pilots called it an aluminum overcast. It flew comparatively low and slow, but, like an army mule, it always managed to get there and back.

I was aboard the second Globemaster to take off from Harewood, a New Zealand Air Force base outside of Christchurch, October 20, 1956. Our destination was the ice runway at McMurdo Sound. For 10 hours we droned along at 8,000 feet making 185 knots ground speed. The whole crew was exhausted from hours spent getting the plane and cargo ready to go. I took the copilot's seat to let the pilots get some sleep. (I was an Air Force Reserve pilot, currently qualified in troop carrier aircraft.)

"Scanner to pilot. Number one engine is leaking oil, about two gallons an hour." Our flight plan estimated 12 to 13 hours en route. No sweat. We would still have 20 gallons of oil left when we landed — if the leak didn't get any worse.

The navigator was relying on dead reckoning. You either reckoned your heading and ground speed on the nose or you were dead. The *USS Brough*, a U.S. destroyer escort, was stationed halfway between Christchurch and McMurdo as a navigation and rescue vessel. It was nice to hear a friendly voice from the *Brough*. The word was that the *Brough* was caught in a raging storm and could not hold its position. Not that it mattered. All air crews knew that there was no possibility of rescue if a plane had to ditch in these hostile seas.

After 10 hours of plowing over, under and through the ragged overcast, everyone in the cockpit was getting a little antsy. When the navigator called for a 20 degree correction to the right, followed 30 minutes later by another 20-degree correction, the pilots began to pucker.

The Antarctic, the fifth largest continent, bigger than the United States and Mexico combined, is pretty hard to miss. After 12 hours we began to make out the ice floes below and then Cape Adare, Franklin Island, and finally the unmistakable outlines of Mount Terror and of Mount Erebus, the Antarctic's only active volcano, which loomed over the U.S. base at McMurdo Sound like a fiery beacon.

FIRST VICTIMS

As we circled the ice runway in bright sunlight we could see the wreckage of the P2V Neptune bomber, the first plane to crash in Operation Deep Freeze II, killing the pilot and four of the crew and seriously injuring four others.

The Navy relied upon the fast, powerful Neptune, equipped with skis, to lead the way to the South Pole, land and deliver construction crews. Its two conventional engines, two auxiliary jets and JATO pods would enable it to take off from the thin air of the pole.

Lieutenant Davis W. Carey took off October 18 in clear weather from Christchurch in the task force's only Neptune, whimsically named *The Boopsie,* to lead the R4Ds to the ice. By the time he reached McMurdo low clouds obscured the runway. There were no alternate airports. The nearest possible emergency landing spot on the sea ice at Cape Hallet, 350 miles away, was also socked in.

Radar equipment was set up and operating at McMurdo, but it had not been calibrated. The controllers had had no chance to practice vectoring aircraft down to the runway. Reports differ, but witnesses say Ground Controlled Approach [GCA] controllers directed Carey on a letdown through the thin overcast and lined him up with the 6,000-foot runway. He broke out with about 500 feet of ceiling and one mile visibility.

Carey, who had never seen ice or snow before, then cancelled the GCA approach, saying that he would make a "visual approach," meaning that he would switch from flying on instruments to eyeballing it, flying by reference to the ground. He immediately banked sharply to the right, dug a wingtip into the ice and crashed. Wreckage was scattered for half a mile.

The ramp crew and Admiral George Dufek, commander of Task Force 43, the Deep Freeze operation, were all standing by on the ice waiting for the big bomber to find the runway. At the sound of the crash, shock set in. Admiral Dufek, who treated his troops like family, was stunned. He feared the worst and stayed on the ice while the ground crew searched for survivors.

It took the ground crew some time to find their way through the drifting snow to the crash site.

One crewman, Clifford Allsup, was wandering around the wreckage in a daze. Carey was dead. So was Charles Miller, an aviation electronics technician, and Chief Petty Officer Marze. Crewman Ray Hudman was sprawled on his back, twitching.

The base helicopter was down for maintenance. The Navy corpsmen had to haul Hudman by tractor the five long miles across the ice to the base infirmary, pouring transfusions of blood into him on the way. There was nothing the surgeon could do for him. He was broken up inside. So Father John Condit, the Navy chaplain, gave him the Last Rites. He was moved into the library where he quietly bled to death among the books.

The bodies were still in the makeshift morgue while the tiny infirmary was jammed with the four survivors when we finally got to the camp. Volunteers had erected a humble chapel from discarded lumber. Father Condit said a Requiem Mass for the first airmen to die in the name of science in Deep Freeze II. He played the rickety organ for his volunteer choir.

Don Guy, news picture editor for Associated Press in New England, captured the mood in the following eloquent dispatch from the ice.

MCMURDO SOUND, ANTARCTICA The church was a tin Quonset hut almost lost in a land so desolate it seems to be forsaken by all but God. The choir wore beards and the congregation wore boots. But no orator could have equalled the spiritual impact the simple service had on the heartstrings.

A soft-voiced Navy chaplain from Jefferson City, MO, held a memorial service today for the four airmen killed trying to land in an Antarctic storm Thursday.

Father Joseph C. Condit has few material things of life here. Men who plan expeditions have to let spirit look out for itself. Survival of the body is grim enough. But before God took the sun away from these hills last May for four bitterly cold months every man in camp of all faiths or no faith had built the first church in the Antarctic.

Its spire seems puny among the cold grandeur of the surrounding mountains. But there is no need for tall spires. There are three crosses on nearby hills that hold up to heaven the memory of men who died in the Antarctic's greatest air tragedy, Capt. Rayburn A. Hudman, Lt. David W. Carey, Marion O. Marze and Charles S. Miller.

More hymns followed and reading of "The Lord is My Shepherd." The choir, many of them buddies of the lost airmen, then sang "O Guard and Guide the Men Who Fly." It's on page 445 of the Army and Navy Hymnal and the last stanza says: "O God protect the men that fly through lonely ways beneath the sky."

Father Condit closed with a letter written by Dr. Edward Adrian Wilson to his wife. The letter was found a year later on Dr. Wilson's body after he died with Capt. Robert Falcon Scott on his tragic journey back from the South Pole in 1912. "All is for the best," Dr. Wilson had scrawled with cold numbed fingers. "We are playing a good part in great schemes arranged by God Himself."

Seabees and navy airmen walked out into the slanting rays of the October sun. Behind them rose the cross on Observation Hill raised by Scott's men to the memory of their leader and still preserved in the dry cold of Antarctica. As they filed out they had passed a plaque on the wall listing those who died in exploration of this icebound continent. John E. Zegers of David City, Nebraska, had carved the plaque with loving skill, but we will have to add four new names now.

However, the line at the end of the plaque needs no change.

Lieutenant Carey, father of five children, hoped to land his Neptune at the South Pole, the first man there since Scott trudged wearily away 44 years ago.

Yes, the last line can stay just as it is. It says, "In seeking to unveil the Pole they found the hidden things of God."

-end dispatch

The lids on the plain pine boxes were screwed down tight and placed aboard the next Globemaster.

This scene was to be repeated many times over the next 36 years. The Navy and the Air Force don't like to talk about it. They say there is no record of the total number of planes that have crashed and the men who have died trying to conquer this cruel continent. But Commander Bryan White, commander of Support Force Antarctic in 1990 said, "We have planes scattered all over the continent. The wreckage of one Lockheed transport plane can be seen from the base at McMurdo."

One of the Navy's C-130s crashed on a 7,350-foot ice dome December 4, 1971. For 16 years it sat there in deep freeze gradually being buried under 35 feet of snow and ice. In 1987 salvage crews dug it up. Lockheed mechanics patched it up and flew it out under its own power. After further repairs at Christchurch it was flown to Cherry Point, Rhode Island, for overhaul and returned to active duty. It was the last of three wrecked C-130s to be recovered.

The Antarctic is dotted with lonely crosses that hold up to Heaven the memory of more than 35 Deep Freeze men who died from 1956 to 1962 while seeking the secrets of this lost land in the grip of the Ice Age. Antarctic agencies estimate that this cruel continent claimed 135 lives between 1840 and 1962 and the list grows longer with each passing year.

TWO DOWN, SIX TO GO

Our pilot, Captain Henry A. Embree of Portland, Oregon, made a smooth landing on the ice runway. Then the huge plane began to pitch and buck like a rodeo bronco on the rough ice. We pulled off onto a small parking ramp. It was 16:40 (4:40 p.m.) Sunday, October 21. Before the props stopped turning, Navy Seabees in color coded "pumpkin suits" began heaving our baggage in a heap onto a 20-ton sled. Somewhere in the shuffle I lost my sleeping bag and my parka. Snow vehicles scurried in all directions. In the confusion one of them ran over and smashed a photographer's bag full of precious cameras and film.

There was good reason for haste. C. J. Ellen, Air Force squadron commander, and I watched the next Globemaster, Number 995, land with 19,250 pounds of cargo, including an Otter, a single-engine airplane with wings detached. Before Number 995 could get off the ice, the third Globemaster, Number 982, arrived. He couldn't land because Number 995 blocked the runway.

Fortunately he had plenty of fuel so Ellen instructed him to fly practice approaches to give the GCA crew some training. All eyes were on Number 982 as the pilot made a practice approach. But instead of going around he set in a perfect landing, nose high. Then the nose dropped down and all propellers went into reverse, hiding the Globemaster in a dense cloud of snow.

When the cloud cleared away there was that mountain of aluminum plowing down the runway on its nose, like a beagle on the trail of a rabbit. No one was hurt and damage was confined to the nose door and three propellers.

The runway was blocked for sure this time. Two more Globemasters were toiling their way across the hostile Antarctic Sea toward McMurdo. Number 983 was past the PNR (Point of No Return). The pilot had no choice but to stay on course and hope he would find an open runway when he arrived.

He lucked out. Ramp crews hooked all four snocats to the mountain of aluminum and dragged it off the runway in time for Number 983 to land at 04:30 a.m. Monday, October 21 with 27,000 pounds of cargo. By this time the temperature had dropped from 3 above to about 10 below as the sun rolled around the horizon lower and lower. Nearly four hours later Number 983 finally got off the ice.

Thus ended what turned out to be a rather typical day at Old McMudhole, as the irreverent Seabees called it. There was never time for boredom to set in. Christmas trees were flown in from Chee Chee and placed alongside the runway to help break up the blending of snow, ice and sky, to improve the pilots' depth perception. But in the next month two more C-124s "bought the farm."

Captain Warren Fair flew in with a crew of mechanics to repair one of the early casualties, only to make more work for the body beaters (air frame technicians). He wiped out the landing gear on approach. He quickly reversed thrust on all propellers. Number three engine caught fire. The ungainly airplane, like a section of the Holland Tunnel, wound up with its tail high in the air. The pilot broke his ankle sliding down the escape rope. A mechanic broke his heel evacuating the airplane. The next day another mechanic broke his ankle on a tow cable.

DRUMS AWAY

For the next nine days the Navy crews seemed to be stunned by the P2V crash and jinxed by a series of lesser mishaps. Almost every day was pucker time. A Navy gooney bird (R4D) caught fire on the ramp. Another R4D pilot experienced a jolt when one of his skis stalled in flight and nearly dragged him down. The right wing struck the ice, damaged the wing tip and jammed the aileron, but the pilot recovered control and was able to fly back to McMurdo Base.

One engine of a four-engine R5D caught fire in flight, forcing the pilot to make an emergency landing on the ice. A helicopter ferrying passengers from the base camp out to the ramp flew too low over a parked R4D and blew the horizontal surfaces off the tail assembly.

Time was running out. The operations plan called for the Navy to land at the South Pole, select a site and deliver a ground crew to receive the drops. Prefabricated buildings, bulldozers and weasels were to be dropped to them by parachute. Five Globemasters stood loaded and ready to start the drops. But the Navy stalled. No polar landings were attempted. (They had good reasons to be reluctant. Their R4D Dakotas were overweight and under powered. If they lost an engine they would be forced down.)

Enter Major General Chester E. McCarty, legendary commander of the 18th (combat airlift) Air Force. Irked by the delay, he left Greenville, North Carolina, and flew down to Christchurch October 25. At Dufek's request, Ellen wired the general from McMurdo Sound, telling him that it would be another week before the Navy could land at the South Pole and advising him to wait in Christchurch.

The can-do general shot a wire right back: "Let's get this show on the road." And he took off in a Globemaster christened the *State of Oregon*, his home state.

The general's message was like a shot fired across the Navy's bow. The inter-service rivalry that always lay just beneath the surface broke into the open. Navy types were openly bitter. Officers and rates (noncommissioned officers) who had been friendly, glared at me in the mess hall and muttered about the Air Force trying to hog all the publicity.

Dufek's PIO (public information officer), quiet, capable, likeable Lieutenant Commander Robin Hartman, scoffed. "The Air Force couldn't get within 40 miles of the South Pole. The POL [petroleum, oil and lubricants] would be lost. The Pole party would die trying to find it."

General McCarty outfoxed his critics. He landed, loaded 50 tons of lumber and POL, put Commander William "Trigger" Hawkes, Admiral Dufek's air advisor, on the Form 1 as copilot; put the Navy's top navigator, Marine Sergeant Henry Strybing, on the crew along with the Air Force's top navigator, Lieutenant Ernest Schmid. He loaded 44 VIPs and accredited members of the pencil and television press and took off at 14:14 (2:14 p.m.) October 26, 1956.

The great Globemaster groaned for about 400 miles over the ice shelf at 5,000 feet where breathing was comfortable. As we approached the Beardmore Glacier we climbed to 11,000 feet and levelled off while the navigators shot the sun line, turned and counted down the seconds to the pole.

There was nothing to be seen but miles and miles of miles and miles. But after an hour and five minutes of sun shots and calculations, Hawkes and the two navigators agreed that they were over the pole. McCarty turned onto his "bomb run." The loadmasters shoved the pallets loaded with Arctic fuel and diesel oil out the door, the four parachutes deployed and the first air drop over the South Pole was history.

When the construction party finally landed at the pole on November 19 they decided that the drop had been made about eight miles from the geographic pole. The weasel had broken down. They finally got to the pole by dog team just as Roald Amundsen did in December 1911. (The dogs had been included in the program for use in rescue missions.)

Actually, after hundreds of observations over the years, the position of the geographic pole, when I landed there in October 1962, was still marked by a wide circle of drums enclosing the mirrored glass ball dropped gently by parachute early in the project to give pilots a landmark — and visiting photographers a target.

We also dropped a "grasshopper," a device designed to radio reports on the temperature, dewpoint, wind velocity and directions. The radio operator claimed, however, that when he made contact with the grasshopper on the 50-below ice cap all he could hear was: "Kee Rist but it's cold!"

On the return flight we encountered clouds — possibly stuffed with granite. No accurate maps had ever been made. The general climbed to 17,000 feet. By this time everyone was gasping for breath, lips and finger tips were turning blue, and hapless passengers were scrambling for a shot at the few portable oxygen bottles available. (Air Force Regulations limit flight without oxygen to 18,000 feet and then only for an hour.) Chaplain John Condit ruptured an ear drum and two other passengers reported to sick bay where they were treated for hypoxia (lack of oxygen) and complications of the cold virus that was sweeping the camp at the time.

A RECORD FOR RECORDS

We had set a several new records:

1) First flight over the South Pole since Bernt Balchen flew Admiral Richard Byrd over the pole November 29, 1929. (Byrd got all the credit. He was still getting credit for everything from exploration to garbage disposal in 1956. We public relations types were under orders to mention the admiral in every news release, although he never did get near the Antarctic during Operation Deep Freeze. It was embarrassing to professional public information officers to have to give the long-retired admiral credit even for trivia like reports on the problem of disposal of human waste.)

2) First Air Force plane and crew over the pole

3) Secured the pole for the U.S. (Rumors were rampant that the Russians might be sneaking in a flight just to beat us to the pole.) And the oil drums could be spotted on radar to help other pilots find the drop zone.

4) Seventh flight over the pole in the history of the Antarctic. General McCarty was the first general officer to fly over both poles. He flew over the North Pole on October 19, 1956. McCarty also set a speed record. He took off from Christchurch, landed at McMurdo Sound, made the drop at the pole and returned to Christchurch in less than 24 hours.

5) Dr. Paul Siple became the first civilian to fly over both poles. It was his second flight over the South Pole. He was a

Boy Scout with Admiral Byrd's expedition to Little America when he made his first flight over the South Pole.

6) The flight was also a first for some distinguished reporters and broadcasters, including Walter Sullivan of the *New York Times*, highly-respected dean of science reporters; Ansel Talbert, from the *Chicago Tribune* and Patrick Trese, NBC writer. Sullivan was reading proofs on his authoritative book *Quest for a Continent* on the flight to New Zealand.

Pat Trese, an alert television reporter with a lively sense of humor and a refreshingly irreverent attitude towards authority, later wrote a hilarious book, aptly entitled *Penguins Have Square Eyes.*

That doesn't mean that penguins do have square eyes. If you really get eyeball to eyeball with a full grown emperor penguin — and I wouldn't recommend it — you will find his pupil looks sort of star shaped at times. Trese, in a frank disclaimer, warns the reader that he intends to exercise his license to distort truth, embellish incidents and generally cut loose and entertain his readers — which he royally does.

That may explain his comments on General McCarty's drop at the South Pole. Trese quotes a latrine rumor that the 55-gallon drums of oil dropped to fuel the weasels and stoke the stoves of the polar party were actually filled with sewage. The contents of those drums burned with a welcome glow when the construction crews finally recovered them to fuel their oil stoves.

McCarty held a brief press conference at McMurdo before taking off for Chee Chee. Asked for comment, he said the flight was "strictly routine".

That "sound bite" inspired Trese to compose a catchy ballad sung to the tune of "The Daring Young Man on the Flying Trapeze".

Strictly routine! Strictly routine!
Going to the Pole in a flying machine
Now General McCarty flew to the Pole
At seventeen-thousand, so nary a soul
Could see very well while gasping for air,
And nobody's sure if he ever got there.
Strictly routine! Strictly routine!

Going to the Pole in a flying machine.
Right after his flight, he conferred with the press
None of whom seemed to be impressed.
He rolled down the runway with a jolt and a lurch
And in less than twelve hours he was back in Christchurch.

And so on for 10 spoofing verses.

CHAPTER 9

AN AWFUL PLACE

In 1956 the South Pole was the most remote and mysterious place on earth. Scientists knew more about the moon's behind than the earth's bottom.

True, Roald Amundsen, last of the great Norwegian polar explorers, had conquered the South Pole on skis 45 years earlier with the greatest of ease — after years of experience and careful preparation. His dog teams reached the pole December 14, 1911, in comparative comfort. Amundsen's party complained of the heat at the pole and shed some of their clothing during the nearly four days they spent relaxing there. They returned to base in Little America without the loss of a man.

"Success comes to him who has all things in order — luck some people call it," Amundsen later wrote.

Robert Falcon Scott of the Royal British Navy and four companions struggled their way to the pole on foot a month later, January 18, 1912. They man-hauled a heavy sled, only to die of scurvy, starvation and hypothermia on the attempt to return to their base at McMurdo Sound.

After finally reaching the pole, Scott recorded his frustration in his diary. "Great God, this is an awful place and terrible enough for us to have labored to it without the reward of priority."

Petty Officer Edgar Evans, suffering from severe frostbite, lost his mind and died on the Beardmore Glacier. Captain L.E.G. Oates, weak and starving, deliberately walked out into the blizzard and never came back. Scott, Lieutenant H. R. Bowers and Dr. E. A. Wilson pitched their tent for the last time, March 19, 1912, only 11 miles from a depot containing a ton of food and supplies. Their frozen bodies and Scott's diary were found the next spring.

Scott's was a story of fatally flawed judgment, poor leadership, wrong equipment and stubborn pride. Yet Scott is still honored as a hero whose tragic tale overshadows Amundsen's heroic achievements. His epitaph is engraved on a cross high on Observation Hill overlooking the U.S. base at McMurdo Sound:

"TO STRIVE, TO SEEK, TO FIND AND NOT TO YIELD."

Amundsen and Scott's journals left a lot of vital questions unanswered: What was the altitude of the pole and the mountains that rimmed the polar plateau? How cold was it? Amundsen did report temperatures of 72 degrees below zero Fahrenheit on the ice shelf during his first attempt to cross the ice shelf, September 7, 1911. (He was smart enough to turn back and wait for warmer weather, October 19.) What would extreme temperatures do to the snow? Would it support the weight of an airplane or a bulldozer?

Some polar experts thought that the snow in the dry, cold air at the pole would be fluffy like feathers, that aircraft would sink out of sight in the powdery snow. Scott had, indeed, reported that snow at the pole was so soft in 1912 that he could thrust a tent pole into it full length. Others thought the sastrugi (sharp-edged drifts hard as rock) would tear the landing gear off any plane that attempted to set down there.

Dufek, a veteran of three other Antarctic expeditions, was haunted by fear that the Russians, who also were establishing an Antarctic base, would beat him to the pole. So the Navy, out of necessity, chose a tired gooney bird older than its pilot, leaking oil in both engines, overloaded by 10,000 pounds, unable to fly on one engine, fitted it with skis and assigned it to the improbable if not impossible mission. They chose the right pilot to man the throttles — gutsy Gus Shinn — with Captain Douglas Cordiner as copilot, both experienced arctic pilots.

Lieutenant Commander Conrad "Gus" Shinn, the Navy's most experienced arctic pilot, took one look at the weary R4D Dakota gooney bird, a gutless wonder, the worst of the fleet, (but the only one available) and dubbed it *Que Sera Sera*. It was as if to say, "What the Hell? Who wants to live forever anyway? Whatever will be, will be."

Gus managed to coax the *Que Sera Sera* into the air at 00:56 GMT October 31, 1956 after using the whole 6,000 feet of runway. John P. Stryder was flight engineer, and Rear Admiral George Dufek, commander of Deep Freeze II was observer.

Hawkes was on board Major C. J. Ellen's Globemaster. Ellen took off two hours later loaded with emergency gear. I was aboard Ellen's plane.

Gus and C. J. were buddies. They were attracted by mutual respect before they discovered that they had attended the same flight school in South Carolina. The faster C-124 reached the pole and circled for nearly an hour waiting for the admiral and his crew. Contrails from our engines gradually wove a veil of clouds that cast a broad shadow over the endless ice and snow down below.

Finally we saw the red wings of the gallant gooney bird flying low across the icy plateau, trailing clouds of glory in the frigid air. Gus made a low pass to check out the surface, then eased the aircraft down for a rough landing parallel to the sharp-edge sastrugi. It was a tolerable 35 degrees below zero at 300 feet above the ice, but when Dufek stepped out of the plane he was slapped in the face by a blast of prop wash which registered 58 degrees below zero.

They were making history. They were the first Americans ever to stand at the South Pole. Only 10 men had ever stood there before and four of them perished on the way back. This was "one giant step for mankind." The only historic words to mark the occasion were Gus Shinn's gasping, "Cripes, is it ever cold!" as he opened the cockpit windows to prevent rime ice from forming on the windshield.

Time was bleeding away. The admiral and his crew of six found their faces freezing within minutes. They hurried to plant the American flag and leave a note that had the effect of claiming the South Pole for the United States. The snow was as hard as concrete. They were barely able to chip a meager hole for the flag staff with an ice axe. Both movie and still cameras froze. Only one black and white picture was useable.

Aerial photos of the flag planting taken from the circling Globemaster provided proof that the Navy had indeed reached the pole. I got a black and white shot of the landing on my Recomar, which the Navy and Air Force released to the press. I didn't get so much as a byline. The Navy's Lieutenant Halsema took color pictures which he sold to *National Geographic* for a tidy sum.

DO SOMETHING!

Now it was pucker time for Gus and his crew. The VIPs scrambled aboard. Hydraulic fluid, red as blood, leaking from every seal, stained the snow. Gus Shinn, who had kept the engines turning, eased the throttles full forward. He had to reach 30 knots before firing his JATOs (Jet Assisted Take Off) bottles, to avoid damage to the airplane.

The ship shuddered and shook, but didn't budge. The teflon covered skis were frozen to the ice.

Gus fired four of his 16 JATO bottles. The blast rocked the ship, but didn't break the grip of the ice. So he fired four more. The reluctant gooney bird seemed to bounce, then lurched forward. Gus couldn't be sure. His breath had coated the windows with ice and the JATOs had kicked up a cloud of smoke and snow that completely hid the grounded plane from the orbiting C-124.

Gus jettisoned 1000 pounds of fuel. Then as a last resort he fired the rest of his 16 JATO bottles and staggered off the ice with barely 60 knots of air speed. "And that ain't flying speed," his flight engineer noted. Gus jettisoned all of his spent JATO bottles, shedding about another 1,500 pounds of weight and reducing drag.

The instrument panel was lit up like a Christmas tree. Gus was getting a red warning light on the number one engine. The oil pressure was low, too low. The fire warning light was burning brightly on number two engine. The gear wasn't coming up worth a darn and the windshield was iced up inside and out. They were flying on instruments.

"Do something, Stryder," Gus told his engineer. So Strider

227

did something. He pulled the circuit breakers, which put out the warning lights. That didn't fix anything, but it kept the admiral's mind off the impending disaster.

When the *Que Sera Sera* disappeared in a cloud of grey smoke and powdery snow, C.J. came on the air. "How you doing, Gus? If you can't get that bucket of bolts off the ground we'll belly land alongside you and give you a home," he drawled. "We Tarheels have to stick together."

Dufek later said that pep talk came at the right time to boost morale. He admitted that the thought of being stranded in deep freeze at the pole even took his mind off his frozen nose.

The *Que Sera Sera* skimmed low along the polar plateau, limping toward the Liv Glacier. Ellen swung his Cargomaster around and fell in behind the little R4D, making S-turns to stay behind the slower plane. They made it to the foot of the Beardmore Glacier where they refueled and limped on to the base at McMurdo.

A couple of holes had been burned in the belly of the old gooney bird when the JATOs were fired in desperation. The main spar in the horizontal tail surface was broken and had to be replaced. It took 11 days for the blacksmiths to patch it up to fly again.

The admiral cancelled all efforts to reach the pole until the weather warmed up. "It's too cold for men or machines," he declared.

Gus Shinn was a real hero. He deserved the Distinguished Flying Cross for his feat. His skill, judgment and sheer guts was all that saved the lives of all aboard the battered R4D. But his name wasn't even mentioned in the Navy press releases announcing the historic landing. Dufek got all the glory. The admiral did recognize Gus's vital role — in his book Operation Deep Freeze, published in 1957.

In 1963, I nominated Gus for the Harmon Trophy, top award for an achievement in aviation. But without the Navy's endorsement the nomination wasn't even considered.

Paul Siple was a big St. Bernard of a man, as hardy as a polar bear. He had probably spent more time below zero than anyone in the task force. He had the manners of a Boy Scout — which he was. He had been chosen to accompany Rear Admiral Richard Byrd's expedition to the Antarctic in 1934.

He went on to become a recognized authority on geography, especially of the polar regions. I spent hours listening to him explain the mysteries of the universe.

When the mercury hit 20 below and the rest of the denizens of McMudhole shivered in their boots and wore huge gauntlets to protect their hands, Siple wore knit gloves with the fingers cut off. He was the most controlled man I ever met. He only lost his cool once. That was when he learned that Dufek had flown to the pole and returned to call off the project because it was 58 below. Siple, who was to be scientist in charge at the South Pole, responsible for the lives of 16 scientists and Navy housekeepers, had not been invited to make the first landing. He had not even been told.

In language that threatened to melt the Ross Ice Shelf, Siple pointed out that polar explorers, including Siple himself, had been surviving 50 below weather for 100 years or more. If Siple had made the flight he could have driven a special thermometer into the ice which would have told him the temperature, yesterday, last week, and last month and would have predicted the temperatures for the coming winter. "That 58 degrees might have been only 20 or 30 below the day before," he said.

Performing another simple test, within five minutes he could have determined how hard the surface was, whether it would support the weight of a bulldozer, what equipment would be necessary to dig into or level off the surface. "That would have been a lot more important than planting the flag!" he declared, with fire in his eyes. His previous experience in the Antarctic told him that the best flying weather would come in the next two weeks — and it did.

Navy Lieutenant Richard Bowers, head of the construction party responsible for building the station at the South Pole, also was in a snit. He resented the implication that it was too cold at the pole for him and his men. "Hell, we've been working in cold like that all winter," he growled.

Que sera sera. Navy types took off for Chee Chee for a week of R and R in the middle of the night. The sun shone bright under cloudless skies; melt water trickled down the main street of McMudhole, and the Ross Ice Shelf began to sag under the weight of heavily loaded C-124s waiting to take off for the pole.

The day drew nearer when the ice would begin to melt from beneath; seals would pop up through the ice, and the runway would threaten to drift out to sea. The construction party finally reached the South Pole on November 19. The Globemasters started dropping their loads as fast as the eight-man advance ground party could handle them.

Some of the early drops were damaged. The South Pole began to look like the city dump as drop loads piled up faster than the construction crew could move them. An air drop specialist was urgently needed. Enter T/Sergeant Richard J. Patton, 31, of the First Aerial Port Squadron of the 18th Air Force. Sunday,

November 25, 1956 he completed the first parachute jump ever made at either pole. He took over the job of drop zone controller and the aerial delivery speeded up.

Eight Globemasters dropped 800 tons of prefabricated buildings, equipment, oil and other supplies with 962 parachutes in 64 missions during 40 days and nights of urgent activity. The second weasel dropped to the construction crew was a "streamer." The parachutes failed to open. The weasel dug a 25-foot hole in the snow, which was hard as ice, but two delicate glass balls, silvered inside, were dropped without breaking. One of them still marks the official position of the South Pole.

Unsung hero of the air drops was M/Sergeant George McNamara. The weasels, bulldozers and other pieces of heavy equipment were too big to be launched out the rear cargo doors. McNamara figured out a way to use the emergency jettison system to drop the dozers on their pallets through the center cargo hatch.

By Herculean effort the pole station was made habitable by December 1, and I saw Dr. Siple off for the pole with a cutleaf philodendron under his arm. "We're going to need a touch of green to remind us of the real world during the long winter buried alive under the ice cap," he explained.

CHAPTER 10

FROST FROGS, SNOW SNAKES and THE BIG EYE

It isn't true that people down here at the bottom of the world walk upside down, hanging by their heels. But everything else is upside down. There is no rust, no rot, no bugs, no parking meters, no lawns to mow —and no night. No liquor either, by Navy ordinance. When the ban on booze was announced, one of the Deep Freeze sailors was heard to lament: "What, all that ice and no bourbon!"

Water swirls clockwise as it goes down the drain, as anyone who lives north of the equator knows. Not so. It swirls counterclockwise Down Under. Coriolis Force, the geographers call it. Maybe that's why they speak with strange accents down here and why summer comes in December and Christmas comes in June.

The Aurora stages its ghostly display over the South Pole. The Kiwis called it the Borealis Australis, Southern Lights. Sometimes they seemed to form a solid wall as we turned our backs on this Lost Continent and headed back to Chee Chee.

It was a million years ago or more that the Lord locked away the Antarctic in a vault of snow and ice — and threw away the key.

The sun rolls around the horizon endlessly, blazing out of a brilliant sky, reflected by endless snow and ice. Stick your head out of your Atwell hut and you can't tell whether it is 2 a.m. or 2 p.m. First timers get the Big Eye — can't sleep, can't stay awake.

Not that it matters, work goes on around the clock in sunshine or in storm — like the one that hit McMurdo November 1, 1957, during Operation Deep Freeze III.

I was in the infirmary under medication for "polar fever," when the "bitch box" came to life. "Now hear this, Set Condition One!" Everyone was confined to base and expected to take cover. A blizzard had suddenly kicked up. We had a Globemaster from Chee Chee due to land in a few minutes.

I hopped a six-by (six-wheeled heavy duty truck) with Chuck Moore, U.P. correspondent, and headed for the airstrip, about two miles out on the floating sea ice.

The driver had to feel his way down the road, rubbing his way along the five-foot snow banks that bordered the sunken truck trail. The driver had to get out and feel for the turn leading to the control tower. By that time we could hear a plane overhead, unable to land. The pilot was diverted to Cape Hallett, where he would have to make a forced landing on the sea ice.

We started back to base in a tracked weasel without a cab. We almost tipped over a couple of times when we hit the steep banks on either side of the truck trail. Finally we came within a foot of hitting another weasel which had thrown a track in the middle of the ice road.

There we were, eight stranded men, two of them without parkas. We found two ropes, to keep the men together, four to a rope. We were lost in a swirling white cloud of blowing snow. We could barely see the man ahead of us as we stumbled along in lock step, feeling our way in the sunken roadway.

After a few minutes one man stumbled and fell down crying, more from fright than from the cold. This young sailor had not worn his parka. So I took off the six-foot wool survival muffler that my wife had knitted for just such an emergency and wrapped the frightened lad in it.

The guys were on the verge of panic — except for one tall black Seabee. He and I exchanged banter to buck up the rest as we stumbled along. It took us about an hour to grope our way the mile and a half to the base.

There was no rest in any kind of weather for the color coded ramp crews that unloaded the cargo, hauled it to the base and maintained the bulldozers, forklifts and snocats. Navy cargo handlers wore international orange coveralls over their arctic gear. Cat drivers wore green; Air Force APO specialists wore yellow.

Old hands warned incoming crews to beware of snow snakes. "They are white and hide in the snow," old hands explained. "If you don't watch out they'll sneak up your pant leg. That's panic time." So ramp crews began tieing up their coveralls at the ankle with red ribbons, leaving a tag end of ribbon trailing out behind.

Next the Navy types reported an invasion of frost frogs. "They lurk in the rime frost when the mercury coasts down to 10 below or colder. They will get into your bunny boots and freeze your socks off. The foggy days and blizzards bring them out in force. You gotta lace your boots with blue ribbons to scare off the frogs," they will tell you with solemn earnestness.

Trail parties used to report epidemics of ice worms poisoning the snow they had to melt for drinking water. Ice worms are also a familiar sight in Greenland and the Arctic.

Anyone who survived a few months in Greenland in the depths of the winter soon found otherwise normal types talking to the rocks. I used to talk at night to Oscar, my pet rock. Smart rock, too. Oscar was smarter than the average rock; smarter than some of the people that I met up there. When the rocks started talking back it was time to start thinking about a transfer to warmer climes.

The light is brighter in the Antarctic than anywhere else on earth. There is no measurable humidity. The air is so dry, so lacking in water vapor, that you can see forever, or 400 miles, whichever comes first.

There were no women during those first rugged days when the Seabees fought to establish a beachhead. For a few glorious seasons the Antarctic was the only place in the world reserved for men only. Those early cadres, goaded by the threat of being frozen in for the winter, left sleeping bags and arctic gear strewn over the ice, abandoned in their haste to escape the long cold winter.

The scuttlebutt was that the secret purpose of the Deep Freeze experiment was to see if men could live without women. The guys found that they could — but they would rather not. The first men to spend the winter under the snow at the South Pole are reported to have rushed outside at the first opportunity and made a bunch of snow women.

By 1962 South Pole City boasted its own hostess — South Pole Suzie, a mannequin with long blonde hair who stood out by the "South Pole International Airport," her flimsy red dress fluttering in the breeze, leering a welcome with cherry red lips.

Even time seems frozen like the landscape in this Deep Freeze. Hike a quarter mile down to Hut Point and you find Discovery Hut, built by Captain Robert Falcon Scott in 1902 when he was able to anchor his ship the *Discovery* just a stone's throw away. You find sea biscuits, hard as hockey pucks, scattered about the hut, unchanged by 54 years of exposure. Scott and his men ate so many penguins that their stomachs rose and fell with the tide. A few feathered remains were still scattered around the hut.

A second monument to the early explorers who tried and failed to reach the South Pole, is the hut at Cape Royds on Ross Island, 25 miles further north where Sir Ernest Shackleton built his hut in 1908.

The third ghost hut stands about 50 miles north at Cape Evans where Captain Scott built his second hut in January 1911 when thick ice prevented him from reaching Hut Point. Here he wintered over before making his fatal dash to the pole. Shackleton's party used it in 1917 while awaiting rescue by sea.

Shackleton's men all dashed out the door, 40 years earlier, leaving their lunch half eaten on the table. A bottle of wine stands on the table, half empty, neatly corked. A loaf of bread, partly sliced, a cut of cheddar cheese, half eaten, a coffee pot, and cups, bowls half-filled with porridge all stand preserved by the dry cold of the aseptic Antarctic, like a slice of living history. Chunks of seal blubber four inches thick filled a box alongside the cast iron kitchen range. They were used for fuel. Dufek declared all three huts "international shrines," and ordered them off limits to all personnel.

Cleanliness is next to godliness. But in the Antarctic cleanliness was next to impossible. General orders allowed everyone one shower every week — a three gallon Navy shower. You stripped, pulled the chain, barely got wet, soaped and rinsed.

The Antarctic, world's fifth largest continent, boasts more than 90 percent of the world's ice and snow. But one day in November we ran out of snow at McMurdo.

"Now hear this," came booming over the public address system: "No more showers, no washing of outer clothing."

The front loader that roared around camp at all hours of the endless day, had scooped up the last vestige of snow from our side of Observation Hill and was forced to invade the Kiwi side of the hill.

No water meant no flushing of toilets. The first Chic Sales was a plain box on the beach with a great view of Mount Erebus and nothing else. By Deep Freeze II the Navy had devised an indoor-outdoor Chic Sales. Oil drums were cut in half and strategically placed. When full, the "Honey Bucket" hauled them out onto the ice and prayed for an early breakup.

When nature called in those early days it had to shout at the top of its lungs. It was 80 degrees at the ceiling, but the blast of air from below was enough to blow you off the throne. In cold weather frostbite would get you in the end.

Those temperatures were courtesy of Sir George Hubert Wilkins, one of the least known, but most able polar explorers ever. He made the first extended flight in the Arctic in 1924, from Point Barrow to Spitzbergen. Wilkins, an experienced navigator, flew to the North Pole, skirted the pole and landed on the sea ice at Spitzbergen.

He could have flown directly over the North Pole, he said, but he had promised Admiral Byrd that he would leave that honor for Byrd. Wilkins said that he could have flown over the South Pole 30 years before, but again he had promised to leave that honor to Byrd. Wilkins finally made his first flight over the South Pole in Dufek's R5D (DC-4) in November 1956.

Wilkins visited the base in 1956 during Deep Freeze II. He had the busiest thermometer in the Antarctic. He also lived by lore acquired in 50 years of polar exploration. When he got sick he wandered out onto the ice where seals had been slaughtered to feed the dogs. He selected a piece of raw liver, ate it, and soon recovered. He said it had a sweet flavor, like pudding. I took his word for it.

Only the Chapel of Our Lady of the Snows, with its modest spire, dwarfed by mighty Mount Erebus, upholds the dignity of Man in this continent of ice that seems forsaken by all but God.

CHAPTER 11

WHITE CHRISTMAS

These reflections appeared in the "Forum" section of The Oregonian *Friday, December 22, 1992.*

"I'm dreaming of a White Christmas just like the ones I used to know."

Those words can be the saddest of tongue or pen when heard on the eve of Christmas on a sunny foreign strand far from home. Every time I hear Bing Crosby lamenting "the tree tops glistening, the children listening for the sound of sleigh bells in the snow" I get a lump in my throat. That haunting ballad takes me back 36 years to a lonely Christmas spent in New Zealand, where the seasons are reversed. December 22 is like June 22 in Oregon.

That was the International Geophysical Year, 1956. I was serving with the U.S. Air Force, helping to establish the first scientific station at the South Pole. I also wrote a series of articles for *The Oregonian.*

I had covered the first landing at the South Pole, October 26, 1956 by Commander Gus Shinn and Admiral George Dufek. We orbited the pole in our air force cargo plane while Dufek planted the American flag in 58-below-zero weather.

The December sun began to melt the runway, which was scraped out of the floating sea ice on McMurdo Sound. We had to board our Globemasters and return to our base at Harewood Airport, 10 miles outside of Christchurch, 2,500 miles away across hostile seas, to wait for colder weather.

The trees in their bright spring foliage were swaying in the balmy breezes. The geraniums were blooming joyfully. The redolence of roses permeated the air. The sun shone hot on the Army tents which formed our home 10,000 miles from home. It was shirt sleeve weather. Off duty crews in shorts kept the tennis courts busy.

But over the midsummer scene from the public address system floated the haunting strains of "I'm dreaming of a White Christmas with every Christmas card I write." It was a little late for Christmas cards via our uncertain air mail. The nearest thing to the sound of sleigh bells in the snow was the tinkle of bells on the forlorn Christmas tree in the officers' club.

Finally Air Force Colonel Harry A. Crosswell, detachment commander, issued orders to cut out the Christmas carols. "The men are depressed and homesick enough without rubbing it in," he said.

The cooks made a valiant effort to conjure up the spirit of Christmas with a juicy turkey and all the trimmings on December 25. But no one had much appetite somehow.

It isn't what's on the festive board, but who's around it that counts. Christmas is not a date on the calendar. Christmas is where the heart is.

CHAPTER 12

GREAT PENGUIN CHASE

When someone mentions The Great Penguin Chase I don't know whether to crow or eat crow.

In 1957 I persuaded the Science Foundation, the Army, Navy, Air Force, agricultural authorities and New Zealand officials to permit the Washington Park Zoo in Portland to bring some penguins back from the Antarctic. There was a vast surplus of penguins. Hundreds of thousands had been sighted in preliminary flights. That was, of course, before the environmental extremists took over the world.

So when the weight of the paperwork equaled the weight of the penguins, we brought back 30 Emperors and 36 Adelie penguins in November 1957. Most of them died of aspergillosis, a lung fungus that also attacks chickens and turkeys. Their deaths are still on my conscience.

I got the idea from Al Capp's Li'l Abner cartoons. Remember the schmoos, the comical little critters who just lived to make people happy by hopping into the frying pan and sacrificing themselves?

Well, baby Emperor penguins are perfect schmoos. Emperors are the true emperors of the Antarctic, lords of all they survey — but stupid. No bird with an ounce of brains would lay an egg the size of a man's head, roll it into her lap and then sit in her own lap for the next two months waiting for it to hatch while temperatures dropped to 80 below and blizzards buried the whole colony under snow.

Actually the female Aptenodytes forsteri (penguin to the lay person) is not so dumb. She rolls her egg over to her mate and lets him turn the heat on the egg atop his feet while she waddles maybe 20 miles to the nearest open water to get a bellyful of krill, a tiny crustacean rich in protein, and bring back enough to regurgitate for the baby schmoo.

The zoo sent Jack Marks down to do the dirty work — and it was a dirty job. Penguins in the pristine Antarctic look like pompous head waiters in their tuxedos with shiny white shirts. But before he was through with the Great Penguin Chase Marks put it bluntly, "I never saw a bird so full of crap!"

Marks was a friend of mine — at least he was before encountering the penguins — and I had told him that the Emperor is no pushover. A mature bird stands four feet high and weighs up to 95 pounds. He can't fly with his stubby wings, but he can break a man's arm with a single blow and his four-inch beak is sharp and deadly.

So Jack, who became known far and wide as The Penguin Man, came prepared. On a bright sunny day we boarded a single-engined Beaver equipped with skis and flew the 25 miles to the edge of the Ross Ice Shelf. We stepped across a crack onto ice that rose and fell with the waves. There we were greeted by a stately parade of Emperors, true relics of the Ice Age. They stood their ground with ridiculous dignity, unafraid. There was danger in the water, but nothing to fear on the surface of the ice.

Marks had invented a pair of penguin pajamas which he attached to a loop at the end of a long pole, like a big butterfly net. He slapped it over the head of the nearest Emperor, leaving the bird's neck sticking out a hole in the top. Upending the struggling bird Marks detached the penguin persuader from the hoop and tightened the draw strings at the bottom, trussing up the regal bird like a sack of potatoes, while his imperious victim squawked indignantly.

A helicopter was required to reach a colony of 30,000 Adelie penguins on rugged Cape Royds. The Adelies, about the size of a mallard, but with the disposition of a tiger, lay their eggs, sensibly, in the spring. The pappa penguin woos his intended mate in much the same way we penguinated people do. He gives her an engagement stone, a lot of stones, in fact.

He picks up pebbles and lays them at the feet of the object of his affection. If she accepts the engagement stones, pappa goes into ecstacy and mamma goes into seclusion. She builds a nest with the pebbles and lays a couple of oversized eggs.

Marks denies it, but sometimes reliable witnesses say that one ardent Adelie mistook Marks for a potential mate and waddled all around the rookery laying pebbles at his feet.

Nesting Adelies fear nothing and won't leave their nests. Try to move one and she will grab you by the finger and try to swallow you. All of which made it easy to select 36 birds not busy incubating.

The makeshift pens on the ice below the camp were soon full. Marks waited for a chance to hitchhike with his dirty birds on a C-124 Globemaster returning empty from the ice to Christchurch and on to Portland.

The order to load, lock and leap came on short notice. All hands turned out to help load. It was hand-to-hand combat. Marks and his helpers waded into the tightly packed Emperors, grabbed them by the flippers and hoisted them aboard the four-foot box.

As they bounced across the rock-like snowdrifts toward the waiting Globemaster, the Emperors began fighting their way over the top of the four-foot boxes, despite screens nailed to the top. I stopped one with a flying tackle while Marks took him by the end that wiggles and I carried his feet. As we ran to catch up with the sled we saw two more desperate birds scramble over the top, drop onto the snow and start scooting miles an hour on their bellies, propelled by their stubby feet and powerful flippers.

As the big box full of penguins was being hoisted through the cargo hold, one side of the box gave way. The dam broke, a flood of black-backed birds sluiced out, flowing in all directions like globs of mercury. The scene resembled a medieval battlefield as spectators struggled with the big birds. Angry outcries from the Emperors mingled with the shouts and imprecations of the volunteers. It took two or three amateurs to subdue each sea-bound Emperor. Marks emerged with a bloody lip and a deep cut on his chin, thanks to an uppercut from a flipper as he hurled himself headlong onto one of the fleeing birds.

The birds all survived the quick trip to Portland. This was the first successful effort to transplant the primitive birds. Early explorers had tried, but the penguins could not survive the long trip by ship.

The caper was repeated in 1962 after Matt Maberry, zoo veterinarian had been assured that the birds could be protected from aspergillosis. A few did survive for about 20 years, but the rest again succumbed to aspergillosis.

THE REST OF THE STORY

The Great Penguin Chase was headline news in the Portland press and television, as well as in New Zealand. That is primarily why *The Oregon Journal* sent Rolla J. "Bud" Crick, their crack aviation and military writer, to the bottom of the world, accredited to Operation Deep Freeze III, the third year of the assault on the Antarctic.

Bud and I were friendly rivals. He had covered the same aviation and military beats for *The Oregon Journal* that I had covered for *The Oregonian* for 20 years. He took pride in getting the story, getting it first and getting it right. This time, as a public relations man for the Navy and Air Force, I was working for Crick and the other correspondents.

Bud was waiting for the Navy to assign a light plane and pilot to go looking for penguins when he was invited by Commander Coley, commander of the Navy's aircraft detachment, to go to the Scott Amundsen Station at the South Pole. They were to land on skis, drop off some scientists and pick up some of the wintering-over party. He was promised 20 minutes at the South Pole, time enough to run around the barber pole with the glass ball on top, erected by the scientists to satisfy tourists.

It was only October 26, five days earlier than the first landing at the pole in Deep Freeze II. But Coley, new to the Antarctic, was out to set a new record. It was reported to be 60 below zero at the pole, too cold for man or machine. I warned Bud that the P2V Neptune, even with all its RATO (Rocket Assisted Take Off) bottles and auxiliary jet engines, would never get off the snow at the 9,000-foot elevation of the pole at 60 below. Snow becomes as hard as concrete and as sticky as sandpaper at those temperatures.

But Bud, dedicated reporter that he was, took off anyway with Commander Coley at the controls. At the last minute I loaned Bud Crick my Rolleiflex camera and a supply of film to shoot black and white pictures. (He had only a small .35 millimeter camera loaded with color film.)

Coley estimated arrival at the pole in four hours thirty minutes. His radioed position reports indicated that he was lost. After five hours, thirty minutes he was reported near the pole station, but it took him another hour to find the narrow landing strip scraped in the snow. He landed, ostensibly to let off some of his passengers, take on others and take off, all in less than 30 minutes. Two hours later he tried to rev up his engines for takeoff and promptly blew out an oil cooler. His oil had turned to asphalt in the intense cold. There sat the pride of the Navy for the next 21 days, waiting for the weather to warm up.

Bud Crick and Tom Abercrombie of *National Geographic*, stranded at the South Pole, missed the Great Penguin Chase. But they had exclusive stories and pictures of the first men to spend six months at the coldest spot on earth.

My Rolleiflex, carefully winterized, continued to function up to speed at 50 below, but froze at 60 below. My camera covered their story without me.

248

SECTION III

Drama of Disaster

CHAPTER 1

I SAW A CITY DIE

It was in the month of May 1948 that I saw a city die. Photographer Hugh Ackroyd and I had just returned from Clatskanie, Oregon, on the lower Columbia where a dike had broken, threatening the town.

It was one of those lazy days when the world seems asleep under the Sunday sun. We were almost out of gas and film, in a hurry to land. But as we headed for the seaplane base at Swan Island we saw airplanes circling Vanport like a bunch of buzzards waiting for the kill. We flew over in time to see the backed-up waters of the Columbia and the Willamette Rivers pouring through a wide breach in the railroad tracks that formed the western dike around the wartime city of Vanport on the outskirts of Portland.

The flimsy two-story hastily built apartments were already beginning to float, smashing into each other like battering rams. One apartment fell apart as we watched, exposing a table set for dinner with the roast half-carved on the table. A baby's crib teetered on the edge of disaster in another apartment.

We could see father, mother and a child perched on the porch roof of one building, just barely out of reach of the rising water. A floating building nudged the porch, which crumpled in slow motion. On our next pass over the area there was no sign of the family.

Two men paddled desperately in the current, half submerged, on a section of boardwalk. Another lay flat on his stomach on a mattress, paddling frantically with both hands.

The current shoved most of the buildings into a splintered huddle in the corner of the dike near the Denver Avenue fill, the only exit from Vanport. The roof tops were dotted with refugees. Some jumped from roof to roof as we watched. An old man pulling a child in a little wagon ran toward the exit. The water overtook him. On the next pass he was gone.

Our instinct was to land and lend a helping hand, but I had to fight off the impulse. The water was full of debris which would have wrecked our tandem Piper float plane.

There was some initial panic, but in the end Vanport died quietly.

By the time we refueled, the 600-acre basin was completely filled with 12 feet of water. At 5:44 p.m. a wandering apartment building, goaded by the dying current, nudged the flagpole that stood at the entrance to the silent city. The tall pole wavered, hesitated, then went down with colors flying — at half mast. (It was Memorial Day, May 30, 1948.)

That was the end of Vanport.

I was on general assignment that spooky night, covering the command center on Denver Avenue where volunteers were still searching for flood victims. Soon the flood waters began to break through the Denver Avenue fill, the only north-south artery between Oregon and Washington. It was Main Street for the whole West Coast. Huge apartment buildings began to crash through the breach.

The road was closed to all but emergency vehicles. About 9 p.m. officers thought they heard a siren wailing faintly above the noise of the crashing buildings. We saw flashing red lights bearing down from the north — only to disappear into the breach. It was days before the victim was identified. He turned out to be a lineman for the Portland General Electric Company. Apparently in the dark of the night he never saw the break in the road.

Ackroyd and I were sure that we had seen scores of victims die. Initial reports estimated 2,000 missing. But when the water finally receded, two months later, the remains of only 15 victims were found in the wreckage. Seven more were reported missing.

The problem was the transient nature of Vanport and its residents. Many were Bowery bums brought out by the trainload from the streets of New York. Many of them had no one to miss them — no friends or relatives and no permanent addresses. Many may have simply walked away, uncounted, in the panic and confusion.

At 4:15 p.m. on Memorial Day, 1948, Vanport was a city of sleepy suburbanites dozing in the Sunday sun, lulled by the laughter of children at play. But by 5:15 p.m. Vanport was a city of silence, covered by the black waters of the flooding Columbia River.

Never has a city grown so big so fast, lived so short a life and died so suddenly, yet with so little loss of life.

Vanport was a war baby, born of the necessity of housing some 40,000 workers for Kaiser's shipyards in Portland and Vancouver. Construction was started on the 700 temporary buildings with wartime urgency on September 1, 1942. The first shipyard workers swarmed into the wooden apartment buildings December 12, 1942.

Within a year Vanport was a city of nearly 40,000, second biggest city in the state of Oregon, biggest war housing project in history — a city that wasn't a city, a city without a mayor, a council, a court of law, a chamber of commerce, or a single homeowner; a city without local taxes or local government; a city without a head, a heart, or a soul.

Five and a half years after this drab war baby was born she was dead — drowned, disheveled, demolished, obliterated. By that time her population had dropped to 17,500.

It is still one of the major miracles among modern disasters that the death toll was so low. It was one of the ironies of fate that the very fickleness of nature that destroyed Vanport also worked to save the lucky thousands who escaped. The lazy weather lured most of Vanport to the beaches, the mountains or the old fishing hole. If the dike had broken at night on a week day the flood could have taken a heavy toll of lives.

Signs warning of the Vanport flood were there for all to see, but were not heeded until too late. For 30 days the sun had shone down out of a cloudless sky. Warm winds licked at the winter snow. Warm rains hastened the melting of the heavy Canadian snow pack at the headwaters of the Columbia River and the Snake River in the east.

As the flood rose the water literally piled up in the center of the raging Columbia. The river got a hump in its back like a buffalo bull. Each day as I patrolled the river with a photographer we saw more and more uprooted trees, bridges, remains of houses and the carcasses of cows and horses caught in the grip of the current. Logs, small buildings and half-ton rolls of newsprint tumbled end over end in the maelstrom as the rising river tore away docks, mills, bridges and levees.

That's a sight I will never forget. But there were some minor tragedies, too. Flying low over the Lewis River at Woodland a couple of days before Memorial Day, photographer Hugh Ackroyd and I saw a fresh break in a dike threatening a farm house below the dike.

A little dog was running frantically back and forth along the dike. Impulsively we landed and nosed into the dike. The little dog kept running back and forth to the farm house, whining and scratching at the porch. We could hear her pups whimpering. But the water was rising so fast that she couldn't reach the pups. Neither could we. In a matter of moments the house was under water. But the distraught mother kept dashing back into the flood, whining for her pups.

Twice we picked her up and put her in the plane. Twice she struggled free. Finally we had to leave her on the levee, her eyes fixed on the farmhouse, now being tilted by the rushing current.

There will never be another Vanport flood, not in the next 100 years and probably never, engineers say. Engineers manning the U.S. Army Corps of Engineers' flood control center say that they can knock 10 feet off the worst flood on record — thanks to more than 20 major dams on the Columbia River and its tributaries, now controlled by computers to absorb even the flood of 1894 which crested in Portland at 34 feet. The Vanport flood crested at 31 feet at Vancouver.

Nevertheless no one lives below the dikes on the site of Vanport or ever will if existing laws prevail. Only the scream and roar of race cars and motorcycles on an oval track is heard where once children played in the streets.

CHAPTER 2

BIG BLOW

Friday October 12, Columbus Day 1962 dawned bright and clear. It was lazy weather, remarkably balmy for an autumn day. It promised to be a dull news day.

I was covering the weather for *The Oregonian* and having trouble finding a lead. A front page story reported the dying gasps of "Typhoon Freda" which had hit Gold Beach in southern Oregon Thursday, smashing a grade school, eight homes, and a number of trailers. But by Friday morning Coast Guard stations reported all quiet along the coast. There was no hint of the impending "worst natural disaster in the history of the West Coast", which would leave an unprecedented trail of death and destruction.

Then about 9:30 a.m. the warning bells rang on the Weather Bureau teletype in the news room. The meteorologists had issued a bulletin warning of possible winds up to 60 miles an hour for the Willamette Valley. Forecasters based the warning on a single report from a Navy radar picket ship at sea about 350 miles west of Eureka, California, reporting a sudden drop in the barometric pressure to 28.41 inches of mercury, followed by winds clocked at 92 miles an hour.

That barometer reading would be an incredible 1.51 inches of mercury below the 29.92-inch standard sea level pressure. But barometric pressures remained normal along the coast and winds were light. Forecasters thought the report must be in error.

Then barometers everywhere in the Willamette Valley began to dive dramatically. Turkey farmers reported their easily spooked birds began to huddle in panic. They knew something mere men did not. All doubt in the minds of the forecasters was removed when the 11 a.m. hourly reports came in from six merchant ships reporting steady winds of more than 60 miles an hour headed for the Oregon coast. A few minutes later a Brazilian freighter radioed an emergency message reporting violent winds of 83 knots and heavy rain.

A wild nor'wester was on the way, but neither the forecasters nor any other official thought it would be the killer storm that it quickly turned out to be.

The storm hit the coast at Crescent City, California, and Gold Beach, Oregon about 11:30 a.m., wiping out everything in its path, including phone lines, radio and television stations and Coast Guard communications. Reports in the wake of the storm were sketchy. By 12:30 p.m. a U-2 pilot flying at 55,000 feet reported "the most severe turbulence ever experienced."

By 1 p.m. the Cape Blanco Loran Station reported the anemometer had been blown away, but estimated winds of 150 knots, gusting to 170 knots. The Mount Hebo radar station also reported 170-knot winds before the station was evacuated. About 3 p.m. the storm hit nearby Corvallis with peak winds of 125 miles an hour. The Coast Guard abandoned its lookout tower at Yaquina Bay when the anemometer hit the peg at 120 miles an hour; peak gusts were estimated at 140 miles an hour.

Winds of unrecorded force blew the life-sized 35-ton bronze statue of the Circuit Rider off its pedestal on the capitol grounds in Salem. Farms throughout the Willamette Valley were brutally battered. Barns collapsed, trapping and killing cattle. Most spectacular was Case Boredrecht's dairy barn near Rickreall, which collapsed at milking time, trapping 60 cows in their milking stalls and crushing 55 of them. Altogether 81 head of dairy cattle were reported killed — not counting beef cattle in the open hit by falling trees.

Barns at the race track in Portland were shattered, freeing race horses to run wild before the storm. Some 5,000 chickens were blown through the air at one ranch when a chicken house overturned. Orchards were uprooted and fields of corn and grain flattened.

An air of hushed expectancy hung over Portland as airports in the path of the storm were warned to start tying down airplanes or flying them east of the mountains.

By 5 p.m. an ominous black cloud loomed in the southern sky, undershot by a weird greenish-gray light along the horizon. The demon wind hit the city with an unearthly banshee howl, uprooting centuries-old elms in the park blocks, ripping the roofs off buildings, knocking out most power and phone lines.

Stunned by the violence of the wind, I debated whether to plunge into the storm, covering the biggest story of the year, or call my wife, Virginia, at home in Vancouver, Washington. We lived on the brow of a hill overlooking the Columbia River, exposed to the full fury of the south wind. We were surrounded by big Douglas fir trees, neatly placed to crash down on us.

An urgent premonition told me to call home. Luckily our phone line survived the storm. "I'm all right," Virginia insisted. She was in my study on the southeast corner of the house answering the phone with one hand while trying to hold the door shut against the force of the gale with the other hand.

"One big fir just hit the roof above the study and damaged the door," she said in the same matter-of-fact voice she would use to report that we were having ham hocks for dinner.

"I was just going down to the driveway to move the Plymouth when the phone rang," she explained.

About that time over the phone I could hear a new note in the roar of the storm. "What was that!?" I asked.

There was a pause then Virginia came back on the line. "That was another big fir. It just crashed down on the old Plymouth, crushing it completely," she calmly reported.

My phone call may have saved her life. Another two or three minutes and she would have been behind the wheel of the Plymouth, crushed to a pulp. When the winds died down we had two big trees through our roof besides the one that flattened the car. We were without heat or lights for days, but we had fireplaces — and lots of firewood.

When the storm let up a little, Virginia ran across the street to call our neighbor Chic Scarpelli to the phone. When he finished the call she asked him to help her get a heavy electric typewriter out of the smashed car so that she could work on the high school paper. (She was advisor to the student staff.) Chic carried the 49-pound typewriter into the dark house and plugged it into a wall socket.

Virginia, who taught at Hudson's Bay High School, and Chic, a veteran professor with more degrees than Carter had pills, stood there in the dark, wondering why the stupid machine wouldn't work. It finally dawned on the two of them at once that electric typewriters don't work worth a darn without electricity!

The storm hit Vancouver's Pearson Air Field a knockout blow. Planes were tossed around like toys. Hangars were blown apart. Sheet metal flew like scythes before the storm. One came within three feet of decapitating Herman Parsons as he tried to save some of the tied down planes. Three planes wound up on a hangar roof. One airplane wing was found half a mile away. Some 59 of the 75 planes on the line were wrecked.

Freakishly, while planes securely tied down were wrecked, a V-tailed single-engined Beechcraft which had just landed faced into the wind and never budged during the peak gusts that followed. A traffic reporter aloft in a single-engine light plane, unable to land, rode out the storm over Hillsboro in violent turbulence. A later survey showed 226 planes damaged and 56 totally wrecked at 13 airports.

As the newsroom went dark I teamed up with a photographer to hit the streets. We groped our way down the stairs and forced our way out the door. Strips of metal from the auto repair shop across the street were flying through the air like guillotine blades, threatening to decapitate anyone in their path. Huge limbs were being torn from the historic old elms in the Park Blocks, smashing parked cars and blocking the streets. The metal siding was being ripped off the tower of the Congregational Church.

All traffic lights were out, but motorists and pedestrians acted as volunteer traffic cops at key intersections and a few cars continued to wend their way through the debris.

As we approached the Multnomah Athletic Club stadium, knocked around by violent gusts, we were startled by an unearthly shriek, loud above the roar of the storm, as a peak gust of wind, well over 100 knots, screamed across the sky. Sections of the roof spiraled up like autumn leaves, only to be snatched away by the wild wind and disappear in the murky distance.

Gusts of 93 miles an hour were reported at the nearby KGW-TV building and 116 miles an hour on the Morrison Bridge before the anemometer blew away.

The St. Johns suspension bridge over the Willamette River had to be closed when it began to dance in the wind, rocking and rolling in 15-foot oscillations. A truck driver, caught on the wildly gyrating span, abandoned his truck and slid down the long arched deck to solid ground.

In the heart of the city ships and boats, big and small, broke their moorings on the Willamette River and went skittering before the wind. A big LST, tied up at a repair dock, broke loose and crashed into the Hawthorne Bridge.

Back at the city room the lights were still out. But we had manual typewriters and I was able to write my first stories on the old Underwood in the dark, thanks to the touch typing that I learned in high school. Emergency generators supplied power for the presses and the city edition came out pretty much on time.

The Big Blow made headlines for months. The survivors licked their wounds, counted their dead and started to rebuild. The final count showed 48 dead, 24 of them in Oregon, three in Clark County, Washington. The storm devastated an area 125 miles wide and 1,000 miles long. Damage was estimated at $210 million.

The Metropolitan Life Insurance Company rated it as the nation's worst natural disaster of 1962. Forests throughout Oregon and Washington were hard hit. More than 17 billion board feet of timber was blown down. By comparison the eruptions of Mount Saint Helens on May 18, 1980, destroyed just 1.6 billion board feet of timber. W. D. Hagerstein, executive vice president of the Industrial Forestry Association, called it "the worst forestry catastrophe within the memory of living man."

The Weather Bureau, in a detailed analysis of the "Columbus Day Windstorm," concluded that "it caused more destruction in the Pacific Northwest than any other windstorm in recorded history."

CHAPTER 3

EARTHQUAKE

"The veil of the temple was rent in twain...
The earth did quake and the rocks rent."

So it was written in the Book of Matthew of the first Good Friday. And so I found it when I landed at Anchorage, Alaska, the morning after Good Friday, March 27, 1964. I was on the first plane to land since the terrifying earthquake that left 131 dead and destroyed $750 million worth of property.

At 5:36 p.m. the quake struck northern Prince William Sound with a force of 8.4 on the Richter scale, at least twice the power of the 1906 quake that destroyed San Francisco. First reports over the radio and television treated it as just another tremor. Alaska was always shaking nervously. By the time we tuned in to the evening news it began to sound more like the disaster it was.

I called the city desk and suggested that we rent a plane and take off for Anchorage with a photographer. William "Bill" Hilliard, was on the desk that night, but he couldn't get the brass to approve. I called back later to see whether Sitka was hit. My brother was federal commissioner there. Then I went to bed with the phone at my elbow.

At 3 a.m. the phone jerked me awake. Hilliard said the Navy had called to invite me to fly to Kodiak with them. I had accreditation from the Department of Defense and clearance to fly with the Navy. I got Herman Parson, flight base operator at Pearson Field, out of bed and asked him to fly us to Whidbey rather than rent one of his planes and leave it at Whidbey.

I put on my winter woollies, grabbed my sleeping bag and emergency rations, borrowed $100 from Herm and we were airborne by 4 a.m. We landed at Whidbey Island at 5:30 a.m. alongside a Lockheed Electra loaded with tents, blankets and medical gear for Kodiak. But all communications had been knocked out and the Navy postponed the flight.

Wally Turner and Larry Davies, crack *New York Times* reporters, and I persuaded the Navy to fly us to Seattle-Tacoma Airport where we boarded a Pacific Northern jetliner. We took off at 10:50 a.m., not knowing whether we would be able to land. As we approached the Kenai Peninsula we could see a column of black smoke two miles high rising from the terminal at Whittier where tidal waves had smashed the fuel tanks and set them afire. Red flames could be seen licking at the stricken town of Whittier as our jetliner soared high over the Chugach Range. They burned for the next two weeks.

Early news flashes had reported a five-foot crack in the runway at Anchorage, but we found only a small crack. The control tower lay in a splintered heap across the terminal building. One controller had been killed in the crash and two others were seriously injured.

All was chaos on the ground. Rumors were rampant. I managed to catch a bus which took us through the apparently undamaged suburbs. We began to doubt reports of the damage — until we dropped into a deep crack in the road and nearly broke an axle. Then we passed the six-story Four Seas apartment complex, still under construction, lying in a heap on the ground.

Alaska's heartland was still quivering and smoking in the wake of the quake that laid it low on Good Friday. A cold, clammy fog hid most of the damage. The Westward Inn, biggest and best in town, didn't look too bad, except for a big crack in the third floor level. That floor was closed.

It was 15 hours after the quake had struck and the city seemed to be deserted, paralyzed. There was no heat, light, water. I was lucky to get the last room available at the Westward Inn, dumped my gear and started walking. You couldn't call a cab. As I groped my way up Fourth Avenue I gradually made out one of the freaks of the quake.

The whole north side of Fourth Avenue had dropped down about 10 feet, leaving the roofs of the one-story buildings level with the street. Fourth Avenue was devoted to pawn shops, bars and taverns frequented by the Olys (Eskimos, so called because they were always drinking Olys — Olympia Beer). They wondered what had hit them when they found themselves slowly sinking into the ground.

> "I was just sitting down to a VO when the quake struck," said a pilot friend that I met later. "I thought: Boy this stuff really packs a wallop'."

I finally found the makeshift command post in the Public Safety building. Eskimo Scouts patrolled the street, while police, civil defense, state patrol, army and volunteers awaited dispatch. An emergency generator supplied power for lights, which failed when you needed them.

Everyone had a story. I found a cab to take me to the Alaska

Communications Center in Elmendorf Air Force Base. I phoned in some stories; made a cup of hot chocolate. Then it was back to the command post where I got my first hot meal in 30 hours — C rations from an army field kitchen.

I hitched a ride out to the exclusive Turnagain Arm area on a bluff overlooking the Knick Arm, which had suffered the worst devastation. The development, highest elevation in the city, was built on a thick layer of what proved to be a form of thixotropic clay, which turned to liquid when vibrated. When the earth began to shake, the whole hill turned to pudding and started moving in waves down the bluff onto the mud flats. A succession of furrows literally ploughed under the expensive homes on the bluff, including the mansion owned by Bob Atwood, publisher of the *Anchorage News.*

Survivors said the earth waves were so violent that they were knocked around, bounced against walls or knocked to the ground.

"I came within one step of being killed," said Roberta Austerman, whose mother lived in Portland.

"I was in the basement of the Hillside Apartments when the quake struck. I ran to get the baby and headed for the street. The quake shook me off my feet and I fell flat, just as a big chunk of concrete fell a foot in front of my face. Another step and I would have been killed."

Sunday I finally found a plane for rent at Merrill Field in downtown Anchorage. Bill Barton, an Oregon pilot, flew me over Whittier and Seward. Whittier, ice-free port at the north end of an 11-mile tunnel, only 40 miles from the epicenter of the quake, was still marked by a column of black smoke rising two miles into the air. The quake had split the big oil storage tanks, which burned for more than two weeks. Some 13 workers were killed by the tsunami (seismic wave) that picked up a four-ton boulder from the bottom of the harbor and tossed it 125 feet onto the railway tracks near the terminal, 26 feet above the water level.

Seward looked from the air like a city that had been skinned alive. And it had been. The tidal wave which struck after the quake, ripped the hide off the business and industrial district. Nearly half the city was scalped clean. Million dollar docks just completed at this sea terminal for the Alaska Railroad were ripped out. Five-ton locomotives were tossed a block inland.

Seagoing fishing boats were tossed into trees, one almost a mile from the normal harbor line. One rested on top of a house three blocks from the vanished dock. A half dozen houses were washed inland. The airport was scoured clean of hangars and airplanes. Yet only one life was reported lost initially. Fire followed flood, wiping out two oil tank farms. A tank car was still burning Sunday. Great pillars of black smoke hung over both Seward and Whittier like funeral pyres.

This became known as the year of the black snow in the Chugach Range south of Anchorage. For 20 miles downwind from Whittier and Seward the pristine snows were smudged with black like a shroud over the half-dead cities. Thirteen were dead or missing in Whittier, which bore the brunt of the tsunamis.

Nature's incredible violence was vented with equal spite on the Alaska Railroad, which runs like a jugular vein from Seward up the Homer Peninsula to Anchorage and on to Fairbanks. The tidal wave ripped out sections of fill, leaving naked rails dangling over the breach. The earth writhed as if in agony, tearing some bridges apart, compressing others until they buckled upward like accordions, pulling others apart.

Great avalanches poured down every draw through the sparse timber and far into the valley. The quake was so violent on the Kenai Peninsula that the tops of trees were snapped off like twigs.

The rails leading to Seward at the tip of the Kenai Peninsula were twisted and heaved in permanent waves, 22 bridges were destroyed. The tsunami that struck Seward had wiped out the docks, tossing locomotives around like toys and killing 11 residents.

Valdez, in the southeast corner of Prince William Sound, about 50 miles from the epicenter of the quake, was the victim of the most spectacular example of the fury of the great earthquake. There was nothing to do in Valdez but watch activities at the town dock. The Motor Vessel *Chena* was unloading that Friday afternoon and about 30 townspeople were standing on the dock watching the action.

Suddenly the earth began to shake so violently that it knocked people off their feet. The dock began to sink into the sea and a great "mound" of muddy turbulent water appeared several hundred yards offshore. Within two or three minutes the 10,815-ton *Chena* was lifted about 30 feet above the pier on an incoming wave and heeled over landward 45 to 50 degrees into a whirlpool of mud and debris where the pier had been. Captain Merrill D. Steward, the *Chena's* skipper, recalled that "the ship was slammed onto the bottom and rolled wildly from side to side like a rag doll by a rapid succession of waves before it finally slithered off the mud bottom through the wreckage of docks and cannery to reach safety in deep water." Water 110 feet deep covered the site of the missing pier.

Where ebb tide used to leave tide flats bare, there was now 70 feet of water. Soon after the dock disappeared with 30 spectators a surge of water shot into Valdez Arm and Port Valdez, setting new records. Huge waves destroyed wooden buildings at Cliff Mine near the entrance to Valdez harbor and deposited debris 170 feet above sea level. The highest wave reached an incredible 220 feet above the water level.

Freak waves in Prince William Sound destroyed all but the school and one house in the native village of Chenega and swept 25 of the 76 inhabitants to their deaths. The wave struck within three minutes after the quake ended. The highest surge entered a school building on a knoll above the village, 90 feet above the water level.

Tsunamis, which can travel 400 miles an hour in the open sea, hit Crescent City, California repeatedly, leaving 10 dead and 16 missing. One wave tossed a motel from the Oregon coast line onto Highway 101, blocking this main north south highway. Four children were swept out to sea when a wave hit a sleeping family on a beach near Newport, Oregon. Prompt warnings by the Sea Wave Warning Service probably saved many other lives.

Those who lived through the great Good Friday Quake had weird and wonderful tales to tell. One man said that he was sitting in the basement supply room filled with heavy auto parts when his little dog began to run around and bark frantically, trying to get out the door. About that time the quake struck:

> "I was sitting there looking at shelves piled with heavy parts when the shelves actually jumped off the floor, then came back down with a crash."

Damage to the Westward Hotel would seem to prove a vertical component. The vertical steel beams which form the main supports for the building were bent into an S-shape as if they had been lifted up and dropped. Part of Chenega Island dropped

11 feet during the turmoil of the earthquake, while other areas rose. This vertical component of the earth's vibrations has, rarely, been reported by Japanese seismologists, who probably have more experience with earthquakes than anyone else.

Horses in pastures outside the city of Anchorage were reported to have run wild in terror minutes before the quake struck, while a dairy farmer east of town reported his cows all suddenly quit eating and headed for the pasture gate. The Japanese have long noted this behavior and incorporated it into their seismic warning system.

I finally got a ride up Knick Arm to Portage Glacier where the land had sunk five to seven feet and numerous spectacular mud spouts had been reported as cracks opened up and then were squeezed shut again. Rumors of people being trapped in these cracks were never confirmed. Mrs. George Larson of Portage reported seeing a small mud fountain grow into a sheet of mud 75 to 100 feet high and 100 feet long. It played for some time like a dirty geyser, then subsided and continued to bubble like a champagne spring. Seal hunters 140 miles southeast of the epicenter in Controller Bay reported seeing "fountains of muddy water squirting from the ground."

Airline pilots and ship's captains reported hundreds of thousands of red snappers died during the quake and floated to the surface. These were big snappers, weighing up to 30 pounds, not like the ordinary run of 10-pounders fishermen were accustomed to catching. One plausible explanation for the disaster is that fish, extremely sensitive to rapid pressure changes, were forced up off the bottom where they normally live by the turbid current triggered during the seismic shaking.

The quake damaged the Navy's runway on Kodiak Island, killed 19 civilians in Kodiak and destroyed the waterfront and the fish processing plant. Scores of fishing boats were lost.

By the time I got back to *The Oregonian*, Gerry Pratt, business editor and a natural promoter, had lined up a freighter and was busy soliciting building materials to fill the ship. The ship was filled by volunteer donations, without government assistance. In June, I flew back to Kodiak with a photographer to cover the arrival of the relief ship with enough material to build a small town.

CHAPTER 4

SPY SHIP *PUEBLO*

On the eleventh of January 1968, the USS Pueblo put out to sea from the United States Navy base at Sasebo, Japan. She was chubby and squat. She was gray and nondescript, like some tramp steamer — except for the white numerals on her bow that identified her as a U.S. Navy ship.

The *Pueblo* was no stranger to those waters. As a freighter, vintage of 1944, she had served the South Koreans until laid up in the reserve fleet. She was taken out of mothballs in 1966 and converted into an AGERS, Auxiliary Geographic and Environmental Research Ship. Now she was steaming north into the Sea of Japan, through heavy weather so severe that she had to detour to the east.

The steering mechanism kept failing — 60 times in two months, her skipper, Commander Lloyd M. Bucher reported. There was trouble, too, with some of the navigation gear. But below decks her two diesel engines droned on flawlessly, thanks in part to Fireman Duane Daniel Hodges, one of four Oregon men on the crew of 83 aboard the *Pueblo*. Those engines were his babies. His crew had torn them down three times and put them back together again, just for practice.

"Then when the engine didn't sound right, he made them tear it down again," his father, Jesse Hodges, recalled. "When he was just a kid he used to tear down his old car and put it back together again. He'd spend a whole weekend rebuilding his transmission or his clutch."

The Pueblo, *once clear of the storm north of Tsushima Straits, headed northeast through the Sea of Japan to 42 degrees north latitude, close to North Korea's border with Communist China. Ice caked the deck and rigging of the waddling old converted freighter. It took up to half an hour to get the canvas covers off the two 50 caliber machine guns, one mounted fore and the other aft, for firing practice.*

On the 16th of January the Pueblo *headed west toward Chongjin, a North Korean port far to the north. There she lay dead in the water for two days listening and taking samples of the ocean water.*

Duane was born September 5, 1946 on the outskirts of the tiny town of Creswell, population 1,145, in a one-story frame home that his father was in the process of building with his own hands.

He was the last of six children, five boys and one girl. All but one still lived within 30 miles of the home place, where Mr. and Mrs. Jesse Hodges still lived. Duane, like his sister and brothers, never ventured farther than 30 miles from home until he joined the navy. He had a happy childhood, doted on by his mother and his sister, Sheila.

The Hodges were a God-fearing family and at the age of nine, Duane accepted the Lord. Reverend J. J. Beshears, who "set the church in order" at Eagle Point, Oregon, remembers confirming Duane in the Church of God of Prophecy in 1955.

"He was a real nice boy, real serious about the church, very active in church work. About everything that was going on he was a part of it."

"It pays to raise your children in a church which believes in repentance of sin," said his father. "Then you know what track they are on.

"Duane was always a good hand around the house. You didn't have to drive him to work, just mention we needed to change spark plugs or points in the car and he was out there doing it.

"I was running the barker at the veneer plant and would come home tired. Duane would find me working the rototiller, and he would just take the handles and go right ahead with the job.

"He was always willing to help. When his mother had to go to the hospital for an operation Duane laid off his job and stayed home to can the tomatoes and corn so his mother wouldn't fret. Duane spent some time in the Boy Scouts and in Four-H work."

By now the Pueblo *was working her way south off the coast of Communist North Korea, flying no flag, showing no lights "except when necessary to prevent a rules-of-the road incident."*

Still in severe icing conditions she arrived off Chongjin on the eighteenth of January, 1968, where she lay for a day and a half "noting very little activity."

On the nineteenth she moved south off Mayang Do, another North Korean port. Here a North Korean sub-chaser passed her at 500 yards, but failed to spot her.

Duane was inclined to be short and fat around the ages of 10 to 12, then he began to grow up rather than out. He was 6 feet 2

when he entered junior high school in Creswell. Lampshire Hyde, who taught Duane language arts and social science, remembered him well.

"He was at the awkward age then, tall and gangly, with big feet. He was a quiet, earnest boy with a good attitude. He wasn't a good student, but he always did his best."

Duane had been singing in the church choir since he first found his boyish tenor. Now his rich baritone was welcomed in the high school choir. He turned out for track, basketball and football. A sprained ankle early ended his football career. But wrestling was his favorite sport, from the beginning.

He had fixed up an old Chevy that he used to race on weekends at the Cottage Grove track. He was handy with tools, but not so handy with the books. In his sophomore year he dropped out of school for the spring quarter.

"I think he got bored," his brother Marion said.

"He came back to school with a complete change of attitude," his wrestling coach, Eldon Hodgins, recalled. "He was like a new man. He brought his grades up and got back on the wrestling squad.

"Duane was the epitome of American youth — an all-American boy.

"He had strong latent religious principles, not ostentatious, just part of his makeup. He had no vices, didn't smoke or drink. He was a good sportsman, a good leader. He was chosen co-captain of the wrestling team in his senior year.

"He really found himself in wrestling. He was strong and fast as lightning.

"He would never hurt anyone, yet he was aggressive. He made the fastest pin on record. He pinned a man from Culver in 5.5 seconds.

"He won his first six or seven matches to help Creswell win its first league and district championships in 1965, his senior year. He weighed 178 pounds in those days and stood 6 foot 2."

His rich baritone helped swell the music of the school choir at graduation exercises in June 1965. Then he was cast adrift, with this inscription on his diploma:

"You have each been given a bag of tools, a formless rock and a book of rules. And each must make, ere life has flown, a stumbling block or a stepping stone."

On the rain dark night of the twenty first of January 1968, the blacked-out Pueblo *slid south toward Wonsan, arriving the morning of the twenty-second, about 25 miles from the island of Nanbo. Later she shifted north to the vicinity of Ung Do.*

At noon she was approached by two government fishing boats, gray, without numbers, apparently unarmed, manned by civilians. They circled the Pueblo *at about 100 yards, withdrew to 9,000 yards, then returned to circle her at 30 yards.*

Commander Bucher decided that he had been detected and at 5 p.m., started trying to file his first situation report, breaking the radio silence he had maintained for 11 days. It was more than 12 hours before the Pueblo's *message finally got back to Japan, thanks to poor conditions for radio transmissions.*

That night Commander Bucher moved out to sea 25 miles off the nearest land.

Duane's "stepping stone" was a job with his brother Marion, a building contractor in Eugene. He had been working Saturdays and summers during his high school days and was soon a top carpenter.

He had joined the Naval Reserve unit at Eugene January 21, 1966, at the age of 19. The Hodges were a navy family. Duane's brother Roy had served in the Marines. Brother LaMerle had served in the navy. So had brother Ron. Brother Marion had served as chief petty officer on ammunition ships. His sister Sheila's husband had also served in the navy, as had his mother's two brothers.

After working as a carpenter for a year, Duane decided it was time to serve his tour of active duty with the U.S. Navy. He volunteered and was called to active duty October 29, 1966.

On November 28, 1966, his brother Marion wrote: "Just a note to say things I never seemed to take the time to say when you were around.

"...You have progressed faster than any man I have ever seen. The boys have all told me how well you have done. I have had compliments on you from customers.

"...I hate to see you have to leave for awhile, but the time will go fast. I hope you intend to stay with the business. You have a place in it when you come back.

"Actually, I had told Duane he was good enough to make it on his own as a contractor," Marion recalled.

Duane told his folks he planned to go back to college when he had finished his two-year hitch in the navy, get a degree in business administration and architecture, then go into business for himself.

On the morning of January 23, 1968, Commander Bucher moved the Pueblo *back to a point about 15 nautical miles off*

the island of Ung Do, which lies in the mouth of Wonsan Harbor. There he lay dead in the water while his oceanographers took a deep water sample.

Just before noon a North Korean subchaser hove into sight, closing on the Pueblo at high speed, and commenced circling the ship at 500 to 1,000 yards. She was at general quarters, with her deck-mounted guns manned and pointing at the Pueblo.

She asked the Pueblo her nationality and Commander Bucher answered by hoisting the stars and stripes. Watching through binoculars, Bucher saw the agitation on the bridge of the enemy ship. Soon she signalled: "Heave to, or I will fire."

By this time three PT boats were approaching from the west, with their deck-mounted machine guns manned and aimed at the Pueblo. A little later a fourth PT boat appeared on the scene.

Commander Bucher passed the word to prepare to destroy classified material. He sent two situation reports to the commander of the naval force in Japan saying that he was being harassed by Communist craft but intended to remain in the area.

By this time two Communist MIGs were circling overhead. A few minutes later one of the PT boats began backing toward the starboard bow of the Pueblo, with fenders rigged and an armed boarding party standing by.

Commander Bucher ordered the engines started and headed out to sea, slowly at first, then at flank speed — a mere 13 knots, flanked by the PT boats, with the subchaser following a mile astern.

After a few minutes the subchaser closed up on his port quarter and opened fire with its .57 millimeter guns. Most of the first salvo of 6 to 14 shots went overhead. But one shell hit the signal mast, and spattered the bridge with shrapnel. Commander Bucher was hit in the legs and rectum and knocked to the deck, but got to his feet within five seconds and ordered the bridge evacuated. At the same time he gave orders to start destroying classified material. Commander Bucher and three other wounded men dived over the side and took control of the ship from the deck wheelhouse.

The Communists continued to fire 10 or 12 salvoes of 6 to 14 shots each. One shell went through the wheelhouse, slightly injuring one of the officers on duty there. The PT boats sprayed the ship with 30 caliber machine gun bullets, which bounced off the hull.

Commander Bucher gave the order to stop the ship — and the firing ceased.

After boot camp at San Diego, Duane was assigned to the *Pueblo* as a fireman. The old freighter, being rebuilt at Bremerton Naval Shipyards had no boilers, hence no fires. Duane's fireman duties turned out to be boss of the diesel engine crew, with a chance to pitch in with his own hands. It was on the *Pueblo* that Duane met Fireman Michael O'Bannon of Beaverton, Oregon. They became fast friends and used to make the long drive from Bremerton to their homes on weekends.

Duane's parents drove up to Bremerton with Merle and his wife for the commissioning of the *Pueblo* May 13, 1967.

"Duane showed us all through the ship," his father recalled. "I didn't see any electronic gear or anything unusual about the ship. I remember thinking she wasn't much of a ship to be putting out in the stormy Pacific.

"Her two civilian scientists told us about her mission to do research to find more food fish that could be used to help feed people in the under-fed countries of the world."

Duane with his mechanic's eye, however, had already begun

to suspect the *Pueblo* was more than a research ship. "She's crammed with electronic gear that wouldn't be needed for deep sea research," Duane told his brother Marion.

The officers knew the top secret mission of the *Pueblo*, but crew members had only been told the cover story. Duane told his buddy Dave Topps, back in the summer of 1967 that she was "an intelligence ship." He swore Topps to secrecy.

About this time one of the two MIGs circling the Pueblo *swooped down and fired four rockets, which hit 8 or 10 miles away. "It must have been an accident. Maybe the pilot got excited," Commander Bucher noted in his log.*

By this time the ship was filled with smoke as the crew began burning secret papers and documents while others smashed classified equipment with fire axes and sledge hammers.

Commander Bucher left the bridge and hurried to his stateroom to check for classified material and to throw his private arms overboard. When he returned to the bridge the subchaser was signalling: "Follow me, I have pilot aboard."

Commander Bucher gave the order to follow the subchaser at one-third throttle back toward Wonsan, escorted by the four torpedo boats close alongside.

Duane was proud of his dumpy little ship and of his shipmates. "I couldn't have got on a ship with a better bunch of guys," he told his parents. And he couldn't have had a nicer skipper than Commander Bucher, Duane told them.

It was September before the *Pueblo* completed her trial runs and left Bremerton for San Diego. She sailed from San Diego November 6, 1967. Duane called his mother the night before she sailed.

They docked at Honolulu Tuesday, November 14, 1967. Duane had the duty and had to stay on board the first day. The second day he and some of his buddies rented motorcycles and drove around the island for four hours. He saw a lot of the island during the four days the officers were being briefed at Pacific Fleet Headquarters.

On December 1, the *Pueblo* put into Yokosuka, Japan. Again Duane had the duty, but he wrote his mother that the boys were looking forward to Christmas in Yokosuka. The ship was going to entertain kids from a Japanese orphanage. Duane took anticipatory delight in listing the elaborate menu Ralph "Cookie" E. Reed was planning for Christmas dinner.

Soon after Christmas the *Pueblo* upped anchor for Sasebo, where they were to get final briefings on their first mission.

Up to this time Duane's letters, scribbled in pen or pencil on bits of note paper, had been full of prosaic details, no news of the *Pueblo* herself. Now in a note dated January 4, he scribbled a postscript in his cramped handwriting:

If you don't hear from me in awhile, don't worry. It might be awhile before I can write. Now don't worry. Everything is fine. Have been here little over a month. Will be here three more days.

Love,
Duane

This was the first hint his parents had of any mystery about the *Pueblo's* mission. "The very fact that he said not to worry, worried me," his mother remembers. "He had never said anything before about anything to worry about." But in the next letter, his last, he was back to his old nonchalant absorption with mundane matters:

Hi Mom & Dad:

How is everyone? We left Yokosuka Jan. 6, pulled into Sasebo the 9th and were supposed to leave today (the 10th by the Japanese calendar) Will be out for awhile this time . . .

You won't have to write for awhile. I won't be getting any mail for awhile.

Love,
Duane.

Back on the Pueblo, *Commander Bucher was taking out his frustration by kicking the deck fittings and "using some appropriate language."*

A half hour had elapsed since he started following the North Korean craft toward Wonsan harbor at one third speed — about five knots — to give his crew more time to destroy secret material. He was confident that he would have everything of importance destroyed long before they reached shore. Then he got words from Lieutenant Stephen R. Harris, in charge of the secret research room, saying that he would be unable to destroy all his classified material, due to the great volume of paper involved and the lack of an adequate shredder.

Commander Bucher gave the order to stop the ship to give more time for destruction of classified documents and equipment while he made an inspection tour of the ship.

The Communist subchaser, which had been about 3,000 yards ahead and moving out steadily, returned to a distance of about 1,000 yards.

Suddenly the Communist guns opened fire again. One .57mm shell penetrated the thin steel hull of the Pueblo *and struck Fireman Duane Hodges, who had been carrying secret material up from the research room to burn in a waste basket in a passageway just outside Commander Bucher's cabin.*

The shell imbedded itself in his right hip and thigh, then exploded, inflicting massive damage in the groin area and lower intestines.

Commander Bucher immediately gave orders to get under way again and no more shots were fired.

"You don't find many men like Duane any more," the words of the girl he left behind. "He had something to offer the world," said Sally Kay Baldwin, a pretty Creswell brunette with long, dark hair and laughing eyes.

"I had an awful crush on him in high school, but he was too shy to notice me. We both matured a lot after we got out of high school. He used to come over to my place, only a few blocks away, and talk or sing. We would go for drives and sing to the radio.

"Sometimes we would take one of my younger brothers with us. Duane was that way — fond of kids and they were fond of him. We used to sing together in the school choir. He had a fine voice. I had a guitar and he later got an electric guitar and we would sing duets together..."

As the Pueblo *steamed slowly toward Communist captivity in North Korea Fireman Duane Hodges lay on a stretcher in the passageway where he was hit. Navy Corpsman Herman P. Baldridge gave him massive transfusions of plasma, "But it did no good. It just went right through him."*

At one point Commander Bucher came by and ordered Baldridge to amputate Duane's leg. But Baldridge refused, explaining that the shock would kill Hodges if he didn't bleed to death.

Corpsman Baldridge gave the mortally wounded sailor morphine. "But he didn't seem to need it. He never seemed to be in any pain. He kept trying to get up and go back to work," Baldridge later recalled.

"I know I am going," he told his buddies. "If I had it to do over again, I would do it for my country."

He died with a smile on his lips, in Cookie's arms.

CHAPTER 5

SURRENDER WITHOUT A FIGHT:
The Story of the USS Pueblo

For 11 months Commander Lloyd M. Bucher and his crew suffered torture at the hands of the North Communists while the eyes of the world were focussed on turbulent times at home: the Tet Offensive in Vietnam; the assassinations of Martin Luther King Jr. and Bobby Kennedy; the trashing of campuses by anti-war protesters; the conviction of Father Philip Berrigan for pouring blood on draft files; rioting at the Democratic National Convention in Chicago and the invasion of Czechoslovakia by Soviet tanks.

Commander Bucher, six other officers, seventy-two sailors, two Marines and two civilian oceanographers of the *Pueblo's* crew were finally released at Panmunjon on Christmas Eve 1968.

Among them were Fireman Michael O'Bannon and Gunners Mate Kenneth Wadley of Beaverton, Oregon. The body of Fireman Duane Hodges of Creswell was returned to his parents who committed him to a grave in the family plot in the town cemetery.

Commander Bucher was called a hero by Rear Admiral Edwin M. Rosenberg, in charge of the repatriation of the *Pueblo's* crew. Was he a hero? Or should he be court martialed for surrendering his ship without a fight?

Questions flew like flak as the Navy kept the crew under wraps: Why didn't the *Pueblo* put up a fight or run for the open sea?

Why was the ship not scuttled? Why was secret equipment not destroyed? Why was the unarmed, 906-ton converted cargo ship, laden with top secret equipment, sent into hostile waters without an escort? Was any effort made to come to the aid of the *Pueblo* during the three hour ordeal? Why was no air cover available anywhere within range? Was the most powerful nation on earth really powerless to save this spy ship from seizure by one the smallest nations on earth? Did the officers and men violate the Code of Conduct when they signed confessions while prisoners of war?

A month after the release of the crew of the *Pueblo*, on Wednesday January 22, 1969, the Navy convened a court of inquiry on the base at Coronado, California. Such courts are convened only "on matters of great national importance," such as the loss of the Navy's nuclear submarines *Thresher* and *Scorpion*.

Captain William B. Newsome, Navy counsel for the board of five admirals, explained to the press that the court of inquiry had no power to try anyone. But it had the power to determine the facts and make recommendations to Admiral John J. Hyland, commander-in-chief of the U.S. Pacific Fleet, who could call for a court martial.

Commander Lloyd M. Bucher had not been on the stand long before Captain Newsome in open court advised the skipper of the *Pueblo* that "the facts reveal you to be suspect of a violation of Article 0730 of the Navy Regulations which provide that the commanding officer shall not permit his command to be searched by any person representing a foreign state, nor permit any of the personnel under his command to be removed from the command of such persons, so long as he has the power to resist." Bucher and his officers may not have been on trial in the eyes of the law, but they were on trial in the eyes of the public. So was the U.S. Navy and the country itself. This was the first time in 160 years that a U.S. Navy ship had been boarded by a hostile power and seized without a fight. Only once before had the nation suffered such humiliation — on June 22, 1807, when the 36-gun frigate *USS Chesapeake* was reduced to splinters by the 50-gun British frigate off the coast of Massachusetts. Commodore Barron, seven times wounded in the shelling, was courtmartialed.

The illusion of a stage trial was heightened by the setting. The court met in the amphitheater used by the Navy's Amphibious School as a classroom. It was a small, intimate theater, with 110 seats stacked up above the pit at the foot of the stage, where five top-ranking admirals sat as judges, flanked by a table for their counsel and a smaller table for Commander Bucher and his counsel. Mounted above the stage was a typical amphibious landing scene, complete with ships, planes, boats and beachhead.

Forty seats were reserved for the press. Each day a new ticket was issued to each reporter and artist. Sketching was allowed, but no cameras or tape recorders. Crewmen of the *Pueblo* were not admitted to the hearing room, since they could be called as witnesses. A tier of seats was reserved for wives and mothers of crewmen.

Sharp at 0900 hours everyone snapped to attention as Vice Admiral Harold G. Bowen Jr., president of the court, strode into the room and the hearing was opened.

Commander Bucher stood and testified with a microphone around his neck most of the time. He was gaunt, sober-faced, hollow-cheeked. His uniform hung loosely on his six foot frame. He lost 100 pounds during his captivity and it showed.

He showed no visible scars nor did he limp from the six shrapnel wounds in his leg and one in his rectum suffered when the first round was fired at the *Pueblo* by a North Korean subchaser.

He had a sense of drama, like an actor on a live stage. He spoke slowly in a slightly hoarse voice. He spoke without notes, but left the impression that he had carefully rehearsed every word. That later appeared to be the case.

Bucher testified that he was knocked down and beaten by the North Koreans who boarded the *Pueblo* and was forced to tour the ship with "Colonel Scar," the Korean commander. He said he saw two mattress covers, 3-by-6 feet in size, still stuffed with classified material which had not been destroyed. When he tried to set fire to it, the guards stopped him. Bucher was startled to discover that the KW7 top secret radio teletype was still operating, although he thought all secret material had been removed.

Bucher and his crew were marched aboard a train for Pyongyang where they were held in a prison and interrogation center.

On the second day of the hearing Commander Bucher testified that when he refused to sign a confession he had been kicked and beaten until he was stiff and sore. He had not slept nor eaten for three days. Then Commander Bucher said that "Colonel Super C," the officer in charge of the prisoners, hauled him into the interrogation room and told him he had two minutes to sign the confession or he would be shot.

"I was somewhat relieved at the prospect of being shot without further torture," he told the court. "Being shot would be a blessing," he said. "During the entire two minutes that I knelt there on the floor, a cocked pistol at my head..."

At this point his voice broke, he stood silent, fighting for control.

"The whole two minutes I merely repeated the phrase: 'I love you, Rose'," he said.

Rose was his blonde wife who sat in the front row of the courtroom about 15 feet away with tears in her eyes. Bucher said, "They tried the same threat again, then said, 'You aren't worth a bullet. We are going to beat you to death.' And they kicked and beat me until I passed out."

He said he came to in his cell, sore all over and urinating blood. "About 10 p.m. Colonel Super C took me to a basement room in the prison, and said he would show me what happened to spies. There they showed me a South Korean strapped to the wall. He was alive, but had been tortured and his right arm was broken," Bucher said.

"He was bare to the waist. He had completely bitten through his lower lip, which was hanging on the right side of his face…"

At this point Commander Bucher broke down again, hung his head and coughed. He asked for a drink of water then continued. "His right eye had been put out. His head was hanging down. There was a lot of black matter running out of his eye socket onto his cheek…"

Bucher said he didn't know what happened next. "I was thrown into a state of mental shock," he told the court. "Next thing I remember was Colonel Super C. in a mood of desperation, saying that they would start shooting members of the crew, one at a time, if I did not sign a confession. So I did."

In his final hour on the stand Bucher said that he was so despondent after signing the confession that he tried to commit suicide by drowning himself in a bucket of water in his room.

The court went into closed sessions and finally recommended trial by court-martial for Bucher for surrendering his ship without a fight and for the ship's intelligence officer, Lieutenant Commander Stephen Harris. Reprimands for dereliction of duty were recommended for Murphy and for Rear Admiral Frank Harris, the Navy's chief of Asian intelligence.

The recommendations were later rejected by John Chafee, Secretary of the Navy, who said that the *Pueblo's* officers and men had suffered enough.

Nevertheless Commander Bucher received a letter of reprimand which essentially ended his Navy career. He retired May 31, 1973. Lieutenant Commander Murphy and most of the rest of the crew also left the service amid bitter charges of whitewash of the Navy chain of command, dereliction of duty and incompetence at high levels of command.

Murphy, second in command of the *Pueblo*, called the *Pueblo* incident a security disaster. "The *Pueblo* was equipped with the most advanced top secret electronics the Navy had developed," he said. "It represented our top technology. Much of the equipment in the secret spaces was destroyed, but we don't know whether the North Korean communists seized enough manuals and spare parts to put them back together again.

"The North Koreans could sell this top secret material to our enemies to buy military equipment. The *Pueblo* should never have been lost," Murphy said in an interview in Portland. "There is no evidence that the communists set out deliberately to capture the *Pueblo*, or knew she was gathering intelligence.

"If, when Commander Bucher first sighted the Soviet SO-1 subchaser about noon January 23, he had turned and headed out to sea, as prescribed in our written and oral orders, there would have been no incident.

"The subchaser could not have boarded us while we were underway. There is no reason to believe that she would have shelled us."

At a Navy ceremony eight years after the *Pueblo* incident, Murphy refused to accept a commendation medal for "withstanding continuing harassment, beatings and malicious propaganda while a prisoner of war."

He called the commendation "shallow and insincere and another attempt at a *Pueblo* coverup, oozing of whitewash."

Then he read a prepared statement making new allegations against Bucher.

In his book *Second In Command*, first book off the press uncensored by the Navy, Murphy dispelled many of the "myths" about the *Pueblo* incident created by Commander Lloyd Bucher. The book paints a picture of Bucher as confused, indecisive, incapable of exercising command in a crisis, disregarding regulations and drinking to excess. Bucher, in his book *My Story* in turn blames Murphy for much of the *Pueblo* disaster.

Murphy says Bucher's story of seeing a South Korean spy strapped to a wall with his eye hanging out of its socket was pure invention. He also questioned Bucher's claim that he tried to drown himself in a bucket of water after signing a false confession.

"When Bucher finally surrendered the *Pueblo* without firing a shot he instructed the men over the public address system, to follow the Code of Honor — give only name, rank and serial number," Murphy argued.

"Yet as soon as he got on board the train to Pyongyang, Bucher started talking, volunteering information to his captors," Murphy said.

But Murphy was most bitter about Bucher's dramatic testimony at the court of inquiry regarding the death of Fireman Duane Hodges. Commander Bucher told the court of inquiry that Hodges died with the words of his favorite hymn "How Great Thou Art" on his lips.

"This was a cruel invention. It never happened," Murphy said. Hodges's death was a personal blow to Murphy. It was Murphy, as medical officer, not Bucher, who was at Hodges's side when he lapsed into unconsciousness after being hit by a .57mm shell from a North Korean gunboat.

When Commander Bucher met Mr. and Mrs. Jesse Hodges, Duane's parents, upon his return from captivity, he assured them, with a great show of emotion, that their son would receive the Silver Star posthumously. "Bucher knew he couldn't award Hodges a Silver Star. The Silver Star can be given for only one reason: gallantry in action," Murphy stated. "I went up and down the chain of command literally begging for the award for Hodges," Murphy said sadly in an interview in Portland.

"Everywhere the answer was the same: 'Bucher had no business making a promise that he knew he couldn't keep.'"

And so the Silver Star engraved upon Duane Hodges's tombstone was never issued.

"Nor have any of the more than 40 members of the 83-man crew received any of the medals Commander Bucher promised them. Most of the crew feel that the old navy axiom applies to the *Pueblo*: 'None required, none desired,'" Murphy said.

CHAPTER 6

THE COOPER CAPER

Boredom hung over The Oregonian *newsroom like a cloud Wednesday November 24, 1971. It was the eve of Thanksgiving. Visions of turkey and football were dancing in the heads of bored reporters and editors in* The Oregonian *newsroom.*

I was about to tackle a stack of obituaries for lack of anything else to do, when the alert bells on the A.P. teletypes began to ring urgently.

Flash: "A Northwest Airliner has just been hijacked by a man named D.B. Cooper. Demands $200,000 in cash. Says he has a bomb. Threatens to blow up the plane and all 42 passengers and crew aboard."

That night a legend was born, the legend of D.B. Cooper. He bailed out of the Northwest 727 with 21 pounds of $20 bills strapped to his waist. And disappeared.

He was hailed as the first in the world to succeed in extorting $200,000 in cash for hijacking a plane, threatening its passengers and escaping with the loot. His is the only hijacking to remain unsolved, having launched numerous copycat acts and terrorism acts in the sky.

Cooper became a folk hero, a "Robbing Hood" who beat the system with his daring caper. To this day he is celebrated in songs like "The Skyjacker's Guide" or "Hold This Bomb While I Go to the Bathroom".

The Cooper caper is still celebrated with beer and bravado every Thanksgiving Day at the Ariel Tavern in Ariel, Washington at Lake Merwin, 10 miles east of Woodland where he was once thought to have landed. Revelry starts at 10 a.m. Thanksgiving Day and continues until 2 a.m. the next morning. There is a Cooper look alike contest and real, live sky divers drop in at the height of the excitement.

Some say that in the dark of the night when the lights are low and the mood is right, Cooper has been seen hunkering up to the bar — or was it his ghost?

Well, the FBI has news for the real Cooper. He is no hero. He's a criminal in the FBI book. Statute of limitations? He was indicted for hijacking and violation of the Hobbs Extortion Act. He will remain a wanted man as long as the indictment stands.

Back in the newsroom details started to emerge:

A man wearing dark Hollywood glasses boarded a Boeing 727, Flight 305 in Portland bound for Seattle. Portland ticket agent Dennis Lysle recalls that the mystery man made sure Flight 305 was a Boeing 727 — with a rear exit door — when he paid $20 cash for a one-way ticket to Seattle. When Lysle asked his name the passenger hesitated as if deciding, then said his name was Dan Cooper.

While the pilot was taxiing out for takeoff the man called Cooper passed a note to Stewardess Schaffner. "I tucked it into my purse," she said later. "I thought he was trying to hustle me. But he said I had better look at the note, that he had a bomb."

He carried an attache case which he opened a crack to show Schaffner what looked like dynamite, a battery and a tangle of wires.

Captain William Scott took off at 2:45 p.m., flew to Seattle, then went into a holding pattern while he relayed the hijacker's instructions to authorities at the airport.

The Oregon Journal sent Rolla J. "Bud" Crick to Seattle on the first available airliner. Crick was held at the Seattle terminal with the rest of the press where they could only dimly see the darkened plane in a remote corner of the airport.

I got Cliff Cernick, regional press representative for the Federal Aviation Administration, on the phone in Seattle. He was one of the best in the business. In fact I had nominated him for an Aviation Writers Association award. Cernick was able to patch me through to an open line where we could hear all communications between the aircraft, the tower and the air traffic controllers along V23 airway.

We heard that four parachutes and the $200,000 ransom had been placed aboard. After checking the bank bag full of $20 bills, Cooper released all the passengers, but demanded that Tina Mucklow, the head stewardess, remain aboard.

We heard the skyjacker's demands that the pilots leave the rear door open and fly no higher than 7,000 feet above the ground. Captain Scott explained that it was not possible to take off with the rear door dragging on the pavement. The skyjacker accepted the explanation and Scott took off with the hijacker alone in the rear of the plane and climbed to 7,000 feet a little north of Kelso, later climbing to 10,000 feet.

At 7:42 p.m. the pilots reported an aft stair warning light, indicating the rear ramp was unlocked. At 8:05 p.m. the crew heard the last word from the hijacker. Asked if he needed any help, he said, "No." At 8:12 p.m. pressure oscillations in the cabin indicated that the jumper probably had left the aircraft.

But the pilots could not be sure. They continued south on V23 airway without any further signs of life from the rear of the plane. They landed at Reno, Nevada, dragging the rear door, and taxied to the ramp. Two of the four parachutes demanded by the hijacker were found — but no bomb.

One parachute was found intact. The shroud lines on the other one had been cut to lash the money to the hijacker's waist. Something else was found, but the FBI has kept this information secret to this day, as a means of testing anyone who claims to be the hijacker.

The FBI estimated that Flight 305 was over Ariel at the foot of Mount Saint Helens when the hijacker bailed out, assuming that he was on course at the time. During the next six months sheriff's deputies, state patrol, Boy Scouts and finally 200 Army troops kept up a foot by foot search of the rugged country around Ariel, aided by hundreds of volunteers spurred by the possibility of finding the $200,000 in $20 bills.

The only clue ever found was a piece of the interior wall of the 727, including a placard which identified the chunk as coming from Flight 305. Apparently the piece of plastic had been ripped off the plane when the rear stairway door was opened in flight.

The skyjacker had jumped into the teeth of one the most violent wind and rain storms in the memory of pilots and old time residents of the area. The pilot of a United Airliner flying four minutes behind Flight 305, reported 100-mile an hour winds at his flight level. Lelooska, Indian artist who lives at Ariel, remembers wind and rain so vicious that he was compelled to pull off the road and wait for a lull.

That coupled with freezing temperatures at 7,000 feet would have been fatal to anyone who, like the hijacker, was dressed in a light suit and slip-on shoes — if he survived the jump.

No trace of the man called Cooper has ever been found. But excitement among Cooper fans reached a fever pitch Sunday February 10, 1980 when soggy bundles containing 294 of the 10,000 $20 bills were found in the sand of Frenchman's Bar on the banks of the Columbia River, about five miles downstream from Vancouver and about 20 miles upstream from the Lewis River. Young Brian Ingram of Vancouver was digging a shallow fire pit when he encountered the loot.

The story broke on *Journal* time, but FBI Agent Ralph Himmelsbach tipped me off to the location of the find in time to make the first edition of *The Oregonian.*

How did the ransom money get there?

Years later the co-pilot admitted flying the aircraft without autopilot due to the strong winds and the tense circumstances. Himmelsbach is convinced that the storm winds had drifted the 727 off course to the east, over the Washougal River watershed where the skyjacker died and some of the money was washed down the Washougal into the Columbia River where it was found nine years later.

"I don't think any trace of the hijacker will be found, not even his bones," Himmelsbach said. But the FBI's Cooper file is still open as long as the indictment stands.

CHAPTER 7

THE MOUNTAIN BLOWS ITS TOP

As we cleared the traffic pattern I got my first good look at the mountain. "That's not St. Helens," I thought out loud. "Where's the rest of it?"

The whole top of the mountain — 1,377 feet — was gone. She was no longer the ermine queen of the Cascades. She was a devil, spouting Hell fire with demoniacal fury. The black cloud that roared skyward was punctuated by the most violent lightning I had ever seen. Short, sharp, jagged flashes of brilliant blue light formed in the ash cloud above the cone and stabbed the earth viciously. Occasionally chunks of white popped up in the black column like popcorn balls. They proved to be fragments of shattered ice from the mountain's many glaciers.

It was about 10:10 a.m. Sunday May 18, a day still vivid in memory. *Oregonian* photographer Don Wilson, a daring skier, but a white knuckle flier, and I were shooting the first pictures of the massive eruption of Mount St. Helens.

It all began two months earlier in the newsroom of *The Oregonian.* Staff Writer Jim Kadera sauntered by my desk with a puzzled expression on his face. "The Forest Service says that an earthquake has triggered avalanches on Mount St. Helens," he casually observed. We had a mutual interest in the mountain. He covered the Forest Service beat and I covered the Cascades.

Mount St. Helens, youngest of the chain of dormant volcanoes that make up the Cascade Range, was the most beautiful by far. It was a perfect inverted cone, frequently compared to Japan's Fujiyama. Its symmetrical contours were reflected in the deep blue waters of Spirit Lake at its feet, making it one of the most popular playgrounds in the Northwest.

Our family claimed Mount St. Helens as our own. We made a pilgrimage to our private mountain every summer, starting in the 1930's when we had to ford the Toutle River in our old Chevrolet. We stalled out once in the middle of the stream. Our favorite campgrounds on the south shore of Spirit Lake were full of deep tree wells. An eruption about 500 years ago had buried the forest 20 feet deep in pumice. As the trees rotted away they left deep holes in the floor of the new forest.

We had scrambled the 17 miles of rugged trails that lead up and over Mount Margaret and clear around the lake and skinny dipped in the icy waters of St. Helens Lake, at the foot of 5,000-foot Coldwater Peak. Our grandchildren had hunted polliwogs in the shallow water of the northeast end of the lake and scrambled up the face of serene Harmony Falls.

We had hiked the trail to the Plains of Abraham on the east side of the mountain marked by the paths of repeated avalanches which started from the very summit of the mountain and hurtled 9,000 feet down the steep slopes and across the plains a mile or more, leaving desolation in their wake.

Every spring we would hike or drive up to timberline and collect stunted mountain hemlock, western red cedar and pine trees. They made ideal bonsai. Every year we would climb up to the foot of Forsythe Glacier and measure its advancing tongue of ice. We had all climbed the mountain's gentle slopes to the top. R. S. Durkee, my father-in-law, had first climbed it in 1924 when the U.S. Forest Service still maintained a lookout station on top. He climbed it again in 1973 at 72 years of age. I went with him, expecting to carry him off the mountain, but he could have carried me.

We took that earthquake report personally. This was our mountain that was under attack. That report from the ranger at Spirit Lake was the first break in the story of the century, the worst natural disaster in the United States in 123 years. But no one got excited. The city desk kissed it off, commenting that "these avalanches happen all the time." That was Tuesday afternoon March 20, 1980.

A couple of days later I flew around the mountain, 50 airline miles north of downtown Portland, with staff photographer Wes Guderian. We saw and photographed the tracks of massive avalanches in the deep snow that covered the mountain. The city desk brushed them off as unrelated to the earthquakes, which were coming faster and with greater magnitude by that time.

Thursday March 27, I took off with staff photographer Mike Lloyd. We orbited the mountain above the clouds for about an hour waiting for a break in the clouds. We were about to give up when we lucked out. We caught the mountain's first plume of steam and ash streaming off to the west. Word of the first ash eruption provoked a panic among media and sightseeing pilots. The airspace over the mountain quickly turned into a dog fight. We maintained 1,000 feet above the peak and circled counter clockwise. But planes recklessly dived in from all directions to get a look at the widening crater. A twin-engine plane dived under us, barely clearing the peak.

For the next two months I patrolled the mountain with a photographer every week or so, while swarms of earthquakes shook the symmetrical cone like a bowl full of jelly. The north face of the 9,677-foot peak began to crack and sag like the belly of a sumo wrestler.

"Our measurements show that the north face has bulged out nearly 500 feet," Bob Johnston, spokesman for the U.S. Geological Survey, told me one day in May. "Something has to give."

And give it did. At 8:32 and 25 seconds a.m. Sunday May 18 all Hell broke loose. Without any warning, an earthquake which measured 5.1 on the Richter scale, triggered a massive landslide, releasing a vertical blast that was heard around the world on listening devices designed to record atomic explosions. The blast shot debris into the stratosphere where it circled the earth for months.

I called to reserve an airplane and headed for Vancouver's airport. Pearson Air Field was besieged by television and press teams clamoring for aircraft. Planes were available but not pilots. TV had usurped the plane I had reserved, but by 10:10 a.m. I was taking off for the first 2.5-hour flight with Wilson, who wasn't afraid to jump off the top of Mount Hood on skis, but was uncomfortable in the air. Only the chance to cover the biggest story of the century overcame his qualms.

The volcano formed its own ominous black cloud in an otherwise cloudless sky. A west wind forced the impenetrable cloud to the east, turning noon to midnight in Yakima, 85 airline miles to the east and obscuring the visibility as far as 220 miles to the east. The Federal Aviation Administration had declared a disaster area around the mountain, restricting all planes, except rescue aircraft, from a 20-mile radius of the mountain. We flew around the mountain under radar control for 2.5 hours, then landed at noon with the first shots of the eruption to go on the wire.

Staff photographer Bob Ellis was waiting. We refueled and took off, trying to circle the mountain. We got close enough on the west flank of the volcano to see some of the pyroclastic avalanches that distinguished this eruption. The French volcanologists called them nuee ardentes, fiery avalanches. We could see them come zipping out of the crater, speeding down the mountain, riding on a cushion of air, at 100 miles an hour or more.

Some of the lateral blasts, hotter than a blast furnace, were clocked at 670 miles an hour. The heat of the lateral blasts killed standing timber as far away as 25 miles northwest of the crater. The Parker family — Donald, Natalie and Richard — were incinerated in their sleeping bags near Meta Lake, about 9 miles north of the crater by one of a dozen fiery avalanches.

The air was full of chatter from the pilots of National Guard and Air Force Reserve helicopters. "Spirit Lake has been wiped out," one chopper pilot reported. "I'm over the lake and see nothing but columns of steam," he said. That report went on the wire, but local pilots who knew the area later that day reported getting a glimpse of the lake, obscured by steam. The lake appeared to be boiling.

It was no wonder that pilots were confused. The landscape had been violently altered. Some 150 square miles of timber —

220,000 acres — to the north, northwest and northeast had been uprooted, sandblasted and burned to death, destroying 1.6 billion board feet of prime timber; 100 miles of streams; killing 2,300 deer, elk and mountain goats; destroying 27 recreation sites; 63 miles of roads; 97 miles of trails and 15 Forest Service buildings worth $134 million.

One cubic mile of the mountain had been ejected, leaving a crater one mile deep and two miles across. The massive landslide had hit the lake at the foot of the mountain, forcing water out of the lake up and over a 1500-foot shoulder of the mountain to the north, wiping out the old growth forest in its path and raising the level of the lake by 200 feet. The same landslide, lubricated by water from the lake, swept 17 miles on down the valley of the Toutle River, burying the valley under 160 to 600 feet of volcanic debris.

We cancelled our flight plan, dropped down below the radar screen and followed the Columbia River down to the Cowlitz River. There a freighter, the *Hoegh Mascot,* with a load of cargo was hard aground in the channel which is normally 40 feet deep. Debris from the volcano had poured 35 miles down the Toutle River into the Cowlitz and into the Columbia trapping 31 deep draft ships up the Columbia and another 50 more stranded at Astoria waiting to come up the river. The Army Corps of Engineers, acting with wartime urgency, had every big pipeline dredge in the West — 28 in all — on the job within hours. They moved 159 million cubic yards of dredging at a cost of about $233 million. It was the biggest operation of its kind in the annals of the Army Engineers.

We buzzed up the Cowlitz River to the Toutle River. That normally peaceful trout stream had turned into a raging demon, laden with a solid mass of logs and downed timber. We watched in fascination as a small building riding the crest of the flood struck the bridge over the Toutle on Interstate 5, the main north-south freeway. The building was reduced to splinters as it hit the bridge. The railroad bridge over the Toutle, 100 yards further downstream, was piled high with logs and debris. Both bridges were closed to traffic.

We followed the Toutle River upstream to the town of Toutle, 25 airline miles from the mountain. The concrete bridge over the river at the edge of town had vanished. The concrete deck was later found a quarter of a mile downstream, mute testimony to the power of the river, heavy with sand, the consistency of wet concrete. The Toutle schoolyard had been turned into a base of operations for rescue crews. Helicopters were taking off to search for survivors and returning covered with gray dust. Gray dust covered the land for 20 miles north and west of the volcano. Gray was the color of death. Survivors who tried to walk out sank waist deep into the fine powder, floundered and died.

We skirted the area to stay out of the way of helicopters and a few light aircraft then followed remnants of the Spirit Lake Highway on up the muddy river. We passed 19-Mile Camp, a major Weyerhaeuser logging center. The river had ripped through the maintenance yard, wrecking shop buildings and carrying away logging trucks.

We poked on up the valley, under lowering clouds, dodging helicopters and aircraft, to Camp Baker, the main Weyerhaeuser logging camp, terminus of the logging railroad, 17 airline miles from the volcano. The camp buildings had been ripped up; trucks, locomotives and logging cars tossed in heaps like so many toys.

On the upstream edge of the camp we saw what looked like telegraph poles lying side by side in neat rows, pointing upstream.

Beyond the camp we saw what looked like a flow of butterscotch pudding. By that time the clouds were getting lower, the visibility was obscured by dust from the mountain and steam from the river and we were busy dodging helicopter traffic.

We turned back. It was not until we saw closeup pictures that we realized we had seen the tongue of the mudflow generated by the landslide — the biggest landslide ever recorded in historic times. We saw a few abandoned trucks and cars along what was left of the Spirit Lake Highway, we had no idea how many loggers or weekend campers had been killed by the blast. First reports listed 20 killed and 60 missing. It was a year before the death toll was finally established at 57.

Volcanologists calculated the force of the eruption as "equivalent to a 400-megaton nuclear explosion, one nearly eight times more powerful than that of the largest nuclear device ever detonated." The volcano's sustained energy output "might better be compared to the aerial detonation of some 27,000 Hiroshima-sized bombs; nearly one a second, for nine hours."

More than 300 homes were destroyed or damaged by the landslide and debris flows; 12 bridges, several logging camps, fish hatcheries and city water systems were wiped out. Millions of board feet of standing timber, including some of the finest old growth Douglas fir in the West, up to eight feet in diameter, was toppled, stripped of its branches and sandblasted. Final cost in local, state and federal funds was more than $1 billion

We landed at Toledo airport a few miles further north, the northern base for rescue operations, where bodies were being taken for autopsies to determine the cause of death. Most had died from inhalation of volcanic dust. But some had been incinerated, melted into unrecognizable heaps. We landed back at Pearson Field at 5 p.m., after logging five hours of flying time.

I had no sooner reached home, hungry and thirsty, than the city desk called to ask me to fly back to Kelso and pick up film from one of the two reporter-photographer teams on the ground. The only plane available was a low-winged clunker not equipped for instrument or night flying. Staff photographer Mike Lloyd joined me on the flight to Kelso on Interstate 5, western base for rescue teams. The sun was setting as we flew past Mount St. Helens. The eruption had finally tapered off after about 10 hours of all-out violence.

The airport was a scene of confusion. Survivors were beginning to come in by truck and chopper. I approached two survivors who were looking haggard and shocked. They told a harrowing tale of death and desperation:

Bruce Nelson and his girl friend Sue Ruff had gone camping on the banks of the Green River near Miners Creek in old growth Douglas fir, 14 airline miles north of the volcano, with two other couples. They woke up early that chilly Sunday morning and were huddled around their campfire waiting for their coffee pot to boil. Their friend Terry Crail had been fishing and was just coming back all excited about the big fish that got away. His girl friend, Karen Varner, was still asleep in their pup tent. Brian Thomas and Dan Balch were just beginning to wake up in their own tent, 50 yards downstream.

Suddenly they became aware of a plume of smoke rising above the valley to the south. "There must be a fire somewhere," Ruff said as she headed back to her tent for a cigarette. Before she could light up, a strong wind whipped up, quickly building up to hurricane force as it whistled through the tall trees. Then a brutal black cloud roared down on them at express speed, laden with sand and volcanic debris, hissing through the trees.

Crail dived for the red nylon tent where his girlfriend still slept as the black cloud blotted out the camp.

Nelson and Ruff clung together between two forest giants. That saved their lives. Huge trees thundered to the ground in a tangled mass. Their two giant trees were uprooted, but formed a roof that protected the two. As the hot wind passed they found themselves in the dark, trapped beneath the tangled blowdown. "I remember groping around and thinking 'My God, Sue. I think we are dead.'"

"We're not dead yet," Sue recalled saying, "Keep digging."

Nelson managed to worm his way out of the tangle of downed trees and shouted for the others in the camping party. But there was no answer. The sky cleared briefly and they scrambled up the hill behind their camp. Then chunks of rock and ice pellets began to fall and they took shelter.

"If we get out of this alive," Nelson remembers saying, "you're going to marry me." Ruff said she would. By that time the fog had begun to lift and they decided to start walking out.

About that time they heard a shout. It was from Dan Balch and Brian Thomas. Balch had badly burned his hands on a hot tree. His arm, scalp and the back of his neck was also burned.

Thomas had a shattered hip that left him helpless. Nelson and Ruff struggled to carry and roll Thomas about 120 feet to what was left of a miner's shack. They built a lean-to out of boards to shelter him and left him there. Thomas begged one of them to stay behind with him. Nelson explained that they were unable to carry him out but would send help back for him. And the three took off down the road. Balch soon dropped out, incapable of taking another step. His feet and shins were badly burned from walking in the hot ash in his stocking feet. *

Nelson and Ruff continued to walk down the ash-covered road, stopping to pet an elk dazed and covered with ash. About mid afternoon they encountered Grant Christens, 59, of Chehalis, who was walking along the same road. He had been with his brother on a ridge above the Green River Valley on his way to recover tools from Camp Baker.

The three walked until dusk and were about to take shelter for the night when they heard a helicopter approaching. They kicked up a cloud of dust to attract the chopper. The pilot spotted them, landed and flew them in to the base at Kelso just as the sun was setting.

Editor's Note: Balch and Thomas were rescued later by helicopter.

The aftermath was a bitter tale of confusion and official obstruction. Nelson and Ruff pinpointed the location of their camp on maps for helicopter pilots that Sunday night. They repeated the directions and their pleas for rescue of Crail and Varner at 7 a.m. Monday at the Toledo search headquarters. They were repeatedly refused permission to go with the helicopters or to conduct their own search. Finally on Thursday, after a TV crew from the NBC network's *Today Show* threatened to expose the Guard's bungling on the national network, Nelson was allowed to accompany a helicopter to the camp site, which he quickly located.

As they approached the camp site they were startled by the sound of barking dogs that came from a pile of trees. Captain Steve Epperson of the Ninth Infantry, their helicopter pilot, saw a spot of red in the dust-covered blowdown. It was the tent they were looking for. Cutting a slit in the tent they found Terry Crail and Karen Varner in the position they had assumed five days earlier when Crail ran back to the camp and dived into the tent with Karen before a tree fell on Crail's head and crushed them both. Crail's dog, Tie, and her three pups were the only survivors. Nelson took them home.

Our copy aide never showed up with the film from the ground teams. But the sun was setting in the west and we weren't equipped for night flying. I phoned a few notes on Nelson and Ruff's story then took off at 7:30 p.m. We landed back at Pearson at 8 p.m. I logged more than eight hours flying time that day. I was to log another 150 hours in the next 30 days patrolling the mountain and about 1,000 hours by the end of the year. Six more explosive eruptions of ash and pumice racked the volcano before it settled down to building a dome about 750 feet high and more than 2,000 feet long.

Gradually the earthquakes faded to background levels, the dome quit growing and the volcano ran out of gas, both literally and figuratively. It has been quiet for more than six years now.

Does this mean the dragon is dead or dying, or is it merely out to lunch? Only time will tell. But the scientists who live with the volcano are not yet ready to write its obituary.

EPILOGUE

All is ephemeral —fame and the famous as well.
                                        Marcus Aurelius Antoninus

It is shocking, a little frightening, to see how fleeting is fame, how fast the world is changing. It was only 40 years ago that scientists conquered the coldest, most hostile, most remote spot on earth — at the cost of hardship, danger and a lot of lives.

Today anyone who has the money can buy his way to the North Pole and, for a little more money, to the South Pole, in comfort bordering on luxury.

Even as the Age of Discovery gave way to the Age of Science in the Antarctic a harbinger of the Space Age appeared like a new star in the southern sky. Our navigators pointed out the strange, faint dot of light low along the horizon in Christchurch, New Zealand, October 1957. It was Russia's Sputnik, first man-made object to orbit the earth. Sputnik, seen as a warning of the intercontinental missiles to come, hogged the headlines, crowding out news of the United States Scott-Amundsen Scientific Station being established at the geographic South Pole.

Time no longer marches on. It rockets on into Cyberspace at warp speed.

GLOSSARY

A

AAR. Air-to-air refueling.

AB. Afterburner which provides a kick in the pants to accelerate jet fighters on take off.

AGERS. Auxiliary geographic environmental research ship anemometer device for measuring wind speed.

Ankus. Elephant hook.

A.P. Associated Press.

APO Army post office.

APU Auxiliary power unit.

Atwell hut. Prefabricated building designed for quick assembly in the polar regions auxiliary, as in auxiliary fuel tanks.

B

Base Ops. Base operations office on the flight line.

Belle-tins. Media bulletins reporting progress of elephant Belle's pregnancy.

BE2. Bluie East Two, located on the east coast of Greenland.

Bingo fuel. Minimum amount of fuel required to land at the nearest airport.

Body beaters. Australian slang for mechanics who repair auto bodies.

BW1, BW8. Bluie West One, Eight, located on the west coast of Greenland.

C

CCC. Civilian Conservation Corps.

Chute. A steep, narrow slide on a mountain.

CMTC. Citizens Military Training Camp.

CPTP. Civilian Pilot Training Program.

Colin Alfa. Call sign used by military aircraft for radio communications.

D

D-ring. D-shaped handle which deploys the parachute.

Drogue. A funnel shaped fixture at the end of a hose trailing behind a tanker aircraft. The fighter pilot thrusts his probe into the drogue to refuel in flight.

E

Extraterrestrial. Not of this earth, coming from another planet.

F

FAI. Federation Aeronautique Internationalle.

Foehn wind. A warm, dry wind blowing down a steep slope into a mountain valley.

Form 1. Form used in the U.S. Air Force to list passengers and crew.

Fox Able. Fighters, Atlantic

G

GCA. Ground controlled approach.

Gooney bird. C-47 or DC-3 aircraft.

Grabber. Colloquial name for an Eskimo "cowboy" who wrestles Musk oxen to the ground.

H

I

IFF. Demands identification as friend or foe.

IGY. International geophysical year.

J

JATO pods. Jet assisted take off bottles.

JP4. Grade of fuel used in most jet engines.

K

KB5OJ tanker. DC-10 modified for use as a tank refueling aircraft in flight.

Kiwi. Slang for New Zealander.

Krill. Tiny crustacean rich in protein.

Kusha. Eskimo word for white man.

Kushapik. Kushapik Eskimo word for Russians.

L

Lanyard. Lanyard strap which would automatically open pilot's parachute at low altitude.

LST. Landing ship tank.

M

May Day. "Help Me" Universal code for used by aircraft in imminent danger to call for help.

MIG. Class of Russian fighter jets.

N

Narsarsauq. Greenland term for "grassy plain".

NASA. National Air & Space Administration.

NATO. North Atlantic Treaty Organization.

Nuee Ardentes. French term for fiery avalanches.

Newfies. Newfoundland civilians who worked on U.S. bases in Greenland, so called by G.I.s.

NOTAMS. Notices to airmen.

O

OD. Officer of the Day.

Operation Deep Freeze. Code name for all-out U.S. effort to establish scientific station at South Pole and elsewhere in the Antarctic.

Ovibos. Ovibos moschatus, scientific name for musk ox found in arctic regions.

P

Paper palace. Pentagon.

Parkway Project. Code name for project establishing a Danish weather base on the East coast of Greenland, with U.S. aid.

Picket Ship Consult. Navy ship stationed in the Atlantic as a check point for military aircraft.

PIO. Public information officer.

PNR. Point of no return.

POL. Petroleum, oil and lubricants.

PT boat. Patrol boat.

Pushers. Crew members who pushed oil drums out of air cargo plane at low level, without parachutes.

Q

R

Rates. Noncommissioned officers.

RATO. Rocket assisted take off.

R.& R. Rest and recreation.

Rime ice. Rough ice, as opposed to clear ice, which forms on wings of aircraft, increasing drag, reducing lift.

S

Sasquatch. Bigfoot, Yeti or Mt. St. Helens's ape.

Sastrugi. Wave like ridges of hard snow found in the Arctic and Antarctic.

Seabee. Short for construction battalion men who built airfields, bridges, docks, etcetera.

Shaman. American Indian medicine man.

Sirk one-zero. Call sign for tanker refueling fighter planes in flight.

Six-by. Six wheeled heavy duty truck.

Skijoring. Norwegian word meaning skiing behind a horse on snow or ice.

Snocat. Large tracked vehicle designed for travel over the snow.

Sprogs. Jet fighter jocks.

STS. Space Transportation System.

T

T-2. Floating ice island in the far Arctic Ocean.

T-3. Fletcher's Ice Island.

TAC. Tactical Air Command.

Tacan. Military air navigation system.

Tarmac. Ramp or parking area at an air base or airfield.

Thixotropic clay. Clay which turns to fluid when shaken, as by an earthquake.

Toboggan. Maneuver used in air to air refueling. The tanker noses down like a toboggan to pick up speed to prevent refueling fighters from stalling out.

Tsunami. Japanese term for seismic waves.

Tyee. American Indian chief.

U

UFO. Unidentified flying objects.

U.P. United Press.

V

V23 airway. Designated air route, the aerial equivalent of an interstate freeway for aircraft.

Vectoring. Directing an aircraft to its target by ground controlled radar or other aids to navigation.

Very Pistol. Hand held flare gun for use in dire emergencies.

VFR. Visual flight rules.

VO. Vodka and orange juice.

VOR. Visual omni range.

W

Wanigan. Small bunkhouse on wheels once used in the woods on construction jobs.

Weasel. Light weight tracked vehicle designed for over the snow transport in polar regions.

Index

-U-

-X, Y-

About the Author

Leverett G. Richards' reporting career began in the 1930s in Southwest Washington and Oregon. He learned to fly a few years later, trained World War II pilots and continues to fly at age 88. He is a retired U.S. Air Force lieutenant colonel.

Richards has covered major stories from the Arctic to the Antarctic and way points. He has retired from *The Oregonian* twice, but continues to contribute to the paper as a special writer. He covered Packy's birth, the eruption of Mount Saint Helens, the D.B. Cooper caper, the *Pueblo* incident and the historic Russian flight over the North Pole. His stories have appeared in the *Reader's Digest, Flying* and other magazines.

Leverett Richards is the author of *Ice Age Coming* "The Story of Glaciers, Bergs and Ice Caps" and *TAC* "The Story of the Tactical Air Command."